Castles in
S·P·A·I·N

A Traveller's Guide featuring the
National Parador Inns

MICHAEL BUSSELLE

PAVILION

First published in Great Britain 1989 by
PAVILION BOOKS LIMITED
196 Shaftesbury Avenue, London WC2H 8JL

Text copyright © Michael Busselle 1989
Photographs copyright © Michael Busselle 1989

Designed by Bridgewater Design Limited

A Cip catalogue record for this book is available from
the British Library

ISBN 1 85145 104 8 (hbk)
ISBN 1 85145 546 9 (pbk)

The Publishers gratefully acknowledge the assistance and
cooperation of Mundi Color with regard to travel
arrangements

4   6   8   10   9   7   5   3

Colour reproduction by CLG, Verona
Printed and bound by Kyodo, Singapore

Contents

I REMEMBER well my first glimpse of Spain – a good many years ago. It was, I imagine, the same as many millions of other travellers have experienced – from an aircraft window at 30,000 feet while on a flight to one of the Costas. I remember looking down at what seemed to be a featureless beige landscape – almost like a desert. I wondered if anyone lived there.

I rather imagined then that, apart from the occasional city like Madrid, there was really nothing much to Spain until you got to the coast. Happily, I now know better but, amongst many, this impression still prevails.

Although Spain attracts millions of visitors most of them go to the coastal resorts. Occasionally a travel magazine will feature an article entitled 'The Real Spain'. This invariably will mean Seville, Barcelona or Madrid. They are certainly more real than say Torremolinos but they are no more the 'Real Spain' than London is the Real England or New York the Real America.

In researching this book I discovered what almost seems to be a secret. The arid brown landscape which I saw from the plane camouflages hidden green valleys, soaring mountain peaks, vast plains patterned by vines and olive trees, limpid blue lakes and fast-flowing rivers.

The exquisite buildings which Spain possesses are not only to be found in places like Sevilla and Granada but all over the country, often hidden away in unknown towns and villages. It is a country of well-kept secrets and constant surprises.

Adjectives like breathtaking, spectacular and stunning are hard to avoid when describing Spain – I have not used them lightly. The landscape – and buildings – frequently make you catch your breath, exclaim out loud or simply gaze in silent wonder.

INTRODUCTION

THE PARADORS

TO MAKE IT REALLY EASY and enjoyable for the traveller the Spanish government had a very good idea: to provide a string of state-run hotels throughout the country, never more than an easy day's drive apart and located in the most beautiful places. They were to be called *paradores*, the name given to an inn which offers shelter and food to travellers.

This wonderful idea is not something new. Indeed the first of the *paradores* was planned in 1926. The site was selected by King Alfonso XIII – a remote ridge in the Sierra de Gredos to the west of Madrid. He was a keen hunter and this was where he would go to hunt the *capra hispanica,* a rare breed of wild goat.

Today there are 76 *paradores* on the mainland of Spain. The latest to be opened was in 1984 in the Conquistador's town of Trujillo in Extremadura. Many of them are situated in historic buildings like castles, convents and palaces. Others have been specially built in spectacular settings. Some have only a few rooms like the ancient castle tower of Villalba with only six bedrooms. Others can accommodate hundreds of people like the Hotel de los Reyes Católicos in Santiago de Compostela. One thing they all have in common is a constant standard of comfort and service, something which cannot always otherwise be found in the more remote parts of Spain.

Booking ahead is wise. Some are extremely popular, the Parador San Francisco in Granada for example often has a waiting list of many months. The parador in which you are staying will always telephone ahead to make your next reservation.

Many people will probably prefer to make advance bookings for the paradors before they leave home. It can be advisable in the peak seasons and for the most popular paradors. My reservations, flights and car hire were made for me by Mundi Color, a tour operator which specializes in both parador holidays and off-the-beaten-track Spain. They provide both a series of set tours and personally tailored itineraries to suit individual preferences. Most of the paradors featured in this book are, or can be, included in tours arranged by Mundi Color.

As some readers will want to use this book to select individual paradors I have devised a star system in the index to the paradors at the end of the book. It is unavoidably subjective. It is also not like the usual hotel guide based on standards of service, cuisine and comfort. These elements are, in any case, fairly standard throughout the parador chain.

My stars are based on a combination of the ambiance of a particular parador, its setting, its outlook and the interest of the building or its immediate surroundings. In this way an isolated but atmospheric castle like the Parador Marqués de Villena at Alarcón rates the same as, say, a modern building overlooking a stunning beach like the Parador Cristobal Colón at Mazagón.

The *paradores*, like Spain, are very informal. Even in magnificent hotels like the San Marcos in León it is not necessary to wear a jacket and tie for dinner.

*O*pposite: *A fortified gateway at Ciudad Rodrigo.*

Castles in
S·P·A·I·N

FOOD AND WINE

SPANISH FOOD is less familiar to most people than, say, French or Italian cuisine. It is also very different. Much of the best Spanish food is simple and straightforward country cooking.

You have only to wander round a country market to see just how good the ingredients are in Spain. Glossy fresh fruit and vegetables with damp soil still clinging to their roots, bunches of fresh mountain herbs and mushrooms from the forests. In the fishing ports the variety of seafood is overwhelming. Fish is extremely popular and wherever you are in the country there will be a standard selection of fish dishes, like *merluza* (flaky white hake), or *rape*, firm meaty monk fish.

Meat is good too: the countryside teems with pigs, goats, cows and sheep, and chickens cluck around every cottage doorway. Game is also abundant: part-ridge, quail and wild rabbit are commonplace items on the menus. Contrary to popular belief, excellent cheeses are made in Spain. The delicious Roncales from the Pyrenees, for instance; San Simón, a smoked cheese from Galicia; or Cabrales, a creamy blue-veined cheese from the Picos de Europa are only a few of those you will encounter.

The cuisine is strongly regional in character. In Valencia, for example, there are numerous rice-based dishes like *arroz abanda* or *paella*. In Galicia there are the *empanadas* (pies with a variety of fillings) and *fabadas* (rich bean stews). In Andalucía there are chilled soups like *ajo blanco* and *gazpacho* and in Murcia fish baked in salt. In Cataluña there are fish stews such as *suquet de pescado* and *zarzuela* and in Navarra dishes like *Truchas a la Navarra* (trout with ham), and *cordero al chilindrón* (lamb cooked with peppers and tomatoes). La Mancha has dishes like *migas* (fried breadcrumbs), and *Pisto Manchego* (mixed vegetables), while in Castile there is *cochinillo asado* (roast suckling pig) and *sopa de ajo* (garlic soup enriched with eggs).

The *paradores* are proud of their regional cuisine and

each has a selection of local specialities on the menu along with more familiar dishes. Some of these country dishes are not customarily served with vegetables. If you don't like the idea of, say, an unaccompanied meat dish, it is best to ask specifically for vegetables.

Spanish wine is just as interesting and varied as it is in France and Italy. Wines from Rioja and Penedés are now quite familiar but many others are less well known. Cariñena, Ribeiro, Rueda, Priorato, Ampurdán and Mentrida, for example, are all wine-growing regions which are greatly appreciated in Spain and their wines are well worth looking out for. The wine lists at the *paradores* will usually have local country wines on the list – like Torreperogil and Cebreros, for instance – and these will often be available *a la jarra* (in the carafe). Many *paradores* have a separate wine list with a wider choice, but you will often have to ask for this.

TRAVELLING IN SPAIN

I HAVE PLANNED THE ROUTES to make minimal use of main roads. It's far more enjoyable to travel on country roads. They are usually very quiet and more scenic. On many of the roads I have suggested you will see only the occasional car – you're more likely to be held up by a flock of sheep or an ox-drawn cart. The maps I used were from the Michelin series, and I have indicated the relevant map number at the beginning of each tour.

When you do use main roads you will discover that Spanish lorry drivers are exceptionally courteous and helpful and will do everything possible to help you overtake. They will signal when it's safe and then move over and slow down until you're safely past.

When visiting a large town, or passing through, it can help to plan to do so between say 1.00 pm and 4.00 pm. The siesta is between these hours and most towns are very quiet, shops are closed and there is much less traffic. Don't be deterred when you are approaching a historic town and are confronted by ugly suburbs – an unspoilt medieval quarter invariably lies within.

When using country roads it's best to make sure you have a fairly full petrol tank. Sometimes there are many miles between filling stations. It's also important to know that filling stations will not accept credit cards, although they are widely welcomed elsewhere. Petrol stations also dislike traveller's cheques or Eurocheques – only cash is welcome. I was told once on offering a Eurocheque, 'We are not a bank, señor!'

I will never weary of Spain and hope that this book will encourage you to enjoy regions often ignored by the tourist.

The view from close to the Parador at Carmona. Overleaf: The coastline near San Sebastián.

PART ONE

Northern Spain

SAN SEBASTIÁN

1

2   3   4 5

VIGO 6   ● LEÓN

OUR 1 Follows the north-western coastline of Spain, passing through the provinces of Cantabria, Asturias, Lugo and La Coruña. It provides an interesting scenic route linking the airport of Bilbao and the car ferry port of Santander to the coastal resorts of Galicia and northern Portugal. Although the road follows the coast quite closely for much of the way, a number of inland detours are included, enabling you to explore fully this fascinating northern region. Linked with tour 3 it forms a complete round trip from the starting points mentioned.

— TOUR 1 —
MICHELIN MAP NOS. 42 & 441

El Ferrol Ribadeo Gijón
LA CORUÑA
                    Santillana
                    del Mar
LEÓN •

SANTILLANA DEL MAR
GIJÓN
RIBADEO
EL FERROL

The tour begins in Santillana del Mar, one of Spain's most unashamedly picturesque medieval villages and takes you to some of the most remote, unspoilt beaches in Europe. The countryside is a constant pleasure with green rounded hills, quiet country lanes and small villages. Here the wooden-wheeled oxcart is a far more common sight than the tractor. The *hórreos*, small buildings adjoining most homes in which the winter grain is stored, have distinctive regional characteristics. In Asturias they are square, usually built of wood with ornate wooden balconies. In Galicia however they are long and narrow, made of stone and much more functional in appearance.

SANTILLANA DEL MAR

SANTILLANA DEL MAR is within easy reach of Santander or Bilbao. In spite of its name the town is several kms from the sea – amidst steep, rounded green hills with meadows bordered by dry stone walls. Take the N 611 from Santander towards Torrelavega and turn right on to the C 6316 approximately 1km before the town is reached.

Santillana del Mar is a town of rough stone houses and elegant mansions lining steep cobbled streets and small atmospheric squares. On Sunday morning the bells of a lovely 11th-century collegiate church, at the end of the long, sloping cobbled main street, summon the villagers who walk in procession down the hill.

The town, rightly considered one of the most beautiful in Spain, has been perfectly preserved and it is hard to find a street or a square which does not resemble a picture postcard – though its prettiness is quite unselfconscious. During the day, in summer months, tour coaches arrive and people throng the narrow streets. Alongside the inevitable souvenir and craft shops many of the old houses still have dairies and stables on their ground floors and cows are still led down the main street to graze in surrounding meadows. Some houses offer fresh milk, home-made cakes and biscuits

to visitors. One of the pleasures of staying in the Parador is in sharing the atmosphere of the town in the evening and early morning exclusively with its residents.

Parador Nacional Gil Blas is situated in a graceful manor house facing the Plaza Ramón Pelayo around which are several lovely arcaded buildings. The house was once the home of the Barreda-Bracho family. The name Gil Blas is derived from the French author Le Sage's fictional character whose imaginary exploits took him to the town of Santillana. The atmosphere of the Parador is in harmony with the town itself. The entrance leads into a large hall with hewn stone walls and a floor of pebbles in a mosaic pattern.

The menu has a good selection of the local Cantabrian cuisine. El Cocido Montañes is a stew of white beans, potatoes, meat and chorizo. Fish is an excellent choice in this region and two dishes which were on the menu during my stay were Merluza a la Cantabria, hake cooked with asparagus and prawns, and Hongos de Monte con Langostinos y Jamón, smally spiny lobsters cooked with wild mountain mushrooms and ham. I chose a dry and delicate rose wine from the list, Bodegas Peñascal from Tudela de Duero, near Valladolid.

One of the most famous historical discoveries in Europe is only 2km from the Parador, the Caves of Altamira. Well-preserved 12th-century BC paintings have been found here. Regrettably, fear of deterioration has resulted in access to the caves being restricted and application for a visit from the Museum of Altamira must be made several months in advance of your visit. However it is sometimes possible to take advantage of a cancellation by simply turning up and enquiring.

If you plan to stay at least two nights at Gil Blas you will be able to tour along the coast to the east: continue along the C 6316 towards Comillas for 1km and turn right to Suances. Soon you will be in sight of the sea. At Tagla, a small inlet between two grassy headlands, there is a fine sand beach the colour of ripe corn. Suances is a small resort with several beautiful beaches. Small roads lead from the main (N 611) road to a number of delightful beaches between Suances and Santander. Playa de Mongro and Liencres are especially fine beaches but there are many others such as Playa de Portio and Somo Cueva. Tracks leading to these beaches thread their way through small farms and meadows – it is a region where it is easy to get away from the crowds. My visit was during the haymaking

The main street of Santillana del Mar.

A square in Santillana del Mar.

season and the hillsides were dotted with small wooden donkey carts and entire families were busy scything, raking and stacking the hay. The air was suffused with the sweet summery smell of fresh-cut grass.

Santander is soon reached, an attractive, elegant seaside town with the ambience of the best of the great traditional resorts like Deauville, San Sebastián and Brighton, in its stylish shops, broad tree-lined avenues, promenades, numerous gardens and parks shaded by palm trees and mimosa. It also has a vast crescent of fine sand at the beach of Sardinero.

From here continue the coastal route by taking the N 634 to El Astillero. Beyond, after crossing the river, a road to the left, the S 430, leads to a succession of small coastal towns along the other side of the estuary with views across to Santander. Pedreña is a little fishing village at the mouth of the estuary where there is a harbour and ferry boats which cross to Santander. A cluster of wooden buildings include restaurants offering freshly caught *bonito* (striped tunny), *besugo* (sea

bream) and *sardinas* (sardines), cooked over the embers of a wood fire – seafood at its best and very popular with the locals at weekend lunches. The landscape is flatter here than to the west of Santander and there are a number of large beaches backed by sand dunes, such as the Playa de Galizano where a river creates a delightful quiet sandy creek. Beyond, at Barreyo, is the pretty Romanesque church of Santa María. The route continues through Isla, Quejo, Ris and Noia, all with beaches, to Santona where there is a busy fishing port, some interesting old houses and a beautiful 12th-century church, Santa María del Puerto.

From Santona the road follows the estuary of the river Asón to rejoin the N 634 where the route continues eastwards to Laredo, another attractive seaside town with a large beach of fine golden sand, sheltered within a deep bay. The well-preserved town of Laredo is quite separate from the resort which has developed around it and contains some lovely old mansions, the 13th-century church of Nuestra Señora de la Asunción and an imposing 16th-century *ayuntamiento* (town hall).

From Laredo the steep, winding, scenic main road, the N 634, continues to Castro Urdiales, an ancient fishing port founded in Roman times with a large 14th-century church, Santa María, strikingly sited high on a rocky promontory overlooking the harbour.

From Castro Urdiales an attractive inland route takes you back to Santillana. As well as avoiding the busy main road it provides a rewarding scenic route through the Cantabrian mountains and reveals a quite different aspect of this region. Approximately 1km towards Bilbao along the N 634 a small road to the south, the S 501, leads to Ortañes and Avellaneda where there is a small *castillo* (castle) containing a regional museum of the countryside known as Encataniones. It is lovely countryside, steep rounded green hills covered with meadows and woodlands. The road continues through Villaverde and crosses the pass of La Escrita into the beautiful valley of Carrenza. The route is a constant delight, quiet rural scenery with wooded hills and plunging valleys. This region is sparsely populated with small villages and isolated farms, surrounded by small market gardens and meadowland. The road continues to Ramales de la Victoria, set in a valley overlooked by a rocky mountain.

The route continues towards Arredondo following the course of the fast-flowing river Asón. The villages dotted throughout this region are a picturesque cluster of ancient houses with wooden balconies brimming with flowers. Beyond Arredondo, which has a dramatic rocky setting, the road climbs up out of the valley with a succession of stunning views. This for me was literally the high point of the return journey. The scenery, almost alpine in character, becomes increasingly spectacular, culminating in the Puerto de Alisas. Here a *mirador* (vantage point) provides sweeping

An old farmhouse near Arredondo.

views northwards to the sea. The road now descends to La Cavada and then to Pamanes on the N 634 from where you can return to Torrelavega and Santillana.

GIJÓN

THE NEXT STAGE OF THE TOUR is west to the Parador at Gijón. From Santillana the route continues westwards along the C 6316 towards Comillas. It is a quiet country road winding tortuously round steep green hillsides with frequent glimpses of the sea. At Cobreces there is a sandy beach enclosed by grassy headlands. A few kms beyond is Comillas with a small sandy beach, harbour, castle and plaza surrounded by old buildings. The town is overlooked by an imposing cluster of grandiose buildings including an ecclesiastical university and the 18th-century Seminario Cantábrico. Almost hidden away on the edge of the town is an extraordinary small building by Antonio Gaudí, the Catalonian designer who was responsible for the un-

finished Catedral de la Sagrada Familia in Barcelona. Here he has designed a curious *castillo*-like fantasy known as El Capricho.

Beyond Comillas there is another long sandy beach at Oyambre. A few kms further to the west the road joins the N 634. Continue to San Vincente de la Barquera, most attractively situated on a promontory between two river estuaries – it almost seems to be on an island. Here there is a busy fishing port and arcaded streets lined with many attractive old buildings. There are also the remains of a castle, ramparts and a lovely 13th-century church on a hill above the town overlooking the river.

The road 10km to the west of San Vincente crosses the Ría de Tina Menor. You can make a short detour to the right beyond the bridge by following a small road which runs alongside the *ría* (estuary) towards the village of Pechón. There are some breathtaking views down into the intensely blue water which is enclosed by steep wooded headlands. Returning to the main road the route continues westwards towards Llanes, passing from Cantabria into Asturias. Here the countryside becomes more mountainous with distant views of the Picos de Europa to the south. At Pimiangó there are caves with prehistoric paintings. Llanes is an attractive town with fishing boats moored along a quayside lined with old houses. There is also a castle, the remains of ramparts and a 15th-century church. Nearby is a delightful sandy beach, Playa de Toro, with rocky outcrops and grassy headlands.

A little further to the west is another fine beach at San Antolín overlooked by a steep green headland. Nearby is the small Romanesque monastery of San Antolín. The road continues along the coastline to Ribadasella, a largely modern town on the estuary of the Sella. Nearby are the caves of Tío Bustillo where there are cave paintings and stalactites. Beyond Ribadasella the road becomes quite tortuous, winding its way between and around the steep green hills which reach down to the sea. The route continues to Villaviciosa, a town with attractive narrow streets and old houses, and then on to Gijón, the location of the next Parador.

GIJON

GIJÓN is a large modern town which preserves an old quarter down by the harbour. There is an arcaded *plaza mayor* and a 16th-century church down by the sea overlooking the beach. The delightfully old-fashioned beach, San Lorenzo, is a long arc of firm golden sand with a promenade, deckchairs and bathing tents.

Parador Nacional Molino Viejo is a modern building in the centre of the town beside a peaceful wooded park with streams and ponds. The Parador has a quiet rural atmosphere with peacocks strutting in its garden, although in fact it is adjacent to the town's football stadium. *Molino viejo* means 'old mill' which is what previously occupied the site and the waterway which fed the mill has been preserved within the Parador grounds. Regional dishes on the menu during my stay included Pote Asturiano (a stew with ham, *chorizo*, *morcilla* (blood sausage), pigs ears, cabbage, white beans and potatoes flavoured with garlic and paprika); Rodaballo a la Pimienta Verde (turbot cooked with green peppers); and Alcachofas Naturales Rellenas de Bonito (artichokes stuffed with tuna).

From Gijón a small detour to the city of Oviedo can be made along the Autopista A 66. Outwardly it is a modern and not very appealing city but it preserves a number of lovely buildings and an atmospheric old quarter centred around its 14th-century Gothic cathedral. The *plaza mayor* contains an arcaded 18th-century *ayuntamiento*. The jewel of Oviedo is however a small church in the Sierra de Naranjo overlooking the city, built as a palace in the 9th century and converted

The harbour and Ría of Cedeira.

some fifty years later. It is considered by many one of the most beautiful buildings in Spain. Jan Morris describes it as being 'formidable beyond its scale'. It is elegantly proportioned with exquisite detail and its warm mellow stone almost appears to glow from within its green wooded setting.

Returning from Oviedo to Gijón the next stage of the tour is west to Ribadeo. The route continues along the coast road, the N 632 to Avilés, an unattractive industrial town on first sight but with numerous arcaded streets and some fine buildings in the old part centred around the Plaza de España. There is the 14th-century Gothic church of San Francisco, a 17th-century *ayuntamiento* and several palaces with imposing façades. From Avilés the route continues to Soto del Barco on the estuary of the Río Nalón.

From here you can make another small detour along a beautiful wide green valley to Pravia which contains an 18th-century collegiate church and the Palace de los Montes of the same period. Nearby, in the village of Santianes de Pravia, is the oldest church in Asturias. Dating from the 8th century and the residence of the Kings of Asturias, it was restored in 1977 under the personal direction of King Juan Carlos. From here you can follow a small country road back to the coast through steep wooded hillsides via the village of Somado, from which are sweeping views of the coastline and of the estuary of the Río Nalón.

Cudillero, the next town en route, has a busy fishing port, reached by descending a steep cobbled street down to the harbour from where tiers of narrow wooden houses rise up the hillside like a wall. On the outskirts is a rather grand 19th-century palace in the French style containing a collection of paintings and carpets.

In this region you can't fail to notice the *hórreos*, large grain stores adjoining most houses. In Asturias they are square, made of wood and supported on tall stone stilts to protect their contents from hungry rodents. Many are quite large and elaborate with small balconies and windows looking rather like fanciful granny annexes.

The houses of the picturesque fishing town of Luarca are built in a steep semi-circle around a horseshoe-shaped bay, within which is a busy harbour. A small road from the end of the latter climbs round the headland providing a wonderful view of the town.

The route continues approximately 1km inland. The landscape is particularly pleasing with steep green hillocky hills and frequent glimpses of the sea. Beyond Navia a country lane leads through farmland to the small fishing village of Ortiquera. For me, this is the most appealing of all the Asturian fishing towns. Set at the mouth of a narrow rocky inlet in which a small harbour nestles, small whitewashed stone cottages are ranged along the top of the headland. It has a rather wild, remote atmosphere and is completely unspoilt.

The beautiful beach at Tapia de Casariego is in a narrow inlet bordered by wooded headlands with a small stream threading through the fine golden sand. Trees grow almost down to the water's edge, adding an almost tropical atmosphere.

The road continues to the estuary of the Río Eo, known for its trout and salmon fishing. There are lovely views across the broad expanse of water to Ribadeo, opposite which the old town of Castropol is picturesquely situated on a promontory on the east bank. The road skirts around the estuary crossing the river at Vegadeo and continuing along the west bank to Ribadeo. A bridge across the estuary connecting Ribadeo with Figueras was nearing completion at the time of writing.

RIBADEO

RIBADEO is a small town with a fishing harbour beside the river mouth, the 14th-century convent of St Clara and the mainly modern church of Santa María del Campo, containing a particularly beautiful gilded Baroque 18th-century retablo. There is also a rather severe 18th-century *ayuntamiento* and an 18th-century customs building. A small road leads out to the headland at the mouth of the estuary where there are substantial remains of the 18th-century fortress of St Damian.

The Parador Nacional de Ribadeo, a modern building on the edge of the town, is much larger than it appears since the single storey entrance is in fact the top floor of a four-storey building with the bedrooms on the lower floors. It is built on a ledge overlooking the estuary and the small harbour with its cluster of brightly painted fishing boats is immediately below. The bedrooms have large balconies with fine views of the river, Castropol and the hills beyond. The restaurant is an attractive L-shaped room with a marble floor and wide stone-arched windows. Regional fish dishes are well represented on the menu. I had Rodaballo a la Gallega, turbot poached with potatoes, paprika and garlic. Filloas de Mariscos Gratinadas are pancakes stuffed with shellfish in a white wine and cream sauce and grilled. For desert you might try Tarta de Mondonedo, a rich sweet tart filled with a mixture of ground almonds, eggs and sugar, and flavoured with cinnamon. The wine list included a good selection of Galician wines as well as more familiar names from the Rioja and Penedes. I had a bottle of Vino Costeiro Ribeiro; a dry but fruity white wine which is slightly *pétillant*.

EL FERROL

THE NEXT STAGE of the tour is west to the parador at El Ferrol. The route continues along the N 634 towards

Harvesting hay near Ortigueira.

Foz. Before leaving Ribadeo however there is an excellent viewpoint of the estuary and the surrounding countryside from the chapel of A Atalaia on the pine-covered hilltop of Santa Cruz which is clearly signposted along a small road to the left just after leaving the town. A few kms beyond Ribadeo is the fishing village of Rinlo – little more than a cluster of colour-washed stone cottages with grey slate roofs bordering a narrow rocky inlet. About here you will notice the change from the square wooden Asturian *hórreos* to the long narrow stone versions of Galicia.

Here the coastline takes on a flatter and bleaker aspect, with stunted trees and gorse covering the hinterland. The beach of Los Castros is very appealing, a small sheltered inlet of impeccably fine yellow sand bordered by low rocky headlands. At Reinante, just beyond, is another superb sandy beach which extends for several kms, with a small road running parallel to the sea for some distance and bordered by low cliffs, eroded to create a series of curious striated rocky outcrops. One of the finest beaches I have seen anywhere, it is remote and unspoilt but needs to be visited when the tide is low.

Just before reaching Foz a small road to the south leads to the pre-Romanesque church of St Martín de Mondoñedo. At Foz you can make a small detour to the south along the N 634 to the atmospheric old city of Mondoñedo where an imposing twin-towered 13th-century cathedral overlooks the Plaza de España which is surrounded by old houses with galleries and arcades. On the road between Mondoñedo and Foz is Villanova de Lourenza whose huge 18th-century church has a spectacular Baroque façade.

Beyond Burela the countryside becomes more hilly and wooded with increasingly beautiful scenery. Viveiro, situated on the estuary of the Río Androve, with a busy harbour and an important sardine fishing fleet, is a large town with modern buildings but the old centre is still a maze of narrow streets, largely traffic-free, and four of the town gates still survive. The road skirts the Ría de Viveiro with lovely views abounding. After crossing the Ría del Barqueiro a small road leads

to the very pretty small fishing village of Porto de Barqueiro. It has a small harbour surrounded by small whitewashed stone cottages. There are several small waterfront bars and cafés where you can sit and watch the fishing boats bobbing on the tidal currents. A short distance along the main road another small road leads out along the headland, with stunning views, to Porto de Bares at the very mouth of the *ría*, an unspoilt village with a cluster of small fishing boats pulled up on a crescent of pale yellow sand.

Continuing along the coast road Ortigueira is the next large town, which has a long sandy beach backed by sand dunes and pine trees, the Playa de Cazador. At Mera there is a worthwhile detour on to the bleak and windswept headland of Cabo Ortegal. From Pedra a road leads across a wild heath-covered hill with spectacular views of the coastline to the tiny hermitage of San Andrés de Teixido, where an annual pilgrimage is held each year featuring traditional dancing and songs.

The road continues, via the fishing port of Cedeira an attractive town in a beautiful setting on the Ría de Cedeira, to Valdaviño where there is a huge sandy beach and a lagoon. From here it is just 18km to El Ferrol.

El Ferrol, a large, busy town, is Spain's most important naval base and the birthplace of General Franco. The Parador Nacional El Ferrol del Caudillo is on a natural terrace overlooking the naval dockyard and adjacent to a naval building where sailors stand guard and the bugle sounds as the flag is lowered and raised. The Parador is a modern building but with a traditional seafaring atmosphere in its dark wood panelling, polished brass, and maps and charts decorating the walls. The restaurant menu strongly features seafood with an excellent selection of local shellfish, such as *cigalas* (small spiny lobsters), *centolla de la ría* (spider crab), *necoras* (small crab) and *ostras* (oysters). I had Abadejo la Gallega, cod cooked with potatoes, paprika and garlic. There is a good selection of Galician wines on the menu. I chose a bottle of Pazo Ribeiro, an excellent light, dry, fruity white wine with a slight sparkle.

From El Ferrol there are several interesting towns nearby to visit and the Parador makes a good base from which to make a round tour of the Rías Altas. Allow yourself two days, spending one in La Coruña, Pontedeume and Betanzos and the other exploring the Rías Altas.

Pontedeume is a lovely old town on the Ría de Betanzos, with narrow arcaded streets, attractive small squares, interesting shops, the 15th-century fortified

The old port at La Coruña.

The fishing village of Muxía.

Palace of the Counts of Andrade, the 16th-century church of Santiago and a 15th-century *ayuntamiento*. The town has an appealing waterfront atmosphere with the remains of a 14th-century bridge which once had 58 arches.

Betanzos too is a fascinating old hilltop town with extensive town walls and entrance gates, a labyrinth of narrow cobbled streets, tall houses with glazed balconies, small squares and a fine *ayuntamiento*. Among the many churches worth seeing are the 15th-century Santa María del Azogue and the 14th-century San Francisco.

La Coruña, the largest city in Galicia, was the port from which the Spanish Armada sailed against England in 1588 and has been occupied by the Romans and Phoenicians since its original foundation by the Iberians. Today it is a busy modern city but with many old buildings, streets and squares to explore. The Iglesia de Santiago and the collegiate church Santa María date from the 12th century. Perhaps the most photogenic sight of La Coruña is the row of tall glass-balconied houses which border the old harbour. They create

unique and striking setting for the colourful fishing boats moored below. Another unusual sight is the Tower of Hercules, a 2nd-century Roman lighthouse, now incorporated into a more recent structure of vast scale which dominates the headland and is still in use.

The tour of the Rías Altas can be made by taking the C 552 from La Coruña towards Carballo. From here the route is initially along the L C414 to Malpica de Bergantinos, an attractive seaside town with a good sandy beach, then along the C 430 to Ponte Ceso. The road towards Laxe becomes more interesting with steep wooded hills and splendid views of the Ría de Corme y Laxe. Laxe is a small fishing town with an enormous arc of fine white powdery sand. Towards Camarinas it becomes mountainous with rocky outcrops and pine-covered slopes. Camariñas is beautifully sited on the edge of the lovely Ría de Camariñas. The town is known for its lacemaking. Near the pretty riverside village of Ponte do Porto is the attractive small Romanesque church of Santiago de Cereixo and, close by, a small twin-towered palace called the Torres de Cereixo.

Muxía, a small fishing village with a colourful harbour and two lovely white sand beaches, is beautifully situated at the mouth of the Ría de Camarinas with views across the water to Cabo Vilán. From here the road continues through attractive hilly countryside

covered with bracken and gorse, and tall pine and eucalyptus trees, to the fishing town of Corcubión. It is the most picturesque of all the fishing towns along this route with its small stone and wooden houses decorated with glazed balconies clustered round a lively and colourful harbour.

From here you can make a detour out to Cabo Finisterre. Its name derives from the medieval belief that it was, literally, the end of the earth. The road out to the cape is however surprisingly beautiful, not at all bleak and rugged as one might imagine. Green wooded hillsides dip into a sea as clear and blue as you will see anywhere in the world and frequent crescents of fine white sand nestle between the rocky headlands. The village of Finisterre is also appealing with the delightful small 12th-century church of Santa María and the diminutive castle of San Carlos. The road continues beyond to the cape where a lighthouse commands an almost 360° panorama over the sea from the very tip of the promontory. Here it is impressively rugged and isolated and it would not be hard to imagine there is no land beyond this point.

From Corcubión the road follows the coastline closely to Muros. Here the landscape is much more open and rocky, with fewer trees. This part of the coastline has a quite striking beauty. There is a remote and wild

A secluded beach near Corcubión.

atmosphere and the coast is scantily populated. The beaches are simply stunning with gleaming white sand and crystal-clear blue water backed by sand dunes and rocks. There is access to the beaches almost all the way along this route. The Playa de Carnota is particularly notable and the village is also famed for possessing the largest *hórreo* in Galicia. In a region especially well endowed with enormous *hórreos* that of Carnota, 100ft long, dwarfs them all. The Playa de Lariño is also magnificent with a long sweeping arc of brilliant white sand. Just beyond, Louro also has a superb beach. Muros is an attractive small town with a harbour looking out across the Ría de Muros y Noja.

The route continues along the side of the Ría to Outes. At this point you can take the road north to Pino do Val from where you can continue back towards La Coruña and El Ferrol along the LC 403 via Santa Comba. It is however a quite long circuit and one which you may not want to rush. An alternative plan would be to drive the much shorter distance via Noia to Santiago de Compostela and stay at the Hotel Reyes Católicos (page 26), where you could join Tour No 2.

*T*OUR 2 *Explores the coastal region of Galicia in the north-west corner of Spain. Begins in the province of La Coruña and then leads south into Pontevedra towards the Portuguese border. A region dominated by the Rías Bajas, the steep and deeply indented river estuaries which penetrate the Atlantic coastline. Hidden between green headlands are beautiful deserted beaches of fine white sand and fishing villages where some of the best seafood in the world is to be found. Behind are green mountains covered with vineyards and threaded by narrow lanes where the oxcart is a more familiar sight than the car.*

— TOUR 2 —
MICHELIN MAP NO. 441
SANTIAGO DE COMPOSTELA
Cambados
Pontevedra
VIGO
Bayona
Tuy

SANTIAGO DE COMPOSTELA
CAMBADOS
PONTEVEDRA
BAYONA – TUY

SANTIAGO DE COMPOSTELA

THE ITINERARY BEGINS in Santiago de Compostela, where the nearest airport is located. The nearest alternative parador is at El Ferrol, 95km (page 23).

The Hotel de los Reyes Católicos is now part of the parador network and is much more than a magnificent hotel – it is a unique experience. The building is a royal hospital founded in 1499 by the Catholic Monarchs, Fernando and Isabel, to give lodging and care to the pilgrims visiting the city. Occupying the north side of the Plaza España, also known as the Plaza Obradoiro, a vast paved square which is surrounded by majestic buildings, the hotel has a long imposing façade with a superb Plateresque portal. Inside are four graceful patios, all quite different. Numerous corridors and grand staircases link the rooms. The bedrooms are contained in several wings which extend from the central patios – it's quite easy to get lost. Beautiful antiques are scattered throughout. The restaurant is in a huge cavernous room with a high ceiling supported on massive stone arches.

From the regional specialities on the menu I chose Pimientos de Padrón, tiny sweet green peppers the size of quail's eggs, which are just sprinkled with salt and fried quickly in oil – absolutely delicious. Empanada de Bonito is tuna fish pie. Vieras de Santiago are scallops cooked in white wine with onions, mushrooms and tomato and flavoured with garlic and parsley. Polpo a Feira are small pieces of tenderised octopus cooked with garlic, paprika and olive oil. This dish is traditionally served on a wooden platter. For desert Tarta de Santiago is a tart filled with a mixture of eggs, sugar and almonds and flavoured with cinnamon.

Santiago is a city which exists because of a legend. It is believed that St James's body, after having been beheaded by Herod, was taken by his disciples to Padrón in northern Spain – a miraculous journey of only seven days. The body was lost and forgotten until in 813 a shepherd was guided to its hiding place by a star. The Saint appeared on horseback in a battle against the Moors. He was reputed to have killed over 50,000 Moors single-handed and soon became the Patron Saint of the Reconquest.

The news spread quickly and soon miracles began to happen. King Alfonso III founded a monastery on the site of the tomb and pilgrims began to arrive from all over Europe. They established a route known as the Camino de Santiago, the way of St James. Cathedrals, churches and towns sprang up along the route, which crossed France and northern Spain, to provide shelter and comfort to the pilgrims on their long journey.

During the Middle Ages Santiago became one of the most important shrines in the Christian world, along with Rome and Jerusalem. At its peak it is claimed that up to one million pilgrims made the journey each year. In 1589, when Francis Drake attacked La Coruña, the remains were removed from the cathedral for safe-keeping. They were then mislaid for another 300 years until their rediscovery in 1879. The relics were authenticated by the Pope and are now, once more, the object of pilgrimages.

One of the pleasures of staying at Los Reyes Católicos is that in the early morning and evening, when the tourists have gone, you can stroll out into the empty square and appreciate it in virtual solitude. The magnificent façade of the cathedral overwhelms you with its presence. It is a truly magical sight in the evening sunlight.

The present building was begun in 1078 after the Moors destroyed the original basilica. The cathedral was extended and modified during many centuries. The glorious Baroque façade was not completed until 1750. Inside, the Pórtico de Gloria, the original west front which now shelters behind the 'new' façade, is a masterpiece of Romanesque sculpture. In its centre is St James set on a column carved with the Tree of Jesse. Here the pilgrims have for centuries placed their fingers into holes worn as smooth as marble into the granite.

There are many other buildings of interest, and the numerous atmospheric streets and squares are built on different levels, creating a theatrical effect. The Parador will provide a guide and a map to the city.

A short excursion from the Parador can be made south-east along the N 525 to Pazo de Oca. Here in a

The cathedral of Santiago de Compostela at sunset.

The Plaza de Leña in Pontevedra.

small village overlooking a wide green is a *pazo*, or Galician manor house known as Pequeño Versailles, or little Versailles. It is a large stern building constructed from massive blocks of granite. Inside are enchanting formal gardens with long rectangular pools and fountains. There is a peaceful and almost unwordly atmosphere. Nearby at Carboeiro, hidden in a deep wooded valley, are the evocative ruins of the 10th-century monastery of San Lorenzo.

CAMBADOS

FROM SANTIAGO the next stage of the journey is southwest to the Parador at Cambados. The direct journey is only 54km but I have described a route which first explores the Ría de Arosa. Initially the route is southwest along the C 543 to Noya, an important port in Roman times, with the 15th-century church of San Martín and the 14th-century Santa María Nova. The latter has a fine Gothic rose window and a fascinating

cemetery with many 13th-century tombs. The road follows the coastline closely to Portosín and Caamano. Nearby is the Playa Río Sierra, a magnificent curve of white sand backed by an enormous sand dune and bordered by a heath-covered headland. Further to the south, near the small fishing village of Corrubedo, is another vast crescent of white sand. The sea here is a translucent shade of turquoise blue, as idyllic as any island in the Indian ocean.

The road continues over the headland to Ribeira, a busy fishing port. From here the road leads east alongside the ría to Puebla de Caraminal, with its 17th-century Baroque church, 15th-century church of Puebla del Deán and 15th-century remains of three pazos. A road leads up to the *mirador* of Culota from where there are sweeping views across the *ría* and to the islands of Arosa and Salvora and the promontory of La Toja. To the west you can see the long sandy beaches of Ladeira and Río Sierra. Further east are the fishing villages of Boiros and Rianjo. At the latter are a

The harbour at Combarro.

number of old mansions and the 15th-century church of Santa Columba with a Baroque tower and a 16th-century portal.

The road continues to Padrón, a town dating from Roman times and where St James's body is reputed to have been brought from Palestine by boat. There is an interesting 18th-century *ayuntamiento* and nearby the Palacio de Alonso Peña Montenegro of the same period. The 11th-century church of Santa María a Dina was rebuilt in the 18th century but retains a 12th-century portal and a 16th-century tower. The 17th-century Dominican convent of Carmen contains some fine 18th-century sculptures.

The route continues south-west along the C 550, following the south side of the *ría* to Villagarcía de Arosa, a fishing port and harbour since Roman times with several lovely palaces. The 16th-century Pazo of Rubianes has a fine portal; the early 18th-century Pazo Vista Alegre is Baroque in style; and the Palacio del Rial has a chapel and two small towers.

Further south a road leads across a causeway to the pine-covered Isla de Arosa, known locally for its excellent octopus fishing. Octopus is a very popular dish in Galicia. There are even special *pulperias* where it is served. A few kms beyond is Cambados.

The Parador Nacional El Albariño is situated on the seafront in the town of Cambados. Facing it is a broad palm tree-lined promenade. A modern building constructed from huge blocks of granite in traditional *pazo* style on the site of an original building belonging to the Bazán family, the centre is an attractive courtyard with a fountain. The Parador is named after the local wine, Albariño, a dry fruity white slightly *pétillant* wine made from vines introduced from the Rhineland in the 12th century by Benedictine monks. The restaurant is a large L-shaped room with a lofty wooden-beamed ceiling and decorated with large stone pillars.

Regional dishes on the menu are focused strongly upon seafood. Crema de Cangrejos is a rich creamy bisque made from crayfish. Rodaballo con Almejas is turbo cooked in light creamy sauce with clams. Lenguado al Albariño is fillets of sole cooked in a sauce of dry white wine, cream and mushrooms. The Parador has its own label Albariño wine and Ribeiro Pazo is a local light red wine.

The Parador is only a few minutes' walk from the Plaza Fefiñanes, the centre of Cambados. This wide square is bordered by beautiful buildings – the 17th-century Palacio de Fefiñanes, which dominates one side, with its unusual corner balconies, coats of arms and an ornamental bridge; the Palacio de Montesacro and the Palacio de Figueroa. The 16th-century Roman-

The Plaza Fefiñanes at Cambados.

esque church of Santa Marina de Ozo is now little more than an atmospheric ruin. Close to the sea is the 12th-century tower of San Saturnino.

PONTEVEDRA

THE NEXT STAGE of the tour is south-east to the Parador at Pontevedra: being only 25km away it can be considered as an alternative base to Cambados if preferred.

The route between the two towns follows the coastline around the headland to the island of La Toja, where there is a resort with thermal springs known to the Romans. It is also a centre for excellent shellfish. Beyond is a quiet and undeveloped part of the coastline where fishing and farming are the main activities. Here fields of vegetables and vineyards extend almost down to the water's edge. There are beautiful white sand beaches along this part of the coast, especially the Playa Bascuas and Playa de la Lanzada. Near Lanzada are castle ruins and a small 12th-century church, NS (Nuestra Señora) de la Lanzada. The road continues to Portonovo, a busy fishing town with a lively and colourful harbour. Nearby, at Armenteira, is the 12th-century Cistercian Abbey of Santa María.

Further towards Pontevedra is the curious fishing village of Combarro. Built on a huge rock beside the sea, the streets are simply narrow stone pathways. The old houses all have ancient stone *hórreos*, set along the water's edge. Nearby at Poyo a 16th-century monastery occupied by Mercedarian monks has a fine cloister with a lovely fountain.

The Parador Nacional Casa del Barón is on the western edge of the city, a short distance from its centre in the Pazo de Maceda, which was built on the site of a Roman villa. Although it dates from the 16th century it was periodically reconstructed and its present form is essentially 18th century. It has had a variety of uses, ranging from a school to a masonic lodge and an old people's home. Its quite severe classical façade leads into a hall with a magnificent Baroque stone staircase leading to the bedrooms. An old Galician kitchen has been preserved.

Galician cuisine is well represented on the menu. I chose Merluza a la Gallega, hake cutlets cooked in a casserole with potatoes, onions and paprika. Tortilla de Cigalas is an omelette filled with crayfish. Empañada Gallega is a pie filled with pork, chorizo, onions, peppers and tomatoes. For desert Filoas de Manzana are a local speciality – pancakes filled with apple purée. I had a bottle of Atalaya de Monterrey, a slightly *pétillant* dry white wine from the region.

The provincial capital of Pontevedra, believed to have been founded by the Greeks, is set at the head of the Ría de Pontevedra and has a busy harbour, numerous old houses and mansions, and streets and small squares of considerable atmosphere and character. The Plaza de Leña has an ancient stone calvery and is surrounded by picturesque arcaded houses with glazed balconies. The regional museum is situated here in two 18th-century mansions. The Plaza de la Herrería contains an ornate 18th-century fountain and the Plaza de Tuero has a fine Baroque mansion. The 16th-century church of Santa María la Mayor, built on the site of an earlier Romanesque church, has a beautifully sculptured facade and the interior is also richly decorated. The 18th-century Baroque church of La Peregrina is an unusual building with a curved façade flanked by two tall towers. Adjacent is the church of San Francisco with a 14th-century apse.

BAYONA

THE ROUTE SOUTH to the Parador at Bayona – a direct distance of 54km – follows the C 550 along the southern shore of the Ría de Pontevedra. Beyond Marín, the headquarters of the Naval Academy and a large port, are a sequence of superb beaches, Playa de Lapamán, Portocelo, Mogor Aguete and Loira. A road climbs the Montes de Morrazo to a viewpoint with sweeping views of the Pontevedra and Vigo *rías* and continues to Bueu, where there is a maritime museum, and then round the headland to Cangas and Moaña. The road passes under the Autopista at the point where it crosses the *ría*. There are some very fine views from the bridge of the Ría de Vigo and the city. The C 550 however continues along the *ría* to its head where it joins the N 550. Here the route leads south to Redondela where the C 550 continues around the southern shore of the *ría* to Vigo. You will see dozens of large platforms moored in the *rías*, these are for the culture of mussels.

Vigo is a busy modern city, an important port and the centre of the sardine fishing industry. On the hill above are two 10th-century castles. In the old part of town is an 18th-century collegiate church and in the Plaza Almeida are some old mansions. The road follows the coastline closely beyond the fishing villages of Bouzas and Panjón to Bayona.

The Parador Nacional Conde de Gondomar is situated on an island-like rocky promontory surrounded by fortifications. It has been defended against the Romans, and after them the Visigoths and the Moors held the stronghold. In 1585 Francis Drake and his fleet were successfully repelled and pirates used it as a base for attacks on the merchant ships of the British and Dutch in the 18th century. One of three ships which sailed with Columbus sheltered here on its return, bringing the first news of his discovery. Massive cannons still testify to its torrid past.

The Parador is in an enviable setting. The small peninsula, known as Monte Real, is now a large park which surrounds the building and the battlements create a scenic walk from where you can watch the

Ancient hórreos in the village of Barcia.

local fishing fleet plying the waters below. Beyond are far-reaching views of the Cies islands and the coastline towards Portugal and Vigo.

The Parador is a modern building constructed from massive blocks of granite in the style of a *pazo*, but on a massive scale. Inside there is a cavernous entrance hall and a magnificent stone staircase which leads to the public rooms and the bedrooms which are contained in extensive wings. The numerous lounges and salons are furnished with regional antiques and decorated with tapestries and heraldic banners. It is hard to believe that the building dates only from 1966.

The seafood in the restaurant is superb. I chose Parrillada de Pescado Rías Bajas, a magnificent dish of locally caught fish which included steaks of tuna, halibut, hake and salmon with sea bream, red mullet and prawns. It would have fed four people with ease. Cocochas en Cazuela con Almejas are the succulent slivers of meat from the throat of hake cooked in a sauce with clams. Local wines on the list included Ribiera Pazo and Albariño de Chavas.

In the old part of the town is a Romanesque collegiate church and a number of old mansions. Nearby at Gondomar is the beautiful 18th-century palace of the counts of Gondomar.

TUY

THE FINAL STAGE of this tour is south to the Parador at Tuy, a direct distance of 51km. The C 550 follows the coastline to Oya, where there is a Romanesque monastery, founded in the 12th century by Alfonso VII,

with a lovely 16th-century cloister. A small road climbs up into the mountains with stunning views of the monastery and the coastline. Wild horses are left to roam free among the heathland and eucalyptus trees. The region is famous for the Curros, exciting annual round-ups which take place at the nearby villages of Mougas, La Volga and Torroña in early summer.

The coast road continues to La Guardia, a small fishing town at the mouth of the Río Miño. A picturesque cluster of pastel-coloured houses are grouped around the colourful harbour. There are some good fish restaurants here. Above the town is Monte Santa Tecla from where there are superb views of the river and the Portuguese countryside beyond. Nearby, on the slopes, there is a Celtic settlements, founded *c.* 500 BC. The village contains the remains of nearly 1,000 circular houses of rough stone, and many of the finds have been preserved in a small museum. The route continues along the C 550 following the north bank of the river to Tuy.

The Parador Nacional San Telmo is situated just outside the city to the south. It overlooks the Miño river and there are fine views of Tuy with its ancient cathedral perched above the houses. The Parador is a modern building, constructed of solid blocks of granite and decorated in traditional *pazo* style.

Regional dishes on the menu included Empanada de Bacalao, a shallow pie made with a bread-like pastry and filled with dried salt cod cooked with onions and tomatoes. Fabada is a stew of white beans, cooked in a rich sauce with onions, salt pork, chorizo and pieces of meat and flavoured with paprika and garlic. From the local wines on the list I chose a bottle of Vina Costeira, a dry white wine from Ribadavia.

The city of Tuy was the seat of the kingdom of Galicia during the period of the Visigoths. It was later destroyed by the Moors and has, on several occasions, been taken by the Portuguese. The cathedral was begun in 1120 and not completed until the end of the 13th century. Its exterior resembles a fortress with battlements and towers. The main portal, dating from the 15th century, is approached by a broad flight of stone steps and is richly decorated with numerous sculptures and carvings. There is a fine 13th-century cloister with twin arches and columns with intricately carved capitals. The 14th-century church of Santo Domingo, extended in the 18th century, has an interesting Gothic cloister. The 10th-century Romanesque church of San Bartolomé, has an ancient calvary.

From Tuy an excursion can be made along the lovely valley of the Miño and into the Sierra del Suido. A few kms north of Tuy along the N 550 a road leads east

The Parador at Bayona.

The river Miño seen from the Parador at Tuy.

towards Caldelas, where there is a small spa, to Salva-tierra de Miño, the capital of the wine-growing region of Condado. The road climbs along the side of the valley through vineyards with far-reaching views over the river to Portugal, the scenery becoming increasing-ly impressive as you travel further east. At Filguiera a small road winds up out of the valley through densely wooded hillsides. Near the summit is a quite spectacu-lar viewpoint of the silvery river snaking through the deep valley far below. At La Cañiza the main road, the N 120, is joined.

You can make a short detour eastwards to Ribadavia, a charmingly situated old town on the north bank of the Miño, and the capital of the wine-growing region of Ribeiro. It is threaded by picturesque streets and there is an attractive arcaded square and a castle which belonged to the counts of Ribadavia. The 12th-century church of Santiago has a beautiful portal and a rose window in the main façade. The 13th-century convent church of Santo Domingo is also finely decorated with beautiful Gothic windows in the apse.

Stone *hórreos* are next to almost every home. Near the turning to Ribadavia a road leads north for approx-imately 1km to the primitive village of Barcia. Built on a rock its small houses of rough grey stone are outnum-bered by ancient, picturesque *hórreos*.

A few kms beyond La Cañiza, a quiet country road leads north-west towards Ponte Caldelas. The road climbs high into the mountains with splendid views of the wild landscape dotted with Galician farmhouses and villages, then descends into a rocky valley filled with heather, broom and eucalyptus trees, to Ponte Caldelas. A road leads west to Sotomayor where there is an impressive square turreted castle of grey granite on a hillside overlooking a wide green valley. The road now joins the N 550 and Tuy is about 35km to the south

The nearest alternative Parador to Tuy is at Verín, 178km (page 72).

A farm near Pineiro in the Sierra del Suido.

*T*OUR 3 *Explores the inland region of the north of Spain and runs more or less parallel to the coast. Provides an interesting route for those returning from Northern Portugal or Galicia towards the French border, the car ferry port of Santander or the airport of Bilbao. It also makes a complete circuit when combined with Tour No 1 (page 14). The route crosses the provinces of Lugo, León, Palencia and Cantabria with a broad spectrum of landscape and architecture. The itinerary includes two unique hotels (one among the most beautiful in Europe) mountain ranges of outstanding beauty and villages barely changed since the Middle Ages. It follows part of the Camino de Santiago, or the Way of St James, the name given to the pilgrim route to Santiago de Compostela.*

—TOUR 3—
MICHELIN MAP NO. 441

Villalba

Fuente Dé
LEÓN

Villafranca   Cervera de
del Bierzo   Pisuergo

VILLALBA
VILLAFRANCA DEL BIERZO
LEÓN – CERVERA DE
PISUERGA – FUENTE DÉ

VILLALBA

THE TOUR STARTS in the small town of Villalba in Galicia. It can be reached by taking, first, the N 6 from La Coruña and then the N 634 from Baamonde. The nearest airport is at Santiago de Compostela.

Parador Nacional Condes de Villalba is quite special. Situated close to the small church square, the building – an octagonal tower – is all that remains of the fortress of Los Andrade. Little is known of its history or when it was built. What makes the Parador particularly unusual is that it has just six bedrooms, two on each of three floors and served by a lift. The ground-floor houses a restaurant and the first floor contains the lounge and reception, entered across a drawbridge. It is an enchanting place to stay and the atmosphere is intimate and friendly. If you ask for the key you can go onto the roof and walk round the ramparts (it takes about 45 seconds) and look over the rooftops to the rolling green countryside beyond.

The menu contains a good selection of Galician dishes. Empanada de Raxo is Galician pork pie and Huevos con Zorza is fried eggs with a local sausage made from pork. I had Pollo con Piñones, a delicious combination of pieces of chicken, pine nuts, tomatoes, peppers and onions. The town is famous for its Queso de San Simón, a firm creamy cheese lightly smoked and slightly aeriated. It is made in a pear shape with a golden rind. A sweet to try is Roscón de Villalba, an almond-flavoured cake.

VILLAFRANCA DEL BIERZO

TRAVELLING SOUTH-EAST to the Parador at Villafranca del Bierzo, if you take the C 641 from Villalba to Rábade you will pass through some of the quiet rural country-side which typifies this region and will also avoid the main road, the N 6. This however is joined at the village of Rábade where the route continues to Lugo, an atmospheric old city, encircled by imposing and extremely well-preserved 2nd-century Roman walls. They are nearly 1½ miles in circumference, 50ft high and 15ft thick. The walls are punctuated by over 50 towers and numerous gateways.

The old part of the town, centred around the lovely 18th-century cathedral of Santa María, is a warren of narrow streets, many pedestrianised, small squares, numerous fascinating shops, restaurants and small bars. The interior of the cathedral is beautiful with magnificent carved choir stalls and a spectacular retablo with gilded statues, ornate columns and an enormous silver sunrise-like ornament like a monumental Victorian Christmas-tree decoration. Close by is the 16th-century church of San Francisco with its beautiful cloister and housing the provincial museum. In an adjacent small square is the tiny 14th-century chapel of Santo Domingo.

From Lugo the route continues along the N 6 south east towards Villafranca del Bierzo. At first the road runs straight through fairly flat countryside, but from Baralia there are steep wooded hillsides and deep green valleys with lovely views from the Puerto de Árbol of big, rounded rolling hills patterned by woods and fields of wheat and vegetables. At Becereá there are the remains of the 12th-century monastery of Santa María. A short distance beyond at Doncas the ruins of a castle can be seen down in the valley.

The road climbs steadily upwards to the Puerto de Piedrafita. From here a small detour can be made along the Camino de Santiago to the delightful small pre-Romanesque church of Cebrero. Nearby are a number of *pallazos*, small thatched huts built of rough grey stone, which date back over 2000 years. One has been made into a small museum with ancient furniture and artefacts used to create an evocative interior.

About 20km further along the N 6, at the small village of Ambasmestas, a fascinating excursion can be made into the Sierra de Ancares. The road, signposted to Balboa, climbs alongside a sheltered green valley in which you can see the ruins of the castle of Balboa on a knoll above the village.

The scenery becomes incredibly impressive as the road ascends to the pass of El Portello. The top of the steep slopes are covered with broom and gorse, a blaze

The Templar castle in Ponferrada.

of yellow in the early summer. The lower slopes however are cultivated with small fields of wheat and vegetables. At Doiras there is a well-preserved castle in a lovely setting on the hillside, overlooking a peaceful wooded valley through which a small river runs.

From Doiras the road continues to climb steadily as the mountains become steeper. It's hard to believe that scenery like this exists such a short distance from the main road. Beyond the small village of Degrada the landscape is magnificent. Looking back along the valley you have climbed you see ridge after ridge fading into the distant haze.

The tarmac road continues to the village of Donís. You can see the small cluster of buildings on the opposite hillside. Although it seems close – less than half a mile as the crow flies – the hillsides are so steep and indented that it takes a good half hour to negotiate the winding road, but the views here are incredible. You can see a number of tiny villages perched far away on the other side of the steep wooded mountains. Although very steep the slopes are thickly wooded with huge chestnut and oak trees. The hedgerows are deep and lush with enormous bushes of brilliant yellow broom, bracken, long grass and wild flowers. Dotted between are small meadows where haymaking takes place at a dizzy angle. You will need to return to the main road by the same route. The distance from Ambasmestas to Donís and back is about 100km and will take you at least three hours.

If you have lingered in Lugo, or simply wish to spend more time in the Sierra de Ancares, you may prefer to make a separate excursion on the following day. The Parador at Villafranca del Bierzo is only about 20km from Ambasmestas.

The town of Villafranca was an important staging post on the pilgrimage route to Santiago and, as a result, has several lovely churches. The 12th-century Romanesque church of Santiago gave indulgences to pilgrims. The old or infirm who were not able to continue their journey to Santiago were allowed to pass through the door here as if they had completed their pilgrimage. The 13th-century convent of San Francisco has a Romanesque portal and a vaulted Mudéjar nave. The 17th-century Jesuit church of San Nicolás has an imposing façade and close by is the massive fortified palace of the Marqueses of Villafranca. Other churches worth seeing are the Colegiata de Santa María and the Convento de la Anunciana.

The Parador Nacional Villafranca del Bierzo is close to the main road on the edge of the town, only a short walk to the centre of the old town. It is a modern two-storey building with spacious bedrooms and bright airy public rooms.

The restaurant is a long room with attractive small alcoves created by brickwork screens. The cuisine is essentially that of Castile but with Galician influences.

Empanada Berciana, for example, is a pie filled with meat and mixed vegetables. Botillo con Chorizo y Verduras is a local pork sausage and chorizo cooked with vegetables, and Truchas Fritas con Unto y Pimientos is trout fried in lard with green peppers. The Bierzo is wine-making country and the wine list at the Parador has a good selection of the local product. I had an excellent bottle of a dry white with a suggestion of spice from the vineyards of Palacio de Arganza.

A small excursion to the south of Villafranca can be made through the rolling vine-covered hills of the Bierzo countryside to Corullón. Here there are two charming small Romanesque churches, San Esteban and San Miguel. There is also a 14th-century castle which belonged to the Marquesses de Villafranca. Just to the east of Villafranca is the village of Pieros with the remains of a fortress. A few kms beyond is Cacabelos with a 10th-century monastery, Romanesque church and archaeological museum.

LEÓN

FROM VILLAFRANCA the route continues along the N 6 to Ponferrada. Though initially it appears ugly and industrialised, once you penetrate the grime and gloom it is a really atmospheric old town. In its centre is a massive, magnificent, 12th-century fortress built by the Knights Templars to protect the pilgrim route. There is also the 16th-century church of NS de la Encina and the 17th-century church of San Andrés. Close to the castle is an attractive arcaded *plaza mayor* overlooked by a 17th-century *ayuntamiento* with a beautiful Baroque façade. On the outskirts of the town is the Mozarabic church of Santo Tomás de las Ollas.

A memorable excursion can be made from Ponferrada to the village of Peñalba de Santiago. A small road, the LE 161 crosses the Río Sil to San Esteban de Val, continues through the beautiful Val de Silencio (Valley of Silence), cutting its way deep into the mountains and climbing higher and higher until, tucked under the stark rugged peak of Monte Aguiana, you suddenly come upon the enchanting village of Peñalba.

Time has stood still here. Centuries-old rough stone cottages with crude wooden balconies and grey slate roofs are grouped around an exquisite small Mozarabic church. On the hillsides surrounding the village are small meadows and cherry orchards. Millions of bees buzz around the primitive hives dotted under the trees.

From Ponferrada to León you may continue along the N 6 via Bembibre and Astorga or take the quieter and more scenic route through the Cantabrian mountains.

At Bembibre there is the 12th-century Romanesque church of San Pedro and a castle which belonged to the Dukes of Frías. In Astorga is the 11th-century Cathe-

The façade of the Hotel San Marcos in León.

dral of Santa María, several churches of note and the Episcopal Palace built of granite by the Catalonian architect Gaudí in a blend of Art Nouveau, Gothic and Moorish styles. It houses the Museo de los Caminos, the museum of the pilgrim route. There is also a fine 17th-century *ayuntamiento* and the remains of Roman walls.

The alternative route takes the C 631 to the north a few kms along the N 6 after leaving Ponferrada. After traversing a coalmining valley, beyond Palacios de Sil the landscape becomes more attractive. The road passes through a deep wooded valley dotted with small meadows and climbs towards the mountains. Beyond Piedrafita de Baba the route follows a high mountain valley along the course of the beautiful Río Luna. The village of San Emiliano is in a lovely setting surrounded by open meadows and impressive mountain peaks. The road follows the river to the Embalse de los Barrios de Luna. The Autopista A 66 crosses over this by an elegantly futuristic suspension bridge. The lake is surrounded by dramatic rugged mountains,

there are small beaches and facilities for water sports. The road then descends to La Magdalena and continues across flat open countryside to León.

León, a spacious, appealing city with broad straight avenues shaded by trees and elegant squares, is built beside the broad Río Bernesga on the northern edge of the Castilian plain. It is the capital of the province with Roman origins.

Of the many interesting buildings three are outstanding. The Gothic Cathedral de Santa de Regla took over 100 years from its inception to completion in the early 14th century. It has an imposing west façade and above the portico is an enormous rose window; on each side two massive towers rise to over 200ft. The south façade is almost as impressive with a beautiful rose window above the portal. The exterior is richly decorated. It is however the 20,000 sq ft of stained-glass windows for which the cathedral is most famed. They are unusual in Spain for the richness and intensity of their colour whose effect within the subdued interior is extremely powerful.

The 10th-century Collegiata de San Isidoro, most of whose present structure is 12th-century contains fine capitals intricately decorated by carvings of strange animals, fierce warriors and wreaths of flowers. Adja-

cent is the Panteon de los Reyes where over 40 of the early kings and noblemen of Castile and León are buried. The walls of the vaults are covered by well-preserved 12th-century Roman frescoes. The treasury and library contain a priceless collection of old manuscripts and religious art.

The third remarkable building in León is the Convento de San Marcos, built in the 16th century by King Ferdinand. The site was originally an hospice, founded by the Knights of Santiago in the 12th century. It is now the Hotel San Marcos, part of the Parador Nacional network. It has had a variety of strange uses in its past, including a barracks and a veterinary college.

When you arrive it is hard to believe that you will be staying here. Extending along the enormous length of

the building is the majestic Plateresque façade, the intricacy of whose carving is dazzlingly complex. It faces a wide square with a large garden in the centre and the Río Bernesga flows past its westerly walls. The interior has a monumental stone staircase and beautiful 16th-century cloisters. The rooms brim with beautiful antiques. In the adjacent church of San Marcos is the provincial museum with a fascinating collection of relics.

The restaurant is beside the river. Leonese specialities included Sopa Leonesa, a light soup flavoured with a most unusual combination of trout, garlic and paprika and thickened with small pieces of bread. Cecina de Babja en Lascas is a local smoked dried beef, served in thin slices. The wine list included a good selection of

massive keep with ruined battlements and a moat.

The route continues along the L 523 northwards to Mansilla de los Mulas. It has extensive 12th-century fortified walls, and the 14th-century church of San Martín, a criss-cross of narrow arcaded streets and several small squares surrounded by ancient galleried houses.

Following the N 601 back towards León for about 1km, a small road to the right leads to the village of San Miguel de Escalada. Just beyond, in an isolated setting surrounded by low wheat-covered hills, is a Mozarabic monastery, an exquisite building whose miniature tower was added in the 13th century. The south face of the building is decorated by 12 beautiful horseshoe-shaped arches of Moorish design. At Gradefes there is the 12th-century monastery of Santa María.

Follow the LE 231 to Almanza and the L 232 and C 626 to Guardo which has some old houses and a 16th-century church; continue along the C 615 to the north for a few kms north to Velilla de Río Carrión, where the P 210 follows a broad valley and climbs a mountainside covered in dense pine forest to the side of the Embalse de Compuerto.

Follow the side of the lake to Camporredondo de Alba and continue to the shores of another lake. The mountains which surround these lakes are wild and heath-covered, the countryside bleak and sparsely populated, but beyond the village of Trollo the landscape becomes expansive and the mountains assume a rugged grandeur.

The village of Santibañez is a picturesque cluster of old stone houses with grey slate roofs. I passed through during haymaking when ancient carts with crude wooden wheels piled high with hay lined the streets. A short distance beyond the road descends into a wide valley with meadows and trees lining the river. The road skirts the shores of a peaceful reed-fringed lake encircled by grassy banks.

The Parador Nacional Fuentes Carrionas, a few kms to the west of Cervera de Pisuerga on a hillside overlooking this lake, is named after the source of the Río Carrión. It commands magnificent views over the lake and mountains to the south and over the wooded mountains of the Fuente Carrionas to the north. Beyond you can see the foothills and distant peaks of the Picos de Europa.

The Parador is a large, modern 5-storey building with an interior which creates the ambience of a hunting lodge. The spacious bedrooms have large balconies with magnificent views. So too does the large terrace which adjoins the restaurant.

The bar and restaurant, decorated with dark wood

Leonese and Bierzo wines as well as some from neighbouring Rueda.

CERVERA DE PISUERGA

FOR THE JOURNEY TO THE NEXT PARADOR at Cervera de Pisuerga I suggest a slight detour to the south of León by following the main road, the N 630, south to Villa-mañán. It is a flat, straight road crossing the Castilian plain with endless wheatfields stretching away towards the distant horizon.

At Villamañán the C 621 branches eastwards to the town of Valencia de Don Juan where you will find an impressive 14th-century castle in the town centre. It has a group of elegant slender towers surrounding a

The castillo of Valencia de Don Juan.

The church of San Salvador de Cantamuda.

panelling and illuminated by big brass chandeliers, evoke a warm, intimate atmosphere. The menu included Cangrejos de Río Cerverana, locally caught crayfish. Chanfaina is a strongly flavoured regional sausage based on lambs blood and tripe. Freshly caught river trout is also an excellent menu choice. For dessert I had Queso de Burgos con Membrillo, a soft, bland cheese with the texture of stiff custard and served with a slice of tangy quince jelly – a delicious combination. My wine choice was Viña Mayor, a crisp dry rose from Tudela de Duero. Local wines include reds from Paramilla and Villamuriel and white from Paredes de Nava.

FUENTE DÉ

THE FIRST PART OF THE JOURNEY, north-west to the Parador at Fuente Dé, is to Cervera de Pisuerga, about 3km to the east of the Parador. Set at the foot of the mountains, it has a 16th-century fortified church, Santa María del Castillo.

Continuing northwards along the C 627 towards the Picos de Europa, the road climbs out of the valley on to mountainsides covered with small trees and meadows and shortly crosses the Embalse de Requejada. Beyond is a small shallow valley bordered by wooded hills.

There are numerous small Romanesque churches in this region. That of San Salvador de Cantamuda, with triple bell towers, is particularly attractive. The road climbs gently through meadows, overlooked by steep mountainsides, to the Puerto de Piedrasluengas. From the 4,000ft summit is a *mirador* with breaktaking views across a deep valley to the magnificent Picos de Europa. The bare peaks are formed from a silvery-grey rock, the tips of which are still snow-covered in the summer months. It's one of the best viewpoints from which to capture your first glimpse of this beautiful mountain range.

From the top of the pass there is a long sweeping descent through woods and meadows to the valley floor. You pass a succession of small mountain villages usually with no more than a dozen old houses and a small church. A small detour to the west to Piasca can be made just before reaching the village of Cabezón de Liébana, where an attractive Romanesque church, Santa María la Real has some outstanding sculptures

decorating its exterior. The building was originally a Benedictine monastery founded in the 10th century. The road to the church provides some fine views of the valley and of the pass which you have just descended.

Soon you will reach the lively town of Potes, one of the main centres from which to explore the Picos de Europa, and quite delightful with its old streets and houses, two lovely churches and an imposing 15th-century fortress, the Torre de Infantado. There are interesting shops, numerous small bars and restaurants, and a fascinating country market on Mondays when the streets and small squares are filled with stalls selling every kind of produce: mountain hams, cheeses, fruit and vegetables, kitchenware and even agricultural implements like ploughs.

A few kms from Potes, along the Río Deva valley, is the 8th-century Monasterio de Santo Toribio de Liébana, one of the oldest in Spain. Although much expanded and altered it still retains some notable elements of its Romanesque and Gothic periods and is impressively sited, high on the mountainside with views over the green wooded valley.

The road continues along the valley, climbing higher towards the towering peaks. Woods and meadows border the small river which tumbles over rocks and

The Mirador above the Parador at Fuente Dé.

weaves between grassy banks overhung with trees. There are a number of pretty villages, such as Camaleño and Espinama line the valley. Their ancient stone houses are roofed with rust-brown tiles and decorated with wooden balconies. The villages echo to the tinkling of cow bells and chicken scratch around the doorways. Mogrovejo, high up on the mountainside, is especially picturesque and completely unspoilt.

The Parador Nacional Río Deva is situated at the head of the valley in Fuente Dé. Behind and around the Parador a spectacular wall of rock rises sheer for 1,000m. The Parador is a large low building with several wings. The bedrooms all have charming glazed balconies reminiscent of the houses in Galicia.

The menu included a local speciality called El Cocido labaniego de Potes, a stew of mixed vegetables with pork, veal and *chorizo*. A local cheese to try is that of Cabrales, a village on the other side of the mountain range – a strong, tangy blue cheese with a rich creamy texture. The local wine, Chacoli – not on the Parador's list when I visited – is a dry white wine made from grapes grown high on the mountain slopes close to the snow line. *Sidra* (cider), is an interesting and popular alternative to wine in this region and there are special *sidrerias* where you can drink it. It is a deep yellow colour, often slightly cloudy, very dry and strongly alcoholic.

About 100m from the Parador is a ski lift where a cable-car whisks you in a matter of minutes across a 750m chasm to the top of the mountain. Here there is a dramatic landscape of rugged rocks and peaks with pockets of snow which remain throughout the summer and stunning views over the valley with the Parador below appearing like a doll's house.

A number of excursions can be made into the Picos de Europa using the Parador as a base, though – as is the nature of mountain country – these will involve going over some of the same routes several times. As an alternative you could stay at other locations for one or two nights. Cangas de Onís and Panes are both ideal places and there are many small hotels and *fondas* (taverns) in other villages along the valleys.

Old houses near Potes.

The first route is via the S 240 from Potes towards Riaño along the Val de Liébano, a steep V-shaped valley with wooded slopes and overlooked by high mountain peaks. From the village of Bores the road climbs the side of the valley in a series of steep winding curves to the Puerto de San Glorio. It is very, very beautiful: intensely green and lush, the roadsides are banked with long grasses, bushes of broom and gorse and all manner of wild flowers. At the top of the pass there is a small road leading to the Mirador de Llesba. Here brown bears, wolves and chamois still roam free, and there is a memorable view of the summits of the Picos de Europa.

The road then descends gradually to Portilla de la Reina, set in a narrow rocky valley, and continues through remote and barren countryside alongside the fast-flowing Río Yuso to Riaño. Here you turn to the north along the C 637 to the Puerto del Pantón.

At this point you have two choices: either to continue along the C 6312 to Cangas de Onís or to turn westwards on to the LE 244 through the Val de Valdeón, which will enable you to return to the Parador at Fuente Dé, completing a comfortable day's drive. The former route however will involve a long day's drive to complete the circuit with little time for the detours de-

The Lago de Enol near Covadonga.

scribed later. To explore this route fully it would be preferable to arrange to stay at least one night en route, at Cangas de Onís, for example.

From the Puerto de Panton the road towards Posada de Valdeón passes through a shallow valley through which a small river runs. Soon the road rises gently to crest the summit of the Puerto de Ponferrada above an enormous deep-green valley surrounded by towering silvery-grey peaks.

The road descends into the valley to Posada de Valdeón a delightful small mountain village, and a small road leads northwards to the village of Cardiñanes. Just beyond, the Mirador de Tombes overlooks a deep narrow valley from which sheer mountainsides rise up at a dizzy angle.

The route continues as a single-track tarmac road into an increasingly narrow valley. It is an idyllic place with a river splashing over boulders and bordered by banks of springy green turf. The valley soon becomes a gorge of quite staggering beauty. There is just room for the road and the river to wind sinuously through.

The road ends at the village of Caín, set in a glen overlooking tree-shaded meadows. The river flows through and finally disappears into the gorge of Cares. It is possible to walk through the gorge to Poncebos on the other side of the mountain. It is, by all accounts, an incredible walk but motorists are obliged to return to Posada de Valdeón.

From here a small road leads to the village of Santa María de Valdeón, set in a peaceful valley bordered by gentle hillsides. The road climbs high along the side of the valley to the Puerto de Pondetrave. Here heathland, with bushes of broom and gorse and clumps of wild thyme, is scattered with small trees. The road descends through a remote rocky valley back to Portilla de la Reina from where you can return to Potes and Fuente Dé.

The alternative route from the Puerto de Pontón leads through the Desfiladero de los Beyos, a deep narrow gorge through which the road winds tortuously following the river course. Cangas de Onís is set in a wide fertile valley beside the Río Sella. The residence of the Asturian kings in the 8th century, it is a quite large, lively resort-like town with a picturesque 13th-century bridge and the Hermitage of Santa Cruz, founded in the 8th century on the site of a Celtic megalith.

The route turns eastwards along the C 6312. After 4km a road to the right leads along a lovely valley to Covadonga, famous as the place where the Spanish, led by King Pelayo in 718, first succeeded in resisting the Moorish occupation. A cave in the rocky hillside above the town contains his tomb. Nearby is the Basilica de NS de las Batallas, a large imposing building in pinkish-beige stone with tall twin spires.

Beyond Covadonga a small road continues higher into the mountains to a region of outstanding beauty. Here the silvery-grey rocks are carpeted with springy green turf and surrounded by towering mountain peaks, with expansive views of the valley from the road. It continues to the beautiful lakes of Ercina and Ernol – a picnic lunch here would complete a memorable day.

The route continues eastwards along the C 6312 through a broad fertile valley. It climbs steadily to the Alto de Ortiguero from where there are sweeping views down into the Val de Cabrales, famed for its tangy blue cheese. At the village of Arenas de Cabrales you can make another detour into the mountains.

A small road follows the Río Cares to Poncebos through a steep rocky valley and climbs a wooded valley alongside a small river to Tielve. It is set at the opening of an enormous deep valley overlooked by towering mountains. The road climbs higher and higher along the mountainside and eventually opens out to reveal a breathtaking panorama. The steep slopes are covered with flower-strewn meadows and dotted with tiny red-roofed farmhouses. The road winds higher still to the mountain village of Sotres, an excellent base for walking. Way below, like an aerial photograph, is the village of Bulnes. It cannot be reached by car, although it appeared that a road was under construction.

On returning to Arenas de Cabrales the route continues eastwards to Panes following the Río Deva, a fast-flowing river which changes from turquoise to ice-blue, green and silver as it crashes over boulders and swirls in deep pools.

Panes is set beside the river in a broad fertile valley ringed by mountains. From here the route leads south to Potes along the N 621 passing through the Desfiladero de la Hermida, a steep rocky gorge carved by the Río Deva and bordered by trees which overhang the water. Just off this road, at Liébena, is the small Mozarabic church of Santa María with its pretty exterior gallery decorated with Moorish arches. The road continues to Potes completing the circuit.

The nearest alternative Parador to Fuente Dé is at Santillana del Mar, 110km (page 14).

The Naranjo de Bulnes seen from Sotres in the Picos de Europa.

OUR 4 Explores the north-east corner of Spain in the provinces of Guipúzcoa, Álava and La Rioja, starting just across the border from France on the Basque coast and then turning inland, first to the foothills of the Pyrenees and then to the plain of Álava and the valley of the river Ebro. Much of this tour is in the Basque region and place-names are written both as the familiar Spanish and in the regional language of Euskera which I have also included in brackets. Within a relatively small area there is a surprising variety of landscape, architecture and industry.

—TOUR 4—
MICHELIN MAP NO. 42
Fuentarrabía

SAN SEBASTIAN

Santo
Domingo de la   Argómaniz
Calzada

BURGOS

FUENTERRABÍA
ARGÓMANIZ
SANTO DOMINGO
DE LA CALZADA

FUENTERRABÍA

FUENTERRABÍA (Hondarribia) is a small town on the estuary of the river Bidasoa which separates France from Spain. The border post is indeed only a short drive away and the French town of Hendaye can be seen clearly from the charming old hilltop town of Fuenterrabía. Charming narrow cobbled streets wind up to the highest part of the town where the church of NS de la Asunción and the Palace of Carlos V are situated.

The streets are lined with lovely old houses, decorated with pretty painted balconies overflowing with flowers. In the lower part of the town is a traffic-free street with café tables scattered under plane trees. On a summer evening it is a place to relax with a drink or take a stroll, and has more of the feel of a Mediterranean than an Atlantic town. To the west is a wide, curving sandy beach and the river mouth is dotted with colourful fishing and pleasure boats.

Parador Nacional El Emperador is situated in the Palace of Carlos V and is one of the most evocative of all the paradors. Placed next to the church, and overlooking a delightful small square, its exterior is rather forbidding, like a huge cube of blackened grey stone. Only the entrance to the Parador and a few small windows relieve the façade. Inside, however, it is both imposing and welcoming. Pools of yellow light from huge lamps on brackets high on the castle walls manage to make the cavernous interior seem quite intimate – but it is not hard to imagine what it must have been like to have lived there in the 11th century from when the castle dates. The walls are so thick that the bedroom windows seem more like small tunnels and the restaurant, with its flagstone floor, tapestries and heraldic flags, has an authentic medieval atmosphere. The Parador only has twelve rooms so it is important to make an advanced reservation to avoid disappointment as it is, understandably, a popular place to stay.

Gastronomically the region has much to offer – Basque cuisine is considered by many to be among the best in Spain. One unusual dish which is a speciality of the area is Kokotxas – the jowls of hake which are poached in a light sauce of olive oil and lemon juice flavoured with garlic and fresh mixed green herbs. The subtle flavour and texture is quite unlike any other fish dish I have tasted. As only two small slivers of meat are used from each fish it is very much a delicacy. Ediazábel is a hard, strong, rather dry, regional cheese reminiscent of young parmesan. Chacoli is a locally produced white wine you might find in the small bars: slightly *pétillant*, it is a good accompaniment to the numerous fish dishes of the region.

An interesting excursion can be made along the coast to the west of the town. A small road climbs the mountain to the lighthouse at Cabo Higuer from where there are dramatic views of the coastline. Nearby another small road crosses Monte Jaizkibel towards San Sebastián (Donostia). This is a particularly attractive scenic drive with sweeping views over green mountainsides to the sea far below. Just before you reach San Sebastián a road to the right leads along the estuary to the atmospheric fishing village of Pasajes de San Juan. A long narrow street lined with old houses runs parallel, and close to, the water's edge. However, the best view of this is to be seen from the opposite side of the estuary at the port of Pasajes de San Pedro, now a suburb of San Sebastián.

San Sebastián is an elegant and attractive seaside town of great character. It has everything you could wish from a seaside resort: a magnificent crescent of sand, almost enclosed by steep wooded headlands, with an island in the centre; esplanades, promenades, fascinating shops, beautiful buildings and tempting restaurants. The route back to the Parador can be made by taking the Autopista A 1 towards Irún.

ARGÓMANIZ

THE NEXT STAGE OF THE TOUR is to the Parador at Argómaniz. I have suggested a route which first detours into the foothills of the Pyrenees. Initially the route is along the C 133 which heads inland along the Bidasoa valley. Steeply sloping mountains rise from each side of the rock-strewn river and every curve of the road brings a new, often spectacular, view. There are a sequence of small villages along the route. Sumbilla is particularly attractive. Set beside the river, its old houses rise sheer from the bank and a steeply arched ancient stone bridge spans the water.

Just beyond Santesteban a turning to the left, the N 121, leads through a peaceful green valley into the Pyrenees. It is a delightfully rural and peaceful region of pretty little villages, dotted over the smooth, rounded hills. The distinctive stone houses of Navarra have decorated corners and window surrounds and brim with flowers. Arizcun, about 1–2km to the east just beyond the town of Elizondo (Baztan) is a particularly attractive example.

The road continues to the French border at the town of Dancharia (Dancharinia) and as it rises higher into the mountains so the scenery becomes progressively more dramatic. The plunging valleys are shaded by huge chestnut trees and the hillsides are covered with bracken, which in the autumn is harvested and stored in small conical stacks with a pole in the centre. The border town inevitably contains a couple of shops for last-minute purchases before crossing into France. Here, though, they are worth a visit, with goods ranging from the region's hand-made wattle baskets and terracotta pots to wild game and, while I was there in the autumn, huge boxes of *setas*, wild funghi gathered from the forests.

Before returning along the valley it is worth making a small detour from Dacharinia to the pretty village of

The village of Ciga in the Val de Baztán.
Overleaf: The fishing village of Pasajes de San Juan.

Zugarramundi. Set up high on the mountainside it is famed for its grottoes and for the inquisition of 40 alleged witches from the village in 1610. On returning to Irurita a very attractive drive back to the N 240 can be made via the villages of Ciga and Berroeta.

On reaching the N 121 the route returns for a short distance towards Irun as far as the town of Elgoriaga where a quiet road, the NA 403, passes through a steep wooded valley to the villages of Ituren and Zubieta and then over the Puerto Usateguieta with memorable views. After descending from the pass the road joins the N 240 where the route continues left to Lecumberri Irurzún and Alsasua. From here it follows the N 1 to Salvatierra, which has a wealth of ancient arcaded buildings, and then onwards towards Vitoria (Gasteiz).

The Parador Nacional de Argómaniz is reached about 15km before Vitoria. It is in quiet, open countryside approximately 1km along a small road to the south of the main road, but clearly signposted. Argómaniz is an abandoned village with most of the buildings derelict, only a few being inhabited. The Parador, a solid

stone building consisting of two modern wings each side of the original 17th-century palace of Larrea, which now houses the reception and public rooms, is on the side of a hill overlooking the plain of Álava and enjoys sweeping views. Inside the atmosphere is one of comfortable elegance. There are flagstone floors and fine antique furniture in the public areas and the bedrooms are spacious and comfortably furnished in the solid rustic Parador style. The restaurant, situated in what was the granary, has a beautiful beamed ceiling.

The regional cuisine benefits from both the neighbouring Rioja and Castile. There are a number of simple country dishes to be found on the Parador menu such as Chorizo con Patatas, spicy sausage with potatoes, and Codornices con Alubias, quail cooked with large white beans. Both of these dishes have a sauce flavoured with garlic and paprika. Tortilla Perrechicos is an omelette with tiny mushrooms and Trucha a la Navarra is trout sautéed in olive oil with *serrano* ham, a delicious combination. The wine list has an extensive selection of Rioja wines including Castillo Labastida, a good full-bodied red from the Rioja Álava.

Vitoria is a city of spacious squares and streets with many fine old buildings. The old town is set on a hill above the plain where the modern city extends. Its centre is the lively Plaza de la Virgen Blanca overlooked by the 14th-century Cathedral of Santa María whose main doorway consists of three arches decorated with beautiful sculptures.

An excursion into the Cantabrian mountains to the north can be made by taking the N 240 for a short distance towards Bilbao and then branching off to the right along the C 6213 to Ullivari beside the Embalse de Ullivari. From here a pretty scenic road leads north via the picturesque villages of Leintz-Gatzaga, perched dramatically on the hillside above a steep-sided, green valley. Continuing along the valley to the industrialised towns of Aretxabeleta and Mondragón, just beyond the latter a road to the right, the C 6322, climbs up the valley to the town of Oñati. It was at one time the capital of a small republic within the province of Guipúzcoa and has some beautiful buildings, an inheritance of its former importance. The Universitas Sancti Spiritus founded in 1542 by the Bishop of Ávila has a magnificent Plateresque façade and the imposing 15th-century church of San Miguel has a Baroque bell tower

The mountain village of Zugarramundi.

The Universitas Sancti Spiritus in Oñate.

and a lovely Plateresque cloister. There is also an ornately decorated 18th-century Baroque town hall.

It is worth making a brief detour higher into the mountains to Arantzazu a town 1,000m above sea level in a truly dramatic setting. An imposing basilica houses the shrine of the Virgin of Arantzazu who appeared to a shepherd boy in 1469. Returning to Oñati the route continues via Bergera and Durango to Bilbao along either the N 634 or the Autopista A 8. Bilbao is a large, busy city with a colourful old quarter.

From Bilbao the route returns towards Vitoria along the N 625 via Llodio, Amurrio and Orduña and then crosses the mountains over the Puerto de Orduña. Just beyond the town of Espejo a road to the east leads for a few kms to the curious town of Salinas de Añana, set in a small valley filled with ancient ramshackle salt pans built on a series of stilts. You can return to the Parador by continuing east along this road until it joins the Autopista A 1 which leads north-east to Vitoria.

SANTO DOMINGO DE LA CALZADA

THE NEXT STAGE OF THE TOUR is to the Parador at Santo Domingo de la Calzada. I suggest a route which first explores some of the countryside and villages to the west of Vitoria. Initially this runs south-west along the Autopista A 1 towards Miranda del Ebro; the C 122 leads north-west to join the N 625 where the route continues for a few kms to the north; a road to the west leads alongside the Embalse de Sobrón, a beautiful lake ringed by steep rugged mountains.

After about 20km, at the village of Quintana Martín Galíndez, a road to the south leads to the village of Frias, one of the most spectacularly perched villages in Spain. Set overlooking a shallow green valley its lovely old houses lining steep cobbled streets are built along the very edge of a rocky bluff, their walls rising sheer from the cliff face. Surmounting it are the remains of a castle, moulded like a cake decoration on to a precipitous spike of rock high above the village.

The route continues to the old town of Ona with its imposing 11th-century Monastery of San Salvador, many fine old houses and the Gothic church of San Juan. Travelling south along the N 232 for about 25km leads to the Briviesca with arcaded square, atmospheric streets and shops where you can buy the local speciality, caramelised almonds – absolutely delicious, a perfect gift to take home.

The route now leads north-east along the N 1 to Pancorbo, a picturesque village of old houses with brown-tiled roofs nestling in a rocky ravine through which the N 1, the Autopista A 1 and the Madrid/Irún railway traverse the rugged Montes Obarenes.

A little before Pancorbo the N 232 leads south-east to the village of Fonzaleche which contains the 12th-century Palace of the Condesa de Berberana. From here you can continue to Villaseca where there is a Romanesque church. A short detour to the north is well worth while to visit the ancient village of Cellorigo. Known as the pulpit of the Rioja, it is perched on a steep mountainside and surrounded by wild country-side over which it commands sweeping views. A little to the south is the village of Sajazarra, with its well preserved 13th-century castle, ancient gateway and fortified church.

It is only a short distance to Haro the capital of the Rioja Alta, an ancient town with narrow streets, some interesting shops including many where the local wines can be tasted and bought, and fine old buildings such as the 16th-century church of Santo Tomás with its splendidly ornate Plateresque portal, the 18th-century town hall and the Basilica of the Virgen de la Vega.

It is worth making a detour to visit some of the wine villages and vineyards – within a small area are Brinas, Labastida, Vincente de la Sonsierra and Laguardia. As well as being home to some of the best Rioja wines they are also fascinating villages set among splendid scenery. A trip to this part of the Rioja should include a climb up to the Balcon de la Rioja, a stunning view-point from the top of the winding Puerto de Herrera which crosses the rugged Sierra de Cantabria.

If you continue north after descending the pass to Penacerrada, where the church of La Asunción has notable retablos and tombs, you can take a small road, the L 130 to Zambrana where you join the N 232 and return to Haro via Conchas de Haro. Here the river Ebro enters the Rioja through a picturesque gorge.

From Haro the route continues along a small road, the LO 751 to Casalarreina, and from here on the LO 762 to Cuzcurrita del Río Tirón, a pretty village set along the river bank with a beautiful church, San Miguel, an ancient bridge and the 14th-century castle of Los Velasco. This road continues south along the valley of the Río Tirón through remote countryside until the main road is reached at Belorado. From here it is about 20km to the east to Santo Domingo de la Calzada.

This historic town was an important staging post on the pilgrim route from the mountain pass of Ronces-valles in the Pyrenees to the city of Santiago de

The village of Frías.

Vineyards near Laguardia in the Rioja.

Compostela in the north-west corner of Spain. In the Middle Ages this was a journey that every devout Christian was determined to make during his or her lifetime in order to pay homage to the shrine of Saint James whose remains, according to legend, were discovered there under a bush in the 9th century. The town takes its name from St Dominic, a hermit who in the 11th century built a bridge across the river and a road, *calzada,* to aid the pilgrim's progress. The town has been built up around this simple crossing and the hospital which St Dominic also built.

The most important building, is the 13th-century Gothic cathedral: inside, overlooking the aisle, is a gilded chicken coop high on the wall containing a white cockerel and hen. It marks a legend in which a pilgrim was wrongly hanged for a crime he did not commit. When he was later cut down from the gallows he was found to be still alive. When the news reached the Mayor who had condemned him, he was in the process of enjoying a chicken for his dinner. On hearing the news he said that, if it were true, the bird he was eating might just as likely come back to life, whereupon it sprang to its feet on the plate and crowed lustily.

The Parador Nacional Santo Domingo de la Calzada occupies the old hospice built by Santo Domingo and overlooks the small square in front of the cathedral. The interior is breathtaking, the lounge a spacious room dominated, and partially divided, by huge stone arches and decorated with beautiful antique furniture. Magnificent stone staircases lead off to the bedrooms. This Parador evokes a lifestyle of centuries past even in the midst of its luxurious surroundings.

The menu in the Parador restaurant contains both national and regional specialities, the abundant vegetables of the Rioja being a strong feature. Menestra a la Riojana is a dish of mixed vegetables containing carrots, leeks, cauliflower, artichoke hearts, peas and onions, all sautéed together with garlic and ham. Pimientos Rellenos are the small sweet peppers of the region stuffed with minced veal and herbs and served in a rich tomato sauce spiced with paprika. The wine list includes a good selection of Riojas.

An excursion can be made to explore the countryside to the south of Santo Domingo. A road due south of the town follows the valley of the Río Oja to the popular winter resort of Ezcaray. Here there is a decidedly

Landscape near San Millán de Cogolla.

holiday atmosphere with villas and apartments and skiing facilities. A circular scenic road enables you to explore the beautiful mountain scenery of the Coto Nacional de Ezcaray.

Another small road from Santo Domingo leads to the south-east to San Millán de Cogolla where the vast 16th-century monastery of Yuso is situated in a peaceful valley surrounded by steep green hills. Such is the scale and magnificence of this building that it is known as the Escorial of the Rioja. Nearby in a quiet corner of the wooded hillside is the small 12th-century monastery of Suso.

Leaving San Millán to the east along a delightfully peaceful and scenic road brings you to the village of Bonadilla. Here the route turns south on to the C 133 which follows the course of the Río Najerilla through a wild and rocky ravine. After about 16km there is a small road to the right leading to the 15th-century monastery of Valvanera. It is in a beautiful and peaceful setting perched high on the side of a deep and thickly wooded valley through which a small river rushes between grassy banks and silver birch trees. Throughout this region you need to keep a lookout for the huge brown cows which seem to stroll casually along the narrow country roads, outnumbering the cars.

Continuing south along the C 133 for another 11km will bring you to a road junction just before the road enters the Embalse de Mansilla. The route turns left on to the LO 8012 and leads through another more gentle, but equally beautiful, valley to the villages of Viniegra de Abajo and Viniegra de Arriba. The latter is a gem, a remote mountain hamlet of small grey-stone houses linked by a series of steeply winding, narrow streets paved with the same small boulders from which the houses are built. It is completely captivating and virtually untouched by the 20th century.

From here the road climbs out of the valley over a remote and bleak mountain, its stark contours relieved only by a few shrubs, stunted trees and flocks of sheep. After about 20km it joins the N 111 between Logroño and Soria. From here you can return to the Parador by following the N 111 north to Logroño and then the N 120 west to Santo Domingo. The nearest alternative paradors are at Calahorra, 95km (page 60) and Soria, 150km (page 106).

*T*OUR 5 *Explores the Rioja Baja, Navarra and the foothills of the Pyrenees, starting in the province of Longroño and continuing into Navarra and Zaragoza. The countryside is richly varied, ranging from the fertile valley of the Río Ebro to the peaceful mountain valleys of the Pyrenees. The route includes numerous medieval villages, remote castles and secluded monasteries.*

CALAHORRA

THE TOUR BEGINS IN CALAHORRA. The nearest alternative paradors are at Santo Domingo de la Calzada, 95km (page 58) and Soria, 116km (page 106). Calahorra can trace its history back to 200 BC when it was known by its Iberian name of Calagóricos and later as Calagurris after its capture by the Romans. Now it is largely modernised: an important centre for both Rioja wines and the extensive market gardening which surrounds the town. There is an interesting old quarter. The 13th-century cathedral is essentially Gothic in style but possesses some Renaissance features. The interior contains numerous treasures including altars, retablos and grills as well as a collection of paintings by Zurbarán, Ribera and Titian. Other buildings of note include the churches of Santiago and San Andrés.

The Parador Nacional Marco Fabio Quintiliano, a contemporary building with a traditional ambience, is situated in the modern part of Calahorra at one end of the Paseo el Mercadel and adjoins a small park. The rooms are spacious, comfortable and attractively furnished and decorated. The restaurant offers a good selection of regional dishes as well as some from Castile and La Mancha. Chorizo con Alubias is a rich dish of spicy red sausage and beans flavoured with paprika and garlic. Cordero al Chilindrón is a typical Navarra casserole of lamb cooked with red peppers, tomatoes and onions and flavoured with garlic and herbs. Roncales is a delicious regional cheese – firm but creamy – from a small village in the Pyrenees. The wine list is, understandably, biased towards Riojas, available in both full-bodied reds and the whites and also *claretes*, a deep rosé. One of many excellent reds on the Parador list which I tried is Viña Ardanza. Navarra wines are also represented and one to look out for is that from the village of St Martin de Unx.

A fascinating tour to the south of Calahorra can be made by first taking the LO 662 to Arnedo, the site of a battle between the Moors and the Christians in the 9th century. The ruins of a castle still look down over the old town and there are remains of an aqueduct. The road continues along a lovely valley with distant views of impressive mountain ranges to the small hot

CALAHORRA
OLITE
SOS DEL REY CATÓLICO

spring resort of Arnedillo. The countryside has a blissful rural tranquillity with valleys filled with almond and olive trees. Further south the road enters a deep valley surrounded by rugged hills, a region scantily populated with only the occasional village to be seen, each with a small area of market garden around it. Yanguas is a picturesque town with ancient walls surrounding its old stone houses, it also has a Moorish fortress, an arcaded *plaza mayor* and a 12th-century Romanesque tower. It is set in a particularly beautiful part of the Cidacos valley where a fast-running river shaded by green trees rushes over rocks and small boulders.

From here the road continues south along the valley to Oncala a secluded village threaded by steep, rough-cobbled streets, situated at the foot of the Puerto de Oncala. A collection of 18th-century Flemish tapestries based on cartoons by Rubens are kept in the church. After crossing the Puerto de Oncala the road continues to Soria. The Parador Nacional of Soria and the city itself is described in Tour No 9 (page 106).

From Soria the route continues along the N 122 eastwards to Agreda, an old hilltop town beside the Río Cailes and dominated by the Moorish castle of La Muela set above the town. Its churches include San Miguel, NS de la Pena and NS de los Milagros, and there are many old mansions and houses. To the southeast are the imposing peaks of the Sierra de Moncayo rising to 7000ft above sea level.

The tour continues to the east of Agreda along the N 122 for about 5km and then turns north on to the C 101 to Valverde de Cervera. A road to the west leads to the old town of Cervera del Río Alhama, set along the banks of the river under a towering cliff, with an ancient bridge and a ruined castle. From here the route continues north along the C 125 for a short distance and then leads westwards along the C 123 back towards Arnedo. A detour to Cornago can be made by taking a small road to the left, the LO 683, for about 15km. Cornago is a strikingly situated hilltop village with a well-preserved castle and an ancient church perched high above the old stone houses. By continuing along this road it rejoins the C 123, leading to Arnedo where the road continues back to the Parador at Calahorra.

Another excursion from Calahorra is to the old ruined fortress of Clavijo, about 15km south of Logroño which can be reached by following the Autopista A 68 to the west of Calahorra. This was the site of a great battle between the Moors and the Christians in 844. Legend claims that St James appeared here on horse-

The cathedral of Calahorra.

back in support of the Spanish army. It is a romantic and memorable place and the narrow winding road which approaches the hilltop site provides stunning views of the Ebro valley.

OLITE

THE NEXT STAGE OF THE TOUR is north-east to the Parador at Olite, a direct distance of only 70km. Initially the route is south-east towards Rincón de Soto and then north to Peralta. From here the C 124 continues eastwards towards Carcastillo. On the outskirts of the village is the Monasterio de Oliva, a 12th-century Cistercian abbey and one of the earliest examples of Gothic architecture in Spain with a beautiful 15th-century cloister. The route returns westwards along the C 124 to the junction with the N121 and then leads north to Olite.

This small town amidst open countryside was originally founded in the 7th century by the Gothic King Swintila and was also the seat of the kings of Navarra. As a result Olite possesses a magnificent castle, built at the beginning of the 15th century to house King Charles III and largely Gothic in style. It is elegantly and elaborately designed with a fascinating complex of towers, battlements and turrets. Next to it is the lovely 13th century Gothic church of Santa María whose main doorway is decorated with intricate sculptures. The town is an appealing jumble of streets and small squares.

The Parador Nacional Principe de Viana is situated in part of the castle, thus enabling one to explore the building at leisure as well as providing memorable accommodation. Among the regional dishes which the restaurant offers on its menu is Cordonices con Alubias, quail cooked with large white beans in a sauce flavoured with tomatoes, onions and garlic. Setas en Cazuela, which are the large brown wild fungi gathered in the woods and cooked with olive oil, garlic and ham: they are quite delicious with a firm meaty texture and distinctive flavour. Local wines on the list included those of Senorio de Sarria, both red and white, and the young, strongly alcoholic reds of Monasterio de Oliva.

SOS DEL REY CATÓLICO

THE TOUR NOW GOES EAST to the Parador at Sos del Rey Católico, a direct distance of only 50km. However, a short detour first to the west of Olite will allow you to visit the medieval town of Artajona. The route is first along the N 121 to the north for about 7km to the busy old town of Tafalla. From here a small road, the NA 603 crosses open rolling countryside to the hilltop town of Artajona. It retains extensive fortifications with walls, towers and battlements, and a fortified 13th-century church, San Pedro, with a finely sculpted façade.

Returning to Tafalla the C 132 leads eastwards for about 10km through hilly countryside to the hilltop

The Río Cidacos near Yanguas.

town of St Martin de Unx. Known for its wines it is a delightful old walled town surrounded by vine-covered hillsides. Its web of steep cobbled streets are lined with ancient houses. A small road, the NA 537 continues higher into the hills with extensive views to the village of Ujué.

Set high on a hill with far-reaching views over the surrounding countryside Ujué is a village of small stone houses and cobbled alleys, dominated by the huge 14th-century fortified church of Santa María with 11th-century apses and a 12th-century silver Virgin and Child.

The route returns to St Martín de Unx, continues north-east along the C 132 to Aibar and then along the

NA 540 to Sanguesa, an ancient town on the river Aragón, with a lovely 13th-century church, Santa María la Real, set on the river bank beside the bridge and with a magnificently sculptured portal. Other buildings of interest include the Romanesque church of Santiago and the Baroque Palace of Vallesantoro. From here the Parador at Sos del Rey Católico is only 13km to the south. But if you have time you can first make another detour northwards into the Pyrenees.

From Sanguesa a small road, the NA 541, leads to the well-preserved 13th-century Castillo de Javier and then joins the N 240 which after a few kms runs alongside the Embalse de Yesa, a large lake surrounded by steep bare hills. Just before this point a small road to

The village of Oncala below the pass to Soria.

the north leads to the Cistercian Monastery of Leyre whose ancient church with its 12th-century crypt was the resting place of the kings of Navarra. It is set below the steep rugged slopes of the Sierra de Leyre and there are sweeping views over the lake.

Continuing east along the N 240 provides constant views along the lake. The road passes the medieval hilltop village of Esco, perched beside the water. About 1km further the C 137 leads north into the valley of Roncal, following the course of the Río Esca which, in places, flows between sheer rocky cliffs – a most rewarding scenic drive through one of the most secluded and peaceful valleys of the region with a succession of changing views around each curve of the road. In the autumn the poplars, which grow along the banks of the river, are an intense golden yellow, like tongues of flame. There are a number of attractive villages along this route. Roncal is a gem, its ancient cobbled streets lined with houses built from blackened grey stone which cascade with flowers. There is also a lovely old church. The village is famed for its cheese and, a wedge of this from one of the shops, a rough crusty loaf, a bottle of Navarra wine and a choice of idyllic spots by the river make it the perfect place for a picnic.

From Roncal the road climbs higher into the mountains with impressive views of the Pyrenean peaks. Close to the French border there is a junction, to the north lies the Puerto de Larrau, a pass leading into France and south descends into the Valle de Salazar. Just before the junction however there is a spectacular viewpoint over the wooded mountains and the bare peaks beyond.

The route down through the Salazar valley is also full of scenic pleasure, passing through villages and small towns such as Izalzu, Ochagavía and Escároz. For a large part of the journey the road runs close to the wide and fast-flowing Río Salazar. Just beyond the village of Aspuz there is another spectacular viewpoint at the Hoz de Arbayón, looking down into a ravine above which huge eagles soar. Continuing along the NA 211, it meets the main road, the N 240, just beyond the town of Lumbier, beside the Río Irati. The route continues east along the main road for 6km and then south along the C 127 to Sanguesa. From here it is just 13km to Sos del Rey Católico and the next Parador.

Sos has retained the atmosphere of a fortified medieval town to a quite remarkable degree. Situated on a steep hill on the borders betwen Navarra and Aragón, it has magnificent views of the distant Pyrenean peaks. Its name derives from the Catholic King Ferdinand, born there in the Palace of Sada in 1452. To mark this event, and for services rendered by the town, Juan II of Aragón decreed in 1458 that every inhabitant be given the status of a nobleman. It is possible to visit the room in which the king was born as well as the Gothic chapel. The town is a web of steep, narrow cobbled streets, and old mansions with seigneurial crests and sculpted

The Pyrenees seen from near Sos del Rey Católico.

The castillo of Sádaba. Overleaf: The village of Uncastillo.

façades. There is an arcaded square and the Romanesque church of San Esteban next to the castle from whose ramparts you can look down over the brown-tiled rooftops of the village houses to the wild landscape beyond. In the early morning the distant snow-covered peaks of the Pyrenees are tinged pink in the sunlight.

The Parador Nacional Fernando de Aragón is a modern building on the northern edge of the village, built with local wood and stone to blend in with the town's architecture. Many of the rooms have views, and some have balconies which overlook the plain below and the Sierra de Leyre and the Pyrenean peaks. There is a large terrace adjoining the lounge and restaurant which makes a memorable place to watch the sun go down while enjoying a drink before dinner.

Regional specialities of Aragón as well as Castile and Navarra are to be found on the menu. Chuletas de Cerdo a la Riojana are pork chops cooked with red peppers, onions and tomatoes. Conejo con Tomate is rabbit cooked in a tangy tomato sauce with white wine, garlic and wine vinegar and flavoured with thyme; the dish is served cold – rather like a thick, tomato-flavoured vinaigrette. Hinojas al Estilo de Fayos is braised fennel; and for those with a sweet tooth there is Biscocho de Barbastro, a type of cake.

An enjoyable tour to the south of Sos can be made by taking the C 127, a small road which climbs up over the Puerto de Sos with dramatic views over the mountains to the north, including one of distant Sos, perched on its hill with a backdrop of mountain peaks. It is untamed country with little sign of human life between villages. Steep rounded hills are covered with brush and small trees. At the village of Castiliscar the road descends, crossing a flat plain with vast fields of wheat to the town of Sadaba which has an impressive 13th-century castle. At Ejea de los Caballeros, 22km to the south there is a fortified Romanesque church.

From Sadaba a small road to the east, the Z 552, leads along the valley of the Río Riguel to Uncastillo, an interesting old town in a picturesque setting with a ruined castle, the remains of an aqueduct, the Romanesque churches of Santa María and San Juan, and many ancient houses. From here a road to the north leads back to Sos.

The nearest alternative Parador to Sos is at Argómaniz, 140km (page 51).

*T*OUR 6 *Links together three parradors in the north-west of Spain close to the Portuguese border, beginning in the province of Zamora and then leading west into Orense. The itinerary provides an interesting scenic route between central Spain and Galicia. The landscape changes from the undulating wheat-covered hillsides of the Tierra de Campos to the lakes, mountains and rivers of Sanabria and Orense. The three parradors featured include one in a 12th-century castle, one overlooking a picturesque hilltop village and another sharing a hilltop with a medieval fortress. The parradors of Puebla da Sanabria and Verín make convenient bases from which to make excursions into northern Portugal.*

—TOUR 6—
MICHELIN MAP NO. 441
• LEÓN
Verín   Puebla de Sanabria
• Benavente
VALLODOLID

BENAVENTE
PUEBLA DE SANABRIA
VERÍN

BENAVENTE

THE TOUR BEGINS IN BENAVENTE. The nearest alternative paradores are at Zamora, 65km (page 84) and León, 70km (page 42).

The Parador Nacional Fernando II de León, on the western edge of the town of Benavente, is set on the side of a hill and enjoys extensive views over the fertile plain of the Campos. The town centre is only a few minutes' walk away. The castle was built in the 12th century by Ferdinand II to defend himself against attacks by the Moors and neighbouring Portugal. Ferdinand and Isabella stayed here during their pilgrimage to Santiago de Compostela. In 1808 it was badly damaged in a battle between Napoleon's troops and Sir John Moore during his retreat to La Coruña. The only original part of the building remaining is the massive castle keep. It is known as the Torre del Caracol, tower of the snail, because of the steep stone spiral staircase which connects the floors.

The interior has been well restored and extended to provide comfortable accommodation and makes use of some of the remains of the castle. It is decorated with heraldic banners, coats of arms and tapestries creating a convincing castle-like atmosphere. There is a tower bar which is entered by descending a deep dungeon-like staircase and the lofty wooden ceiling is supported on huge beams. A large lounge called the Salón Artesanado has a beautiful Mudéjar ceiling. The bedrooms and the restaurant have wide views of the chequered plain which reaches way towards the Montes of León.

The regional specialities on the menu included: Pastel de Puerros y Gambas al la Esencia de Cangrejos, a delicately flavoured pâté of leeks and prawns served with a crayfish sauce; Bacalao al Tío, literally 'uncle's salt cod' is cooked with red peppers; Presas de Ternera Zamorana, small slices of veal cooked in a spicy sauce.

From the regional wines on the list I chose a bottle of El Cubeto, a deep-coloured dry rosé from Benavente.

In the centre of the town is the church of Santa María del Azoque. King Ferdinand II initiated its construction at the end of the 12th century and it has undergone several restorations since. Its main portal dates from the early 18th century but it also possesses a Romanesque portal remaining from the 12th century. The 12th-century church of San Juan del Mercado with its intricately carved portal contains the first Gothic vault to have been built in Spain. The Hospital de la Piedad is also of interest with an imposing façade and a fine Renaissance portal.

An interesting circuit can be made from Benavente into the Tierra de Campos to the south-east. The route is initially along the N 6 to the old town of Villalpando, with its outstanding 12th-century fortified gateway, the Puerta de San Andrés, built by King Ferdinand; and several lovely old churches including San Lorenzo, dating from the 13th century; the Mudéjar church of San Miguel with a beautiful 15th-century gilded retablo; and the 12th-century church of Santa María la Antigua which had three apses.

A road leads north-east to Villamayor de Campos where the 16th-century church of San Esteban has an interesting altar. The road continues east to Medina de Río Seco, a historic town dating from Roman times which retains numerous old buildings, a fine Gothic gate and arcaded streets with ancient wooden beams. The 15th-century church of Santa María de Mediavilla contains notable retablos, grills, statues and paintings, and the 16th-century church of Santiago is also of interest with an imposing façade and beautiful Plateresque portal.

A few kms east of Medina de Río Seco is the impressive castle of Montealegre set on a sandy ridge and commanding fine views over the wheat-covered hillsides. The massive Gothic castle is built of bleached stone and has large octagonal towers. In the town are the churches of San Pedro and Santa María, both with interesting retablos. A few kms further to the east are two other fine castles at Ampudia, also with ancient arcaded streets, and Torremormejón.

From Medina de Río Seco the route leads back along the C 612 to Villafrechos, where the 15th-century church of San Cristóbal contains a fine Baroque retablo. A right fork leads to Castroverde de Campos whose

The fortified gateway of Villalpando.

beautiful 13th-century church of Santa María del Río possesses a Madonna and Child from the same period. The partially ruined church of San Nicolás also dates from the 13th century.

A striking feature of the Campos is the adobe houses of which the villages are built. They are covered in a coating of reddish-brown clay giving the streets a curious sepia appearance, like an old photograph. On the edge of most of these villages, in the low hills, you will see numerous caves tunnelled into the sandy stone. These are small private *bodegas,* or wine cellars, where the wine is made and stored away from the ferocious summer heat of the region. Here too numerous flocks of sheep are to be seen. In the early morning as many as five or six huge flocks will radiate out from the small villages and disappear into the countryside with long plumes of dust marking their progress. From Castroverde de Campos the C 620 leads westwards back to Benavente.

PUEBLA DE SANABRIA

THE NEXT STAGE OF THE TOUR continues westwards along the C 620 to the Parador at Puebla de Sanabria, a

distance of 84km. At Santa María de Tera there is a 13th-century church and beyond at Mombuey is a curious 13th-century church with a separate Gothic bell tower. As the road leads further east the countryside becomes greener and more hilly with views of distant mountains. The hillsides here are dotted with vineyards and pine trees.

The Parador Nacional de Sanabria on the western edge of the town, is a modern building set back from the road on a slight rise with fine views of the fortified hilltop town. It is simply decorated with marble floors, white walls, wooden panelling and comfortable leather furniture. Stone fireplaces and traditional dark-wood furniture create a rustic ambience.

The menu shows signs of the region's proximity to Galicia with dishes like Caldo Gallego, a substantial country soup made with salt pork, greens, potatoes and haricot beans. Beans also feature in Habas con Almejas, haricot beans cooked with clams in sauce flavoured with onions, garlic and saffron. Merluza en Caldeirada is cutlets of hake cooked in a sauce with

Bringing the sheep home at Montealegre.

An adobe house in Villamayor de Campos.

potatoes, onions and tomatoes and flavoured with garlic, wine vinegar and paprika. Among the regional wines on the list I had a well-made dry white from the cooperative of El Barco de Valdeoras.

Puebla de Sanabria is a picturesque old town perched on a steep ridge beside a small river. On the edge of the hill is a 15th-century castle and a particularly lovely 12th-century Romanesque church with a fine portal flanked by sculpted columns. There are numerous old houses and mansions with escutcheons and an ancient arcaded *ayuntamiento* in the small square. A footpath runs along the remains of the battlements with fine views over the surrounding countryside.

A delightful excursion can be made into the mountains to the north from the Parador to the lake of Sanabria, a beautiful unspoiled expanse of water ringed by green hillsides and fringed with reeds. From the lakeside a road climbs higher with striking views of the lake far below to San Martín de Castañeda. Here, just outside the town, is the Benedictine monastery of San Martín. The Romanesque church was built in the 12th century. The road continues higher still into the mountains with increasingly dramatic views. The same route must be taken back to the Parador.

Another trip along a road to the south of Puebla de Sanabria through bare ridged hills will take you to the Portuguese border, a remote and wild region populated only with a few small villages of ancient stone houses decorated with crude wooden balconies. A road leads to the left to one of the most remarkable villages I have seen during my travels in Spain, Santa Cruz de Abrañes. Dirt pathways connect the crumbling stone houses and the hillsides are dotted with small conical haystacks. Enormous vines, 10–12ft high and grown on trellises, are so old that the stems resemble tree trunks. An old lady showed me an ancient wine press hidden in a barn. It was simply an enormous block of granite suspended on a massive, pivoted wooden beam above a large stone plinth. She said it was centuries old and still in use. Scattered around the village were ancient carts with crude wheels made from large discs of wood.

VERÍN

THE NEXT STAGE OF THE TOUR is west to the Parador at Verín, a direct distance of 98km. Initially the road runs along a wide green valley with meadows and fields of grain, but soon it climbs into the mountains and the views become increasingly more impressive.

The Parador Nacional Monterrey, set on a steep vine-clad hill about 1km to the west of Verín, is a modern building constructed in traditional style of large granite blocks and surrounded by lawns from where there are sweeping views of the Tamega valley. A swimming pool completes a peaceful setting in which to relax. The interior is decorated with antiques and suits of armour.

The menu includes regional dishes like Lacón con Cachelos y Chorizo, pork fillet cooked with chorizo and potatoes; Lacón con Grelos, a similar dish but with pigs trotters and turnip greens in addition to potatoes and chorizo; Pierdo de Cordero a la Orensana, leg of lamb baked with onions, carrots and haricot beans. For dessert, Filloas a la Crema are pancakes filled with a rich creamy egg custard and served cold. A good local cheese to try is Queso de Tetilla. Regional wines are well represented on the list: I had Viña Costeira, an excellent dry white wine from Ribadavia.

The Parador shares its hilltop site with the medieval fortress of Monterrey, ten minutes' stroll away. The 12th-century castle, built on the remains of a Celtic settlement and rebuilt in the 15th century by the Count of Monterrey whose coat of arms still decorates the fortified gate, still has several impressive towers including the massive 14th-century castle keep. There is a lovely courtyard with surrounding arcades of double columns. The battlements also enclose a Gothic church with a fine wooden ceiling and a stone retablo. The 14th-century hospital has a Renaissance portal. The town of Verín set below in the valley has retained numerous ancient houses and mansions in its old quarter.

The Parador makes a good base from which to explore the countryside of Orense. The route is initially westward along the N 525, climbing through heath-covered mountains to the Alto de Estivadas. The road continues to Ginzo de Limia where there is a Romanesque church, old houses and a castle, then south-west along the valley of the Río Limia via Bande to the Embalse de las Conchas at the confluence of the rivers of Cados and Limia. Here on a hillside overlooking the lake is an exquisite small 7th-century Visigothic church. The route leads northwards along the N 540 to Celanova, a large lively town with an imposing 10th-century monastery with a magnificent Baroque façade overlooking the *plaza mayor*.

3km to the north of Celanova is Villanova dos Infantes, an attractive old village of small arcaded houses

The village of Puebla de Sanabria seen from near the parador.

with grain stores and picturesque streets. Overlooking the small square is the lovely Baroque church of the Virgen del Cristal.

A small road now leads north-east to Allariz, with its 12th-century church of Santiago and the convent of Santa Clara which preserves an unusual Madonna and

Child, known as the Virgin Abridera. A small road continues north-east to Junquera de Ambia with the 12th-century monastery of Santa María. The church has a tall Romanesque tower and a fine façade and portal. At Baños de Molgas there is a lovely 18th-century church, Santuario de los Milagros, and near Maceda, the remains of a hilltop fortress.

A few kms further north the main road is joined and the route continues westwards to the provincial capital of Orense on the banks of the Río Miño. The 12th-century cathedral is the finest in Galicia with the ex-

ception of Santiago de Compostela. There are many lovely old squares with numerous arcaded houses, old mansions and churches. An extended visit to Orense would need a separate excursion.

A road follows the south bank of the Río Miño and soon climbs the mountainside with breathtaking views over the river. A small road to the right leads to Ribas de Sil where a monastery founded in 550 and restored in the 10th century has three cloisters, of which one is considered to be the most beautiful in Galicia. The church has a fine Baroque façade and a 16th-century

altar. The huge building is set on a peaceful wooded hillside. The road continues to climb alongside the river to the confluence with the Río Sil.

Here the route leads along the south bank of the Sil through the dramatically beautiful Gargantas del Sil. The road runs high above the river, winding sinuously around the precipitous and indented hillsides with astounding views. Surrounded by alpine-like meadows, villages of rough-stone houses with glazed balconies and brown-tiled roofs cling defiantly to the steep slopes. On the opposite bank the hillsides are patterned with terraced vineyards.

The road continues upstream to where the river is dammed, forming a beautiful lake. Beyond, it joins the main road at Castro Caldes. Here there is an impressive 14th-century castle and old houses with glazed balconies. The route continues eastwards along the N 120 to the Alto de Cardeira from where it descends to Puebla de Trives and Freixido.

The façade of NS de Hermitas.

Farmers in the village of Santa Cruz de Abranes. Overleaf: The view from the hill above Consuegra.

The route now leads south along the C 533 towards Viana del Bollo. A few kms south of the village of Lentellais a small road to the right leads to Las Hermitas, a tiny village set on a bluff overlooking the river. The 16th-century sanctuary of NS de Hermitas has an extremely beautiful Baroque façade, extravagantly decorated with sculptures and ornate columns.

This route is a scenic delight: as the road climbs higher to the Alto de Covelo there are sweeping views of the valley below. Viana del Bollo is an attractive old town set high on a hillside overlooking the Embalse de Bao. It has a tangle of narrow atmospheric streets lined with old houses and a castle tower. The road continues along the valley south to La Gudina where the route leads westwards along the N 525 back to Verín.

The nearest alternative parador to Verín is at Tuy, 178km (page 33).

PART TWO

Central Spain

VALLODOLID

7

8   ÁVILA

MADRID

TOLEDO

GUADALUPE

11

10

9

OUR 7 Explores the central and western region of Castile-León, starting in the province of Segovia and passing into Vallodolid, Zamora and finally the province of Salamanca. It includes two of Spain's most beautiful and historic cities and a wealth of historic buildings. The countryside ranges from the mountain landscape of the Guadarrama and the Sierra de Peña de Francia to the wide plains of Castile where prairie-like fields of wheat stretch away to the shimmering horizon.

— TOUR 7 —
MICHELIN MAP NOS. 442 & 441

Zamora
Tordesillas
Ciudad Rodrigo
SEGOVIA
ÁVILA
MADRID

SEGOVIA
TORDESILLAS
ZAMORA
CIUDAD RODRIGO

SEGOVIA

THE FIRST PARADOR at Segovia is about 100km from Madrid airport. From Madrid the route follows the Autopista A 6 north-west of the city to the town of Guadarrama, where the C 600 leads through the town of Navacerrada before commencing the climb over the Puerto de Navacerrada, crossing the pineclad Sierra de Guadarrama. It is an attractive scenic road with a succession of sweeping mountain vistas. After descending the other side of the pass the road continues to San Idelfonso La Granja, a small town which houses a famous glassworks as well as the magnificent palace and formal gardens of La Granja. The 18th-century building is evocative of a French château and was built for King Phillip III. The gardens are extravagant and extensive, covering more than 300 acres. Among the elegant avenues of chestnut trees and formal flower beds are 26 ornately decorated fountains which, on certain days, are orchestrated to give a spectacular aquatic display.

From La Granja it is only 11km to Segovia, one of the most beautiful cities in Spain. The Roman aqueduct, with 118 arches built of massive stones, is one of the most impressive of all Roman remains and still carries water into the city. The Alcázar is also a memorable sight, a drive around the city's perimeter road providing a viewpoint from which the lofty, turreted building looms high above you like the prow of an ocean liner. Of particular note amongst Segovia's many remarkable ancient buildings are the cathedral dating from 1525, the 10th-century church of St Martín, the 13th-century church of Vera Cruz and the lovely Romanesque church of San Esteban with an imposing tower.

The Parador Nacional de Segovia, a modern building 2km from the aqueduct and the city centre, is built on a site called El Terminillo, once planted with vineyards and olive trees. Set on a natural terrace overlooking the city, known as the Mirador de la Lastrilla, it commands magnificent views and the bedrooms have balconies which make the most of its outlook. Its imaginative and unusual design has created a spacious and bright interior. Built of concrete and brickwork with high sloping ceilings and illuminated by huge windows the public rooms brim with plants and greenery. There is a large circular indoor pool and sauna as well as an outdoor pool with extensive lawns.

The restaurant also has fine views of the city and is an excellent place to try Cochinillo Asado, roast suckling pig. Very much a regional speciality the succulent white meat is covered with a crisp golden skin as thin as a potato crisp. Cordero Lechal Asado is a similarly delicious dish of roast baby lamb. Another Castilian speciality at which the Parador restaurant excels is Sopa de Ajo Castellana, a rich soup of garlic and olive oil thickened with bread and enriched with eggs. The wine list includes a selection from nearby Rueda and Ribera de Duero as well as the more familiar Riojas. An interesting, and delicious, drink is El Ponche Segoviano. Made of hot milk and enriched with egg yolks, it is flavoured with brandy, vanilla and ground almonds and makes an excellent nightcap.

A short detour to the south-west along the N 110 leads to the Real Palacio de Ríofrío, an elegant 18th-century palace set in a large, peaceful green park dotted with thousands of oak trees and inhabited by numerous herds of deer. The palace is now a museum of hunting.

TORDESILLAS

THE NEXT STAGE OF THE TOUR is to the Parador at Tordesillas. I have outlined a route which first explores the region to the north-east of Segovia. The first part follows the N 110 towards Soria. After about 25km a road to the left, the SG 233, leads towards Pedraza de la Sierra, a small, walled hilltop town built on a rocky outcrop and overlooking a steep-sided valley. It is well preserved and unspoilt, the only concession to popular interest being the presence of a few restaurants. Its tangle of narrow streets are cobbled in mosaic patterns and lined with houses built from the same stone. There is an enchanting small square surrounded by arcaded buildings. On the edge of town is a castle dating from the 15th century. A town that makes you want to linger, it houses the Hostería Nacional Pintor Zuloaga, a restaurant situated in one of the town's old houses, the Casa de la Inquisición – so called because it was the home of the inquisitor Escobedo. A speciality here is Cabrito Asado a la Serrana, roast baby kid.

The Alcázar at Segovia.

You can continue northwards to Sepúlveda through remote, hilly countryside planted with sunflowers, wheat and vegetables, with only the occasional small farmhouse to be seen between the small villages. Sepúlveda is in a dramatic setting. Its old houses are tiered up the slope of a steep hillside which overlooks a deep rocky gorge. The town's history dates back to Roman times and it contains many historic buildings as well as remains of its medieval walls and castle.

The route returns for about 12km to a junction with the C 112. Nearby is the impressive 12th-century Arab fortress at Condado de Castilnovo. Continuing westwards to Cantelejo, with a 17th-century church, the route then follows the C 603 south to Turégano where, inside the crenellated walls of a hilltop castle overlooking the town, is a 13th-century Romanesque church.

The tour continues to the west along the SG 222, joining the main road, the N 601, at Navalmanzano.

From Cuéllar the route follows the SG 342 to Navas de Oro where a road to the west leads to Coca. Here is one of the most attractive castles in Spain, built in the 15th century in brick by the Moors it has a moat and four octagonal towers. It is a rare and beautiful example of a fortress in the Mudéjar style.

The SG 351 continues westwards to Arévalo, a fascinating small town with a wealth of ancient buildings, a 14th-century castle, two 14th-century bridges and several arcaded squares. Madrigal de las Altes Torres, 26km to the west along the C 605, was the birthplace of Isabella the Catholic and her home until her marriage to Ferdinand of Aragón. The town is encircled by walls, relieved by lofty square towers. There is a well preserved gate with an archway and tower. The 15th-century palace in which Isabella was born now houses the Convent of Madres Augustinas de NS de Gracia. There is also a hospital with a Renaissance façade and the 12th-century Mudéjar church of San Nicolás de Bari.

The tour continues northwards along the C 610 for 26km to Medina del Campo, overlooked by the impressive 15th-century castle of La Mota. This lively, attractive town has many fine buildings including the Casa de Dueñas with a lovely patio, and the 16th-century collegiate church of San Antolín. The N 6 continues north towards Tordesillas, passing the wine town of Rueda with the richly decorated Baroque church of Santa María.

Tordesillas, an old town with narrow streets and an arcaded *plaza mayor*, is set high on a hill above the Río Duero. The most beautiful of its ancient buildings is the Real Monasterio de Santa Clara, a convent in a palace built for Alfonso XI in 1340. This fine example of Mudéjar architecture has an exquisite small patio framed by decorated arches. The Salón Dorado, the golden room, is richly gilded with an intricately decorated ceiling and containing 16th-century frescoes and paintings and a beautiful 13th-century altar.

The Parador Nacional de Tordesillas, a modern building in a pine forest about 1km south of the town (south of the N 620 in the direction of Salamanca) is a single-storey building of mellow brickwork with spacious rooms and a peaceful shady atmosphere. The menu includes a selection of dishes such as Tortilla de Patatas y Ajetes, omelette with potatoes and baby garlic cloves, and Mollejas en Salsa Casera, lamb's sweetbreads with a creamy sauce. Merluza al Ajillo is cutlet of hake cooked in oil with garlic. To finish the meal Santa Clara con Crocantes is a type of cake with ice cream. The wine list includes Verdejo Pálido from Rueda and also wines from Toro and Ribera del Duero.

The route is now across flat, featureless landscape relieved only by pine trees and fields of sunflowers. About 23km to the north along the N 601 is Cuellar with a 15th-century castle, many ancient houses and several Mudéjar churches. If you have time, visit the castle of Peñafiel, about 30km further to the north-east. Over 200m long, it is one of the largest and most imposing in the region. The walls of the castle are punctuated by twelve elegant circular towers.

San Idelfonso La Granja.

ZAMORA

THE NEXT STAGE OF THE TOUR is west to the Parador at Zamora, a distance of only 65km. I have outlined a circuitous route which first leads 30km north-east to Vallodolid. This large, busy city however would need a full day to do it justice. The main sights include the Cathedral which was completed in the early 18th century, contains a superb 16th-century retablo and fine choir stalls among its many treasures. Numerous churches include the 15th-century Santa María la Antigua and the 15th-century Las Angustias. The Colegio San Gregorio, a lovely building with Plateresque, Gothic and Mudéjar influences in its magnificently decorated façade and a beautiful Plateresque gallery now houses the National Museum of Sculpture. En route to Valladolid you will pass the town of Simancas whose picturesque château-like castle houses the National Archive, containing over 30 million documents.

The medieval town of Sepúlveda.

The Castillo de Coca.

12km to the north of Valladolid is the small town of Fuensaldaña whose well-preserved 15th-century castillo has a square keep and round towers at each corner. A small road, VA 514 follows a small valley to the village of Torrelobatón, dominated by a well-preserved, 15th-century castle. At Mota del Marqués, 16km further west is the lovely hall church of San Martín with a Plateresque portal; the Mudéjar chapel of NS de Castellaños, a Renaissance palace and the remains of a castle.

It is worth making a small detour to the north to visit the ancient, fortified hilltop town of Ureñua, still encircled by crenellated walls with old gateways and towers remaining. Close by, near Villa García de Campos, is the Monasterio de la Espina a lovely old building in a peaceful secluded valley. The villages in this region, formed of adobe houses coated with an ochre-coloured clay, look like old sepia photographs.

Continuing westwards to Tiedra, where there is a

The Plaza Mayor of Pedraza de la Sierra.

ruined castle, then south-west along the C 519 through endless wheatfields to Toro, you pass another ruined castle at Villalonso. Toro, a small, ancient town, is famed for its wines. It has an imposing 13th-century church, the Collegiata Santa María la Mayor, set beside a shady square with views down to the Río Duero far below. Other interesting buildings include an 18th-century *ayuntamiento*, the 13th-century Mudéjar church of El Salvador and a 15th-century palace, now the Convent of Mercedarias Descalzas. The route continues 33km westwards along the N 122 to Zamora.

Zamora, built on a rocky hill, lies on the right bank of the Río Duero and is an historic city, at one time home both to the Romans and the Moors. In the church of Santiago de los Caballeros is the altar at which El Cid is said to have been knighted. The most distinctive of the city's buildings is the Byzantine cathedral which has a cupola tiled in a fish-scale pattern and beautiful doorways, particularly the Puerta del Obispo, decorated with particularly fine sculptures. The interior's treasures include a 15th-century retablo and a collection of

Flemish tapestries. Next to the cathedral is the castle surrounded by gardens with far-reaching views from the battlements.

The Portillo de la Traición, the traitor's gate, commemorates the murder of Sancho II asleep in his tent during a seige of the city in 1072. Other buildings of note include the Romanesque churches of Santa Magdalena and San Cipriano, the 12th-century church of Santa María de la Horta and the 17th-century *ayuntamiento*.

The Parador Nacional Condes de Alba y Aliste, set in a 15th-century palace on a quiet square in the city centre, has been sensitively converted, preserving a magnificent staircase and beautiful cloisters surrounding a courtyard. The decor includes suits of armour, tapestries and banners along with comfortable, traditionally styled furniture and antiques.

The menu includes Dos y Pingada, pieces of pork fillet cooked with eggs; Truchas a la Sanabresa, fresh fried trout; La Sanantonada, a rich dish of stewed white beans; and Chuleta de Cerdo Ahumada, smoked pork chop. The wine list includes some from neighbouring Toro. Sangre de Toro, literally bull's blood, is a full-bodied, highly alcoholic red wine quite different to that of the same name from Penedés in Cataluña.

A detour can be made to the Visigothic church of San Pedro de la Nave by taking the N 122 to the north-west and then forking right after 12km on to a small road to Campanillo. It is an attractive drive through remote countryside of wheatfields and oak trees. The small church, which has fine carved stone capitals, is thought to have been built in about 680. It was moved to its present position in 1932 before its original site was flooded to create the Embalse de Elsa.

Another small detour can be made to the south-east to Arcenillas where the Gothic church contains a collection of beautiful panels painted by Fernando Gallego in 1490. There is also a 13th-century Christ and a collection of religious dolls.

CIUDAD RODRIGO

FROM ZAMORA the next stage of the tour is south-west to the Parador at Ciudad Rodrigo, a direct journey of 151km. I have outlined a route which allows you to explore the countryside bordering Portugal and the valley of the Río Duero. Leaving the city to the south on the N 630, after crossing the river a road to the right, the C 527, leads towards Fermoselle. The first part of this journey is flat with rocky outcrops, stubby oak trees and small, isolated fields of grain. There is little sign of life between the occasional tiny villages.

Around Fermoselle the landscape changes, becoming more hilly and rugged with extensive areas of vineyards. It is a most attractive old town built on a rocky hill, with a castle and a 13th-century church with exceptional groin vaults and a tower. Under the medieval village houses and tangle of narrow cobbled streets there is a maze of ancient wine cellars. I was told by a villager, who insisted on giving me a guided tour, that they were over 800 years old.

The road continues southwards towards Salamanca descending in a series of steep curves into a ravine-like rocky valley, terraced with vineyards, olive groves and almond trees. The Río Tormes flows through it – a delightful spot for a picnic. It is remote, peaceful countryside and on the other side of the valley the ground is strewn with huge boulders. Beyond this is a region of open heathland which gives way to fields of grain and vineyards.

At the road junction the route turns right towards Villariño and Aldeadávila de la Ribera. The road continues southwards across flat heathland to Saucelle, a small, attractive village. About 3km further there is a dramatic viewpoint of the deep, plunging valley through which the Río Duero flows. The landscape here is of immense proportions. At the junction with the C 517 the route leads eastwards towards Lumbrales, with remains of Roman walls. 10km to the south is the ancient walled town of San Felices de los Gallegos, with the impressive remains of a castle surrounded by extensive walls. There is an unusual Romanesque church incorporating a gateway. About 40km to the north-east is Yecla de Yeltes, where there are the remains of an Iberian castle, the 16th-century church of San Sebastián and the Hermitage of NS del Castillo. From San Felices it is only 40km to Ciudad Rodrigo.

Ciudad Rodrigo is an enchanting old walled town set beside the Río Agueda with a splendid 14th-century castle perched high above it. The fortifications are well preserved: massive walls encircling the town are punctuated by impressive gateways and towers. Lining the streets and small squares are a wealth of mellow medieval buildings, many with seigneurial crests. The 13th-century Cathedral of Santa María has magnificent portals (the west in particular is exquisitely decorated), an early 16th-century Gothic cloister and finely carved choir stalls from the end of the 15th century. The 16th-century *ayuntamiento* is also a lovely building as is the Capilla del Cerralbo and the Casa de los Castros. Don't

A medieval mansion in Ciudad Rodrigo.

miss seeing the old post office, which still fulfils its purpose. The original desks and benches, ornate wrought iron grills and decorative panels and ceilings have all been preserved. A lively country market takes place in the square by the Capilla del Cerralbo on Tuesdays where baskets of fruit and vegetables are sold with dark and damp soil still clinging to their roots.

The Parador Nacional Enrique II is situated in the castle and a more enticing place to stay is hard to imagine. It is only a short walk from the *plaza mayor* (main square) which is full of character. I walked down in the evening for a drink before dinner and the sound of animated conversation and laughter reached me long before I arrived – like a distant party in full swing. There is a small garden on the steep hillside in front of the castle which provides lovely views down to the river. The bedrooms of the castle are linked by a series of tunnel-like corridors creating a cosy but fortress-like atmosphere. The restaurant is particularly attractive with a high-beamed ceiling and windows looking out over the river. The menu includes Magras de Cerdo en Cazuela, fillet of pork cooked in a rich tomato sauce and Perdiz Estofada Jardinera, braised partridge stuffed with vegetables. Roscas, delicious almond biscuits, are made in Saucelle.

An excursion to the south-east into the Sierra de la Peña de Francia can be made from Ciudad Rodrigo by leaving the city on the C 515 towards Béjar. Initially the route is quite flat along a quiet country road with a view of distant mountains. At El Maillo the route turns right towards La Alberca. After a few kms a small road detours to the right and climbs up towards the monastery of NS de la Peña de Francia, winding through wooded slopes thickly covered with cork oaks, fir trees and carpeted with bracken, rosemary and thyme. The lovely old blackened stone building could scarcely have a more dramatic setting. It is built on the very summit of a pinnacle of rock which rises more than 6000ft above sea level. It commands astonishing views over a full 360° and a *mirador* with direction signs enables you to identify distant features such as Bejar and the Embalse de Gabriel y Galán.

You can continue on a small circuit through the mountains, firstly to San Martín de Castañar, a small, captivating village with a web of narrow streets and alleys, lined with small rough-stone houses patterned by exposed timbers. They cascade with flowers which hang from wooden balconies and stone arcades. During my visit the villagers were busy with the cherry harvest. Huge brimming baskets of shiny red fruit from the trees on the hillsides around the village were being carried in on mules.

The weekly market in Ciudad Rodrigo.

There are beautiful views all around as the road continues through Sequeros to Miranda del Castañar, which has a castle and Romanesque church. A particularly pretty village with very steep cobbled alleys leading off from the main street, it is entered through a fortified gateway. The countryside is lush and green with orchards, fig and chestnut trees and small market gardens covering the hillsides.

The route continues through Cepedo, Sotoserrano and Madroñal to La Alberca. The road is a scenic delight, winding round the hillsides like a lateral helter-skelter and providing constantly changing views. La Alberca, a slightly larger but picturesque old town, is the capital of the region with an arcaded *plaza mayor* and a 17th-century church. Traditional plays, in which regional costumes and jewellery were worn, take place here in the square in mid-August.

If you do not want to return to Ciudad Rodrigo the nearest alternative Parador to La Alberca is at Jarandilla de la Vera (page 94).

The village of San Martín de Castañar in the Sierra de Peña de Francia.

*T*OUR 8 *Explores the provinces of Ávila, Salamanca and Cáceres in the western region of Castile-León and the northern part of Extremadura, including some exciting mountain scenery in the Sierra de Gredos, the atmospheric cities of Salamanca and Ávila and numerous small unspoilt villages. There are also some memorable castles in this region. The paradors featured include one unusual modern building with a superb outlook, two 15th-century palaces and a remote mountain lodge. The itinerary creates a round trip based on Madrid and the first parador at Ávila is about 120km from Madrid airport.*

— TOUR 8 —
MICHELIN MAP NOS. 447 & 441

SALAMANCA

ÁVILA

Sierra de Gredos

Jarandilla de la Vera

ÁVILA
SALAMANCA
JARANDILLA DE LA VERA
SIERRA DE GREDOS

ÁVILA

FROM MADRID the route is initially along the N 6 to the north-west of the city. At Las Rozas it forks left on to the C 505 to San Lorenzo de El Escorial, set in a peaceful wooded valley. This is the location of a vast monastery built during the reign of King Phillip II to mark his defeat of the French in 1557. The building, completed in 1584, is in the form of a large rectangle with towers at each corner. There are 12 cloisters, over 80 staircases, 16 chapels and 16 courtyards. The exterior is severe but its massive façade is extremely impressive.

The Patio de los Reyes (courtyard of the Kings) is entered through the main portal and decorated by huge statues of the Old Testament kings. The interior is a virtual maze of rooms, ante-chambers, corridors and staircases. The Royal Palace contains a wealth of tapestries, paintings and frescoes which decorate the walls from floor to ceiling and depict every aspect of medieval life. The library too is an extraordinary room: extravagantly decorated, it contains the most important collection of books in Spain. There is also an exquisite 16th-century Florentine planetarium. Most of the rooms can only be visited with a guided tour and it would be easy to spend a whole day here. The visitor's ticket also provides access to two Royal lodges nearby, Casita del Príncipe and the Casita del Arriba. 14km to the north of El Escorial is the Valle de los Caídos where there is a memorial to those who died in the Civil War.

From San Lorenzo the road climbs up out of the valley and over a winding pass through barren hillsides. Beyond, the road descends again through a rocky pine-clad valley to Las Navas del Marqués with its 15th-century Gothic church and a 16th-century fortified palace with a beautiful Renaissance courtyard.

The road continues through an open heath-covered landscape with views of distant mountains towards Ávila, a remarkable town set on a hill overlooking the Río Adaja. It is ringed by massive crenellated walls, the

most complete and well preserved in Spain. They are 2.5km in circumference, over 10ft thick and 40ft high. Every 30m there is a tower, with 88 altogether. The town is entered through 9 fortified gateways, some of which are extremely beautiful.

The 12th-century cathedral was originally Romanesque in design but was continued in Gothic and Renaissance styles. It is still unfinished: the west façade has an incomplete tower. The interior walls are built from an unusual stone with red and white striations. The 12th-century churches of San Pedro and San Vincente, built of a mellow golden stone, are also of great interest. The 15th-century Dominican monastery of Santo Tomás has three cloisters of which the King's cloister is especially beautiful.

Ávila is the birthplace of Santa Teresa and there is a museum dedicated to her life and works in the Convento de las Madres. The Convento de Santa Teresa incorporates the house in which she was born. La Encarcina is the convent where the saint spent 27 years as a nun and a collection of relics are also kept here. Her cell has been converted into a chapel. The old town of Ávila also possesses many ancient palaces and mansions.

The Parador Nacional Raimundo de Borgoña is situated in part of the town walls just inside the Puerto de Carmen and only a few minutes' walk from the main square. There is a lively country market here on Fridays. The Parador is named after Count Raymond of Burgundy who regained the city from the Moors. The public rooms occupy a 15th-century palace known as the Piedras Altas, the high stones. Inside, an imposing marble staircase leads to the bedrooms which are housed in a modern extension built in traditional style. The Parador has a peaceful, secluded garden shaded by pine trees where you can climb up on to the ramparts and walk along the battlements.

Regional dishes on the menu include: Judías del Barco de Ávila, large white beans cooked in a rich paprika-flavoured sauce with *chorizo* and salt pork; and Pucherete Teresiano, a chunky soup with mixed vegetables and pieces of meat. A delicious and unusual local sweet is Yemas de Santa Teresa, candied egg yolks, golden yellow and intensely sweet that melt deliciously in the mouth. An interesting wine from the region is Cebreros: very strong with a distinctive flavour, it comes from a small village in the hills to the south.

*O*ne of the fortified gateways of Ávila.

Landscape near Solosancho.

An interesting excursion can be made into the wild, remote countryside of the Sierra de la Paramera to the south-west of Ávila. The route is initially along the N 110 towards Piedrahita. At Muñogalindo a road leads south through fields of grain bordered by dry stone walls to Solosancho. This region is known as the Wilderness of Ulaca, the site of an Iron age settlement. Solosancho is an ancient village of curious stone houses thatched with dried brushwood. In the centre is the 15th-century castle of Viciosa. Beyond the village an unsurfaced road climbs higher into the mountains where massive boulders are scattered on the hillsides which are carpeted with bushes of yellow broom and heather.

From Solosancho a small road, the C 502, turns back towards Ávila. Shortly a road to the right leads to Mironcillo. From here a rough road leads into a rugged and dramatic landscape to the 15th-century Castillo de Aunque-os-pese set above the village of Sotalvo and belonging to the Medinaceli family. The castle is in an impressive setting, built on a massive border from which its walls appear to be moulded. From here a quiet scenic road leads back via the village of Río Frio to Ávila.

SALAMANCA

THE NEXT STAGE OF THE TOUR is north-west to the Parador at Salamanca. The first part of the route follows the N 501 towards Peñaranda de Bracamonte. After about 1km a road leads to the village of Cardenosa. Nearby is a 4th-century BC Iron Age settlement. Continuing along the N 501 a road to the right leads to San Juan de la Encinilla. Nearby, in the village of Narros de Saldueña is a remarkable Mudéjar fortress complete with its portcullis.

At Peñaranda de Bracamonte are two large plazas surrounded by stone arcades, a large hall church and a Carmelite convent with a good cloister. From here the SA 114 leads south-west to Alba de Tormes, where Santa Theresa died and an important place of pilgrimage. The convent of Carmelitas Descalzas was founded by her in 1571 and contains the saint's relics in a casket beneath the altar. Other churches include San Juan (12th-century), mixture of Romanesque and Mudéjar, and the 12th-century churches of Santiago and San

Miguel also blend Mudéjar and Romanesque styles. A 16th-century tower remains from a palace which belonged to the Duke of Alba. From here the C 510 leads north-west to Salamanca.

The Parador Nacional de Salamanca, just outside the city on a knoll beside the Río Tormes, is aggressively modern in its design, tiered in blocks of white stone like a cubist's impression of a mountain. It commands magnificent views of the city which the bedrooms also enjoy from large balconies. It's worth waking early to see the sunrise over the city and at dusk it is equally memorable.

Among the Castilian dishes on the menu I chose Chuletas de Ternera a la Castellana, veal cutlets braised in sherry and served with asparagus and green beans. Tortilla Española is a potato omelette and has become a staple Spanish dish. It is not just an omelette, however – more like a rich golden brown cake of eggs and potatoes. Sometimes onions, peppers and other vegetables are added but the classic version is just eggs and potatoes cooked in olive oil. Pecho de Ternera con Guisantes is a veal stew with peas flavoured with thyme, parsley and saffron.

Salamanca is a quite magical city, endowed with many of the finest examples of the Plateresque style of architecture. The buildings are of a mellow golden stone which, when seen in the evening light, almost appears to glow.

The Plaza Mayor is arguably the most magnificent square in Spain. Built in the early 17th century it is surrounded by tall arcaded buildings with richly decorated Baroque façades. It is very much the hub of Salamanca and a wonderful place to experience the vibrant life of the city. To sit at a café table with *churros* and a coffee in the morning is to take breakfast in real style.

Nearby are the twin cathedrals. The new in Gothic style dates from the 17th century and the old, linked by a passage, was built in the 12th century. The façade of the early-16th-century University is perhaps the most famous example of Plateresque art. The Casa de las Conchas is also a famous landmark, a mansion decorated with sculpted shells, beautiful windows and coats of arms. The convent of San Esteban has a superb 16th-century Plateresque façade. The massive Roman bridge is also an impressive sight, spanning the Río Tormes on 26 arches and is over 400m long. There is so much more to see that a guide book is necessary to explore it fully.

JARANDILLA DE LA VERA

THE NEXT STAGE OF THE JOURNEY is south to the Parador at Jarandilla de la Vera. The route is south along the

The mountain village of Candelario.

N 630 towards Béjar across open heath and pasture land. Béjar is a large busy town set high in a mountain valley at the foot of the Sierra de Candelario. There are remains of Moorish walls and the 16th-century Alcázar del Duque de Osuna with a Renaissance patio. A road leads high into the mountains to the curious village of Candelario in a lovely setting below a mountain peak. Its steep cobbled streets are lined by houses with over-hanging balconies and unusual double stable-like doors. Curved tiles are used to cover the walls of the houses, giving them a strange ridged appearance. The older ladies of the village still wear their hair in an elaborately coiffured traditional style.

South from Béjar the road begins to descend along the side of the valley. After about 10km a road to the west detours into a peaceful wooded valley to the pretty hilltop village of Montemayor del Río with its castle and Roman bridge. Beyond Baños de Montemayor, a thermal resort of Roman origins, a road to the east leads to Hervás. Set among meadows and cherry orchards it possesses the churches of Santa María and San Juan Bautista, the latter with a fine Baroque retablo. There is also a well-preserved old Jewish quarter. A short distance further south a road to the west leads to Abadía. Here a Templar's castle was first converted into a Cistercian abbey and then into a palace for the Duke of Alba. It contains an exceptionally lovely two-storey Mudéjar cloister with horseshoe arches. The palace was designed in the 16th century by Flemish and Italian artists and once had a beautiful garden and parklands.

A few kms further to the west, overlooking the Embalse de Gabriel y Galán, is the deserted village of Granadilla with a 14th-century castle and a 16th-century church. Once an important town it was abandoned when the valley was flooded and now rests in serene isolation on the banks of a beautiful lake. It was the home of one of the Conquistadores who named two towns in Perú after it.

The road skirts the edge of the lake and then leads south-east to the ruins of Cáparra where an imposing Roman triumphal arch remains. The main road is re-gained after a few kms where the route continues south-west to the medieval town of Plasencia. Set on the banks of the Río Jerte it dates from Roman times. Parts of its extensive walls and towers remain together with the castle. The cathedral dates from the 13th century although the main structure was not completed until the 16th century. There are also many interesting churches and mansions.

The Parador at Jarandilla de la Vera is 56km to the east of Plasencia. There is however an interesting de-

The Plaza Mayor of Salamanca.

Traditional costume in Montehermoso.

houses and atmospheric old streets. Returning to the main road and heading northwards for 6km a road to the east leads to Monroy where there is a well-preserved castle and a lovely 15th-century Gothic church.

The route leads north-east along the CC 912 to Torrejón de Rubio. About 15km along this road you can make a detour to the left to Serradilla, with two old churches, and Mirabel where there are the ruins of a 12th-century castle, a church and a 16th-century palace.

At Torrejón the route leads north along the C 524 to the castle-like sanctuary of Monfrague. This beautiful region is a natural park preserved for its wild life. The road runs beside a lake which is overlooked by towering crags. You can see eagles' nests perched on small ledges and watch the huge birds wheeling lazily around the cliff face. From here the road continues northwards to the Puerto de la Serrana and then to Palencia.

The route to Jarandilla continues eastwards along the C 501 with lovely views of the Río Tietar. About 1km beyond Jaraiz de la Vera, the centre of the region's tobacco and paprika cultivation, a road leads up into the mountains to the picturesque village of Garganta de Olla. A few kms further is Cuacos de Yuste, another unspoilt village of ancient arcaded houses.

A road leads into a peaceful wooded hillside to the Hieronomite monastery of Yuste, founded in 1408 and famous because Emperor Carlos V died here in 1558. You can visit the sombre, black-draped room in which he died. Some of his possessions, including his sedan chair – he suffered from gout – his bed and even the sheets in which he died have been preserved. There are two interesting cloisters and a 17th-century refactory decorated with Mudéjar *azulejos*.

The Parador Nacional Carlos V, on the edge of the town of Jarandilla de la Vera, occupies a 14th-century castle which belonged to the Counts of Oropesa and is one of the most evocative and historic buildings in the Parador network. The Emperor Carlos V lived here for two years while preparations were made for him at the monastery of Yuste. Charles de Gaulle also spent the night here.

An impressive inner courtyard is overlooked by a beautiful Renaissance gallery and imposing round towers. The interior is decorated with antique furniture, tapestries, paintings and ancient weapons. High-beamed ceilings, mellow wooden floors and open fireplaces create a medieval ambience combined with modern comfort.

The menu includes a number of regional specialties: Bacalao al Estilo de Yuste, dried salt cod cooked and combined with puréed potato and butter; Caldereta a la Jarandilla, lamb stew flavoured with paprika and garlic; Huevos a la Extremeña, eggs baked in a white sauce with peppers, onions and tomatoes and flavoured with paprika and parsley.

tour further to the west of the city which I will describe now but which would need a separate day's excursion to complete.

The CC 204 leads west to Montehermoso, a small town famous for its curious local costume which is still occasionally worn. The hats, made of plaited straw, are elaborately embroidered and bejewelled, with a distinctly South American appearance. Local shops sell baskets and other gifts in the same style. A road leads south-west to Coria, an ancient city with extensive fortified walls and towers, a 15th-century castle, a Gothic cathedral with Renaissance additions and a fine Platersque portal, the palace of the Duke of Alba, several interesting mansions, and an impressive Roman bridge spanning the river.

From Coria the C 526 leads south-east, passing the ruined castle of Portezuelo, to join the N 630 beside the Embalse de Alcántara. Continuing south for about 15km a road to the right leads to Garovillas whose spacious arcaded plaza is surrounded by whitewashed

SIERRA DE GREDOS

The Sierra de Gredos near Hoyos de Espino.

THE NEXT STAGE OF THE TOUR is eastwards to the Parador at Navarredonda de Gredos. The route leads along the C 501 through a sequence of small villages similar to Jarandilla with old porticoed houses with wooden balconies and narrow cobbled streets. Candeleda is an attractive little town with timbered houses, balconies and arcades, and a 15th-century Gothic church. Beyond is Arenas de San Pedro, a large, popular summer resort at the foot of the Sierra de Gredos, containing the Castillo de la Triste Condesa (the castle of the sad countess) – a 15th-century castle in which the widow of Don Alvaro de Luna lived after he was beheaded on the orders of Juan II of Castile. There is also an 18th-century palace, a Gothic church and the 18th-century monastery of San Pedro de Alcántara with a fine retablo. Nearby is the village of Ramascastañas where there is an impressive stalactite cavern, the grotto of Romperropas.

From Arenas de San Pedro a small road climbs through impressive scenery to the attractive old village of Guisando set high on the mountainside. A road continues along the course of a beautiful river, which tumbles down through the pine trees over rocks, and via the dramatically sited village of El Hornillo and El Arenal finally descends into the valley to Mombeltran. Here there is the beautiful 14th-century castle of the Duques of Alberquerque with its imposing façades, courtyards and staircases, strikingly set against a backdrop of the snow-capped peaks of the Sierra de Gredos. The town also has 15th-century Gothic church, a 16th-century Renaissance hospital and several medieval mansions with escutcheons.

The route continues northwards along the C 502 to the picturesque village of Cuevas de Valle where it begins to climb towards the Puerto de Pico. The views from this road are sensational. If, like me, you enjoy driving over mountain passes this is one to remember. At the top you can see the remains of the old Roman road.

The route continues north for about 6km and then the C 500 leads west along a shallow valley to San Martín del

Pimpolar. The countryside here is intensely green with small trees and boulders dotting the meadows and mountainsides.

The Parador Nacional de Gredos – the first ever parador – is over 6000ft above sea level in a peaceful, isolated setting surrounded by snow-covered peaks. Built in 1928 on a site chosen by King Alfonso XIII, it is in the midst of some of the finest hunting and fishing countryside in Spain. It has, not surprisingly, the atmosphere of a hunting lodge with polished pine floors, wooden beams and comfortable leather furniture. A long verandah extends along the rear of the Parador with an outlook of pine forests and snow-covered peaks.

The menu included: Truchas con Almejas con Vino de Cebreros, a delicious dish of mountain trout and clams poached in the white wine of nearby Cebreros; and Codornices a la Casera, quail cooked in the oven with ham, white wine, mushrooms and onions. For the sweet-toothed, Tocino de cielo (literally, 'salt pork from heaven'), a rich egg custard coated with a caramel sauce.

An excursion into the Sierra de Gredos can be made by continuing westwards along the C 500 to Hoyos del Espino, where a medieval bridge spans the Río Tormes. Here a road leads south along a wide green valley deep into the mountains. Broad meadows of springy green turf threaded by brooks reach away to the snow-clad peaks and a fast-flowing river crashes over boulders.

From Hoyos del Espino the road continues to a junction where the AV 932 leads north towards Piedrahita. The road winds high along the side of a steep V-shaped valley through which a river rushes. The slopes are patterned with dry stone walls and as the road climbs higher the views become increasingly impressive. La Herguijela is a tiny village of red-tiled rough-stone houses completely untouched by the 20th century. The landscape here has a stark and savage beauty. Beyond at the Puerto de la Pena Negra the views are immense. The road descends to the lovely small town of Piedrahita with a 15th-century Gothic church, an 18th-century palace where the Duke of Alba was born, the 12th-century church of La Asunción and a Carmelite convent.

The route leads south-west along the N 110 to El Barco de Ávila, on the banks of the Río Tormes. Overlooking the town is the 14th-century castle of Valdecorneja. There is also a 14th-century Gothic church with a massive tower and an interior with many fine features. The return to the Parador can be made by following the C 500 to the east.

The nearest alternative Parador to Gredos is at Oropesa, 90km (page 120). The route back towards Madrid can incorporate an excursion into the eastern region of the Sierra de Gredos. From Gredos the route is initially

back along the C 502 to the Puerto del Pico. A few km further south a road leads eastwards into pine-clad mountains to the attractive village of San Esteban del Val. The road continues through dramatic mountain scenery to Pedro Bernardo, perched on the very edge of the mountain, from where there are extraordinary views.

The road descends to join the C 501 where the route continues eastwards to Piedralaves, which has a picturesque old quarter with ancient galleried houses and

El Barco de Ávila.

steep cobbled streets. The road continues through green meadows to Adrada, with its ruined castle, and San Martín de Valdeiglesias. Nearby are the Toros de Guisando, curious granite sculptures of bulls believed to be of Iberian origin. Here too is the 14th-century monastery of Guisando. A few kms to the north is El Tiemblo where there is a large fortress-like 16th-century church.

Here the AV 504 leads westwards through remote rocky hillsides patterned with vineyards to the wine town of Cebreros. There is a 16th-century Renaissance church, the ruins of a monastery and several medieval mansions in the town – as well as several shops where the unusual local wine can be bought. The road continues north-east to join the C 505 between Ávila and El Escorial.

*T*OUR 9 Explores the region to the north-east of Madrid beginning in the province of Guadalajara and leading north into Soria. It includes one of the most beautiful monasteries in Spain, an atmospheric medieval town, a remarkable hidden valley and numerous villages and castles. Linked with tour No. 5 (page 60) it provides a scenic route between Madrid and the French border. The first Parador at Sigüenza is about 150km from Madrid airport.

SIGÜENZA

—TOUR 9—
MICHELIN MAP NO. 442
• VALLODOLID
Soria
Santa María de Huerta
Sigüenza

SIGÜENZA
SANTA MARÍA
DE HUERTA – SORIA

FROM MADRID AIRPORT the route leads first along the N 11 eastwards past Alcalá de Henares to Guadalajara, the capital of the province. It continues north-east along the N 11 for about 20km until you reach a road to the right, the C 201. Here you can make a small detour to visit Brihuega, a picturesque old town on a hill beside the Río Tajuna, with a number of interesting old buildings along its typically narrow streets including four Romanesque churches. There is a festival held here in August when the bulls are run through the streets as in Pamplona.

Returning to the main road the tour continues north-east for another 10km and then turns left on to the GU 184 to Jadraque. The road runs along the almost sheer edge of a high ridge which overlooks a vast plain below with superb panoramic views. As the road descends in a series of wide sweeping curves the 15th-century castle of Jadraque comes dramatically into view. It is set on the summit of a steep conical hill on the side of the valley. A rough track leads up to the castle from where you can see for miles across the vast patterned plain.

Returning a short distance back along the road and then taking a right fork on to the C 101 leads to Hita, a picturesque walled village strikingly set at the foot of a lofty hill. Here there is a well-preserved, 12th-century gate, an arcaded plaza and the ruined monastery of Sopetrán. A small road, the GU 144, heads north to the town of Cogolludo set below a ruined castle. On one side of its large arcaded plaza is the magnificent 15th-century Palacio de Medinaceli, built in Renaissance style with a finely decorated façade of mellow golden stone and a Plateresque portal.

From Cogolludo the GU 151 continues northwards towards Hiendelaencina. The countryside here is peaceful with gently sloping hillsides planted with pine forests and covered in green springy turf and heather. Hiendelaencina is a most curious place, a village of small stone houses set in a wide green valley with few trees and divided by numerous dry stone

walls and dotted with the remains of ancient silver mines, now abandoned.

From Hiendelaencina the GU 152 continues northwards through a small secluded rocky valley covered in brush. Wild thyme, sage and rosemary grow beside the road and a small river traces its course over a rocky bed. The village of Naharros is built out of the grey stone boulders scattered on the slopes, as are the numerous dry stone walls bordering the fields. Just beyond, the medieval walled village of Atienza comes into view at the widening of the valley. Its houses are spread down the slopes of a steep rocky hill and a ruined castle looks down over the village rooftops from the summit and the towers of several old churches are visible. A road goes up to and beyond the village and a small track leads up to the castle where there are far-reaching views over endless fields of wheat and sunflowers to distant mountains. There are seven churches dotted throughout the village.

The route follows the C 114 eastwards towards Sigüenza. Just beyond the village of Imon there are extensive salt pans which are still in use with two enormous, ancient stone warehouses to store the salt. At the junction a little further on a brief detour to the left brings you to the village of Riba de Santiuste where there is an impressive castle on a rocky hill beside the small village.

Returning southwards, about 5km before reaching Sigüenza, a small road to the right leads to the partially deserted village of Palazuelos, with well-preserved remains of its walls, the ruins of a castle and a gateway. Although rather derelict it has considerable charm and atmosphere. Continuing south for a few kms a curve in the road suddenly reveals a dramatic view of the old town of Sigüenza. It is set on a hill in the fertile valley of the Río Henares and is surrounded by orchards and fields of grain.

Sigüenza is a quite magical place. Very old and with a rather faded glory it evokes the feeling of a medieval stronghold and is dominated by its castle which, built by the Arabs in the 12th century, looms high above the steep cobbled streets of the town. The 12th-century cathedral is also fortified. Facing on to a beautiful plaza surrounded by stone arcades, it contains the tomb of a young nobleman ornamented by one of the most important Romanesque religious sculptures in Spain, known as the Doncel. The sacristy contains a beauti-

The cathedral of Sigüenza.

fully decorated ceiling by Covarubias and there are paintings by El Greco and Titian. Many interesting old buildings and the narrow streets provide rewarding hours of exploration. A lively market is held just outside the town walls on Saturdays.

The Parador Nacional Castillo de Sigüenza is situated within the Moorish castle walls and is one of the most magnificent of the historic paradors. It is a few minutes' walk down the hill to the cathedral and the *plaza mayor*. The lounge is an enormous room with a lofty beamed ceiling luxuriously furnished and decorated with tapestries, suits of armour, banners and seignorial crests. The restaurant, situated in the tower of Doña Blanca, is dominated by huge stone arches.

The menu has a good selection of Castilian dishes, including excellent roast meats like suckling pig and lamb; Chuletas de Ternera a la Madrileña, pork chops coated with chopped onion garlic and herbs and roasted; and Cocido Castellano, a stew with chick peas, potatoes, cabbage, salt pork and chorizo. Navercillos appear on the menu in the autumn when in season and are the wild orange-brown fungi found in the pine forests. Cooked with garlic and serrano ham they have a unique flavour and texture. Along with the more familiar Riojas and Valdepeñas wines, look out for those from Ribera del Duero, a wine-growing region to the north around the town of Aranda de Duero. Of these the most renowned is the fine red wine of the Vega Sicilia vineyards.

SANTA MARÍA DE HUERTA

THE NEXT STAGE of the tour is north-east to Santa María de Huerta, a direct journey of only 64km. Leaving Sigüenza on a small road to the north-east leads to the small village of Guijosa where there are the remains of a castle. A fascinating house has been carved out of a huge rock in the nearby village of Alcolea de Pinar, next to the main road, the N 11. It took Luis Bueno 20 years to carve a series of tunnels and chambers to form a small home with a fireplace and even windows.

The route leads along the N 11 north for 17km to the town of Medinaceli. This is reached by a small road leading off about 1km to the west. Set on the summit of a high hill, commanding sweeping views over the plain below, it is an ancient Iberian settlement which subsequently became both a Roman and Arab stronghold. It has an impressive 2nd-century Roman arch, the 16th-century church of Santa María and the Monasterió of Beatario San Ramón. An imposing arcaded plaza is overlooked by an 18th-century Ducal palace. However, the town is now almost completely

The hilltop village of Atienza.

The Palacio de Medinaceli at Cogolludo.

deserted and has a strange, ghost-town atmosphere.

Continuing north-east from Medinaceli along the N 11, the route follows the valley of the Río Jalón to Arcos de Jalón, which has the remains of a castle. It is a richly fertile region with crops of all varieties including orchards. The river flows dark and thick like red mud. Santa María de Huerta is unremarkable but for the impressive Benedictine monastery in its midst. Founded in the 12th century by Alfonso VII, among the features that make it one of the most beautiful in Spain are enormous rose windows, a magnificent Gothic cloister and an 18th-century Baroque retablo. There are also fine Plateresque choir stalls, frescoes illustrating the battle of Navas de Tolosa and a huge vaulted Gothic refactory. The guided tour which is offered provides a fascinating hour or so.

The Parador Nacional de Santa María de Huerta, situated just off the N 11 about 1km east of the town, is a spacious, comfortable and modern, motel-style building. The restaurant, in common with all paradors, offers regional food as well as the more familiar

The fortified gateway of Hita.

Spanish dishes: Potaje de Garbanzos y Espinacas, a substantial soup of chick peas, spinach, salt cod, tomatoes, onions and eggs; and Perdiz Escabechada, partridge cooked in a sauce of olive oil, onions, herbs, wine and wine vinegar, left to marinade for several days and served at room temperature. The wine list includes those from the region of Cariñena, 50km to the east, as well as Ribera del Duero and Riojas.

A further enjoyable excursion can be made into the countryside to the east. Leaving Santa María the route leads to the east for about 25km through a rocky valley which becomes progressively deeper and narrower. The spa town of Alhama de Aragón is situated between two cliffs in the deepest part of the valley, the road passing through a tunnel. A few kms further east is the old town of Ateca which possesses two imposing Mudéjar towers. 14km further to the east is the old town of Calatayud, a castle set among, and blending with, clay-coloured hills within which are troglodyte dwellings – some still populated. The town contains many old buildings including a ruined castle the 17th-century church of Santo Sepulcro and the 16th-century church of Santa María. There are several Mudéjar towers and an old Judería. The Convent of Santo Domingo is just outside the town.

Returning westwards to Ateca an attractive scenic road, the Z 461, leads south to Nuevelos, passing along the side of the Embalse de Tranquera. Although the hills are dry and clay-like the valley is rich and fertile with orange and almond trees mingling with fields of vegetables and grain. From Nuevelos the road continues to the beautiful Cistercian Monasterio de Piedra, founded in the 12th century and now converted into a luxury hotel. The monastery is built on the side of a deep wooded valley into which water cascades from all directions. It varies from a gentle trickle between mossy banks to a raging torrent, bouncing over boulders creating dramatic waterfalls.

A series of footpaths lead down into the valley, into numerous hidden corners and along the shores of lakes and rivers. At one point a pathway is tunnelled vertically into the hillside behind the largest of the waterfalls which is 40m in depth. Halfway down it opens into a huge cavern behind a massive wall of water – a memorable experience.

The route returns to the N 11 at Alhama de Aragón following a small scenic road to the left, the Z 410 just after crossing the head of the Embalse de la Tranquera. The road passes a picturesque village, Godojos, with a ruined castle and a church with a Mudéjar tower. At Alhama de Aragón the route leads west along the N 11 towards Santa María.

SORIA

THE NEXT STAGE of the tour is north to the Parador at Soria, a direct journey of 104km. Leaving the parador at Santa María de Huerta, the route is first for a few kms along the N 11 to the east. Then turn north on to the C 116 to Monteagudo de las Vicarias. Here there are impressive town walls with gateways, a 15th-century castle and a 16th-century church with a Gothic portal.

This road continues north through remote countryside to Moron de Almazán where there is a lovely 15th-century church with a Plateresque tower overlooking a small square surrounded by medieval mansions. After continuing north for 14km the road joins the N 111 at

The cloister at Santa María de Huerta.

In the valley of the Monasterio de Piedra.

Almazán, an attractive old town beside the Río Duero. A bridge crosses the broad river with tall poplar trees lining its banks. It has the 12th-century church of San Miguel, the 18th-century Ermita de Jesús, the Puerta del Mercado and the medieval Palace of Altamira set on the banks of the river.

Just to the south of the bridge a small road, the C 116 leads west to Berlanga de Duero. Here there is a most impressive 15th-century castle set on a stony ridge with vast encircling walls. Narrow cobbled streets radiating from a picturesque *plaza mayor* are lined with many old houses decorated with wooden arcades. A detour of 12km to the south-east leads to the Ermita de San Baudelio, an 11th-century Mozarabic chapel.

From Berlanga the road continues west to Gormaz where there is another vast, impressive castle with extensive walls encircling the steep hill on which it is built. A road winds up the hill towards it and there are magnificent views over the plain below with a patchwork pattern of fields reaching away to the horizon. The road leads west through vast pine forests to El Burgo de Osma, an atmospheric old town with arcaded streets and a magnificent 13th-century cathedral that is considered one of the finest in Spain.

A short detour 14km to the west along the N 122 leads to San Esteban de Gormaz beside the Río Duero, with an ancient bridge and two attractive 12th-century churches with exterior galleries, San Miguel and del Rivero.

From El Burgo de Osma the route continues northwards along the SO 920 towards San Leonardo de Yague, an attractive scenic route along the valley of the Río Ucero, with rocky, pine-clad hillsides and poplar trees lining the river banks. The town of Ucero is picturesquely sited with an impressive castle mounted above it. Beyond the town a small road leads off to the left into the Canyón de Río Lobos, a small, secluded valley bordered by high cliffs and pinnacles of rock which soar above you. A small river runs between grassy banks and pinewoods – a perfect place to take a picnic lunch.

Returning to the main road it climbs northwards up a steep winding pass out of the valley with magnificent views. At San Leonardo de Yague, where there is a 16th-century castle, the route turns right on to the N 234 towards Soria, an agreeably quiet road passing through hills covered in pine forests. At Abejar you can turn to the north on to the SO 840 to Molinos de Duero, town of warm-coloured stone houses set beside the river.

The road continues through vast pine forests to Vinuesa, an attractive old town set on a hillside with narrow cobbled streets and ancient houses. Along this road I stopped to watch an elderly couple collecting Nacillos the large brown fungi which grow wild under the pine trees. They showed me a huge basket which they had collected that morning and were taking to market on the following day.

From Vinuesa a small road, the SO 830, turns to the left to head deeper into the pine forest towards La Laguna Negra de Urbión. Bracken and green springy turf cover the ground under the pines and the peace is undisturbed. You need to follow the road to the very end and from here a rough footpath leads off over rocky ground towards the lake. Nearby a river tumbles over small boulders and is almost hidden by the trees which line its banks. When you reach the lakeside you have to clamber over huge rocks before it is revealed. On the opposite side a monumental cliff towers above the glasslike water and a cascade tumbles down its face. It is rimmed by enormous rocks and boulders, between which pines and small trees grow – a tempting place to linger and there are beautiful walks into the surrounding woods – and would be worth considering as a separate excursion from the Parador at Soria. From here you must retrace the road to Vinuesa and follow the SO 821 until it joins the N 234 18km west of Soria.

Soria, situated on the right bank of the Río Duero between two hills, is an ancient city regained from the Moors by Alfonso of Aragón and later ceded to Castile. Its ancient buildings are of a reddish stone giving it the quality of an old sepia photograph. One of the most beautiful buildings is the 12th-century church of Santo Domingo whose exquisite Plateresque façade is decorated with fine sculptures. The co-Cathedral of San Pedro is situated on the edge of the town close to the river and has a fine Plateresque portal as well as a 12th-century Plateresque cloister. Nearby, on the banks of the river, is San Juan de Duero, an old monastery of the Order of the Templars, which has preserved a most unusual cloister with horseshoe arches. Among many other interesting buildings in the old part of the city is the Renaissance Palace of the Counts of Gomara, an enormous building with an imposing and ornately decorated façade.

The Parador Antonio Machado, a stylish modern building set on the very brink of the hill overlooking the river, just outside the city, occupies the site of the ruined castle and is now a park with sweeping views over the ancient rooftops, the mountains beyond and the silvery Duero far below. The Parador is named

after a renowned Spanish poet who made Soria both his home and his inspiration. The restaurant has large picture windows providing an impressive panorama. The furnishing and decor are a departure from many of the more modern paradors since elegant contemporary furniture is used, together with polished pine floors and pastel-coloured walls which are decorated with modern prints and paintings.

The menu contains Castilian dishes as well as some from neighbouring Rioja and Navarra: Judías del Burgo de Osma, green beans cooked in a casserole with garlic and serrano ham; and Trucha Escabechada, fried trout

The Castillo of Gormaz.

marinaded in olive oil, white wine and wine vinegar and flavoured with herbs and garlic, and served at room temperature. The wine list includes a selection from Navarra and Ribera de Duero as well as those from the Rioja.

From Soria it is only a short distance to visit Numancia, an ancient settlement of the Iberians and the site of a heroically defended siege against the invading Romans. In 134 BC they could hold out no longer and, rather than surrender, destroyed their city and committed mass suicide. It is situated on a hilltop 7km to the north of Soria along the N 111 near the village of Garray. Today there is little left to see other than stones which trace the course of streets and the foundations of dwellings. The site however commands extensive views all around and evokes a heroic sense of history.

The nearest alternative paradors to Soria are at Calahorra, 116km (page 60) and Santo Domingo de la Calzada, 151km (page 58).

OUR 10 Encompasses one region which is associated with Cervantes, the plain of La Mancha. Comprising five provinces rich in Spanish history – Cuenca, Ciudad-Real, Guadalajara, Toledo and Albacete, traditionally known as New Castile and now forming the Autonomous Community of Castile-La Mancha – it also includes the southern environs of the city of Madrid and the beautiful medieval city of Toledo.

CHINCHÓN
TOLEDO
MANZANARES
ALMAGRO

Miguel de Cervantes has probably done more to promote tourism in inland Spain than any other person and through his legendary character, Don Quixote, has helped to impart a romantic, almost unworldly atmosphere to a region of Spain that is, on the surface, the least well-endowed scenically.

The countryside of La Mancha (from the Arabic *manxa* = 'parched earth') is an extraordinarily flat and expansive tableland, starkly contrasting with the hills and plateaux that rise above the plain – almost, it seems, in defiance – and which, by sheer comparison, are as grand and lofty as any mountain range.

The land itself is called *secano* (unirrigated), but ironically it is a richly fertile region. Vast cornfields alternate with the largest areas of vineyards in the country (from whose grapes come the famous Valdepeñas wine) and they combine with the regimental silver-green rows of olive trees to create the uniquely patterned nature of the La Mancha landscape.

The soil is predominantly a rich terracotta brown with occasional patchworks of chalky white, but through the spring and summer months the Meseta is transformed: entire fields of poppies of a colour and intensity which would otherwise only exist in a paintbox; acres of purple-flowering saffron; or small areas smothered in flowers of every colour and hue that nature has to offer.

The tour starts in the village of Chinchón, less than an hour's drive south of Madrid, then west to the city of Toledo. From here the route strikes south to the adjacent towns of Manzanares and Almagro in the heart of La Mancha.

CHINCHÓN

THE TOWN OF CHINCHÓN can be reached by leaving Madrid on the N 3 and then turning right on to the M 302. The latter part of this road provides an attractive scenic drive as it climbs out of the wide, flat valley of the Río Jarama into the rocky hills among which Chinchón is situated.

The Parador Nacional de Chinchón was once an Augustinian convent. The original convent was founded by the lords of Chinchón in the 15th century in a different part of the town and the present site has been occupied since the 17th century. Since then, however, the building, constructed of the slim, ochre-coloured bricks typical of the region, has been used as the town's courthouse and jail. It adjoins a lovely old church, Santa María del Rosario, the entrance of which is next to the Parador.

This elegant building has a large patio and extensive gardens at the rear. Leafy green trees create a cool and shady retreat. Here, on the garden benches, you can relax and contemplate. Nearby is a large swimming pool within a separate walled patio, shaded by a tiled roof.

The interior contains numerous corridors linking a series of staircases and ante-rooms, all beautifully furnished with antiques and decorated with paintings, tapestries, painted ceilings and frescoes. The atmosphere is peaceful and luxurious.

The superb restaurant is lined with painted alcoves on one side and long, garden windows on the other. The menu includes many regional dishes: Sopa de Almendros, a light, creamy soup, delicately flavoured with almond, garlic and lemon, and garnished with lightly toasted, flaked almonds; Lechazo al Horno con Patatas Panaderíos, roast baby lamb served with potatoes; and Merluza a la Cazuela con Almejas, casserole of hake with clams.

Two puddings which are specialities of the Parador are Pastel de Monje, monk's cake, a rich creamy concoction, and Yemas de Chinchón, candied egg yolks. The wine list includes red, white and *rosé* wines from Chinchón and the neighbouring village of Colmenar as well as a selection of Riojas, Penedés and Manchegan wines.

The Parador could hardly be more conveniently situated, tucked away behind one corner of one of the prettiest and most unusual *plazas mayores* (main squares) in the region. It is a circular 'square', surrounded by three-storeyed houses with arcades and wooden balconies supported on ancient timber beams. The square is overlooked by the 16th-century parish church of NS de la Asunción set on a hill above the square. A tree-shaded square next to the church is a popular gathering place for the villagers in the cool of the evening. Here they can enjoy a delightful bird's-eye view of the village rooftops and the square below.

The square has been a venue for bullfights since 1502 and one is still held each year on 25 July. Theatrical performances are also mounted in the square during

The Plaza Mayor of Chinchón.

Holy Week and a lively market takes place every Saturday. Other buildings of interest in the town are the Monastery of the Mothers of St Clare, the Hermitage of San Antonio, and Chinchón Castle which is on the edge of the town. The 15th-century castle is in the Gothic style – four-sided with circular keeps. Although parts of the ramparts have crumbled away, the large stone bridge and drawbridge remain and the building still has a formidable presence.

Chinchón is also famed for its anisette liqueur which is popular all over Spain.

THE ENVIRONS

CHINCHÓN IS NEAR ENOUGH to Madrid for it to be a convenient base for visiting the capital, for those who prefer not to stay in the city centre. Of course, like any major city Madrid has an enormous variety of interests to offer the visitor and a separate guidebook to the city will be essential if you are to explore it fully, or even if you only have time for a brief visit.

Before starting the journey to Toledo, which is the next parador on the route, a detour of some 50km to the north-east is well worth while in order to visit the town of Alcalá de Henares. From Chinchón you take the C 300 towards Madrid and after about 10km turn right on to the C 300 through Morata de Torres to Arganda, which is known for its wines. Here you cross the National Highway 3 and continue along the C 300 to Alcalá de Henares.

There is however an interesting detour which you can make en route – to the ruined 13th-century Castillo de Casaola. At the point where you should turn right for Morata de Torres, turn left, instead. After about 1km you will see an unsurfaced road to the left leading off into the countryside through vineyards and small farms. Crossing a bridge over the river Tajuna, turn right and soon you will see the ruined castle perched up high on a large rock. Although in ruins, its precarious setting and the sweeping views from its precipitous walls make it a memorable place.

Alcalá de Henares is a lively town with a unique character. It has been the seat of a number of Spanish kings as well as the home of a great university, Universitas Complutensis. It was also the birthplace of Miguel de Cervantes Saavedra (1547–1616). His

memory is marked by a square shaded by plane trees, Plaza Cervantes, and also by the Casa Cervantes, a reconstruction of a 16th-century house on the site of his original home.

The most important building however is the Colegio de San Idelfonso, the university building first founded in 1498 by Cardinal Cisneros and completed in 1508. The Plateresque façade (so called because its ornate style of decoration resembles the intricate, embossed work of silversmiths) was built in 1543 and is considered one of the most beautiful in Spain. Among the many other lovely old buildings are the church of San Idelfonso and the Archbishop's Palace. There is also a Hostería Nacional del Estudiante, a restaurant run by the National Tourist Board which is situated in a Castilian hall, once part of the former Colegio de San Jerónimo. In addition to the excellent regional food (you can try the wines of Arganda here), there is an enchanting patio named the Three Languages Patio, because Latin, Hebrew and Greek were once taught in the college.

The route I have suggested from Chinchón to Toledo will take you to a number of other places of interest. 5km to the south of Chinchón along the M 330 is the wine-growing village of Colmenar de Oreja. During my 1986 visit the *plaza mayor* with its arcades and balconies was undergoing extensive restoration. There is also the 15th-century church of Santa María la Mayor.

From Colmenar de Oreja continue a short distance to the south the TO 315 to Noblejas and turn right along the N 400 to Ocaña with its arcaded *plaza mayor*, several interesting churches and the palace of the Dukes of Frías. From here it is only 16km to the north along the N 4 to the town of Aranjuez.

This town is something of a surprise: it is lush and green with broad avenues and gardens shaded by huge trees. Like an oasis in the summer-bleached plain south of Madrid, the town is known for its asparagus and strawberries. It is also famed for its imposing, pink and orange stone royal palace (built in 1727 by Philip V as a summer residence), flanked by pavilions with arcades facing a green, tree-shaded open space. The Parterre, a beautiful formal garden, is to be found to the east of the palace. Two other lovely gardens are the Jardín de la Isla, set on an island in the middle of the river Tajo, and the Jardín del Príncipe, containing many magnificent trees and situated to the north-east of the town. The Casita del Labrador, or the workman's house is a small, classical mansion built by Charles IV with an extravagantly furnished and decorated interior, set within a pretty park.

The Royal Palace at Aranjuez.

Leaving Aranjuez on the N 4 to the north for about 10km and then turning left on to the TO 421 will take you first to the village of Esquivias, where the marriage of Cervantes is recorded in the church register of Santa María, and then to Illescas. The town was a royal residence in the 15th-century and its 13th-century parish church has a 14th-century Mudéjar bell tower. Mudéjar is a blend of Moorish and Gothic architectural styles. The Hospital Santuario de la Virgen de la Caridad contains five paintings by El Greco as well as a wealth of fine sculptures, altar pieces and altar paintings.

From Illescas, after continuing south along the N 401 to Toledo, take a brief detour to the north-west along the N·403 to visit the Castillo de Barcience, a well-preserved castle set on a quiet pine-covered hillside.

TOLEDO

THE NATIONAL PARADOR Conde de Orgaz, situated on a hill overlooking the city of Toledo, is spacious and modern, built in the style and out of materials typical of the region. A small road winds around the edge of the ravine (which encloses the Río Tagus) and the city,

and climbs to the Parador from which there are breathtaking views. The old town is almost encircled by a loop in the river and gives the impression of being on an island, or appears like an impregnable fortress surrounded by a moat.

The Parador takes full advantage of its commanding situation and has been designed to give the majority of the bedrooms memorable views from their balconies. An enormous terrace provides the perfect setting to relax with a drink in the evening and watch the lowering sun turn the ancient buildings below to gold. The building has a rocky garden in front with a small path which winds down to join the road below. The city is only about 3km away so that it is quite possible to walk into the centre without needing to be too energetic.

Among the many Castilian specialities which the menu features is Mojo de Habas Verdes, fresh broad beans cooked in a casserole with onions, tomatoes and eggs. Jabalí Estofado is a stew of wild board simmered in a wine rich sauce. Magras de Cerdo con Pisto is loin

The Plaza Mayor at Tembleque.

of pork served with the typical mixed vegetable dish of the region, similar to ratatouille. Castile is known for its abundant wild partridge and this is an excellent place to try some, Perdiz a la Toledana being the local version. A sweet which is a particularly nice ending to a rich meal is Cuajada con Miel, milk curds with the local honey.

The wine list includes *jarras* (jugs), of the local wine, and other wines to look out for in the area include Yepes, from the countryside surrounding the nearby village of Villasequilla de Yepes and also some excellent wines from Escalona, a village some 50km to the north.

Toledo is a beautiful and historic city – and, unusual for Spain, the old part has been kept quite separate from its modern suburbs, largely because it is virtually self-contained on its 'island'. Indeed from a distance there is little sign of any modern building to mar the vista of its medieval heritage. It is however very popular: its wealth of architectural and art treasures and its proximity to Madrid, 70km away, mean that it is nearly always crowded. For this reason you should book the Parador Conde de Orgaz a day or so in advance.

You could easily fill several days exploring Toledo

The Mudéjar ceiling in the cloister of San Juan de los Reyes at Toledo.

fully and as with Madrid, a separate guidebook is essential. Wandering through its steep narrow streets is a pleasure in itself, as indeed is lingering during the afternoon siesta, or in the evening, at the café tables around the Plaza de Zocodover. However, if time is short there are several features you should make a point of seeing. The Cathedral is the finest example of the Gothic style in Spain after Burgos and its towering spire dwarfs the web of narrow streets which surround it. Built between 1227 and 1493, its interior is virtually a museum both of Spanish history and of Spanish architectural styles.

The church of Santo Tomé, built in the 14th century by the Count of Orgaz, contains a superb example of El Greco's work, *The Burial of the Conde de Orgaz,* and has a Mudéjar tower. Nearby is San Juan de los Reyes: completed in the 17th century it was a Franciscan convent first founded in the 15th century. The cloister has an intricately decorated Mudejar ceiling in the upper part.

The Alcázar is a vast building which dominates the Toledo skyline in distant views. It has had a sad history of burnings and batterings, culminating in almost total destruction during the Civil War, after which it was rebuilt.

It is also rewarding to drive along the winding road which follows the course of the Río Tagus to see the city walls with their numerous gates and bridges. Don't miss a glimpse of the Toledo railway station a short distance along the road to Ocaña – a fanciful blend of Art Deco and Mudéjar.

THE ENVIRONS

A SMALL DETOUR of 10km to the south-west along the C 401 will bring you to the Castillo of Guadamur, the kind of Spanish castle of which dreams are made – well-preserved, turreted building of ochre-coloured stone set in the midst of peaceful pinewoods.

Leaving Toledo on the N 400 towards Ocaña, take the right fork after a short distance on to the C 400 and soon after fork right again on to the N 401 to Orgaz where another enchanting castle is set nonchalantly among the small white houses of the village. It seems to have become just as much a part of the village life as the local grocer's shop and bar.

From here continue south for 10kms along the N 401 to Los Yebenes. From the plain the road climbs a steep hill giving sweeping views over the patterned land-scape through which you have passed. Above the town of Los Yebenes the hill crest is dotted with the pretty, toylike windmills Don Quixote himself tilted against and which are such a delightful feature of the region.

In Los Yebenes take the TO 231/232 to Consuegra. A dramatic stony hill towers above the town upon which a row of ten gleaming white windmills are lined up along its ridge together with an imposing *castillo*. A small road allows you to drive up to this remote, romantic spot from where there are breathtaking views over the surrounding landscape. Here the horizon is as distant as if it were the sea. The town of Consuegra is the centre of the production of saffron. First introduced by the Moors, it is now a valuable crop.

From Consuegra you can join the C 400 for 7km to Madridejos. A detour to the north is recommended along the N 4 to Tembleque, a delightful 'white' town of small single-storey houses and narrow streets with an exquisite *plaza mayor* surrounded by buildings with stone arcades and slender timber balconies, decorated with crests. There is also a pretty, balconied gateway into the square and an interesting 16th-century Gothic church.

Windmills on the hill above Consuegra.

After returning to Madridejos take the N 4 south for 17 km to Puerto Lápice, where a local inn is reputed to be the very hostelry in which Don Quixote was dubbed a Knight by the innkeeper. From here take the N 420 to Alcázar de San Juan, an important wine centre. The town is named after·a Moorish castle, or *alcázar*, later taken over by the Order of St John. Only the restored tower remains. Continuing along the N 420 for 10km will bring you to the atmospheric town of Campo de Críptana, a maze of steep narrow streets lined with dazzlingly white houses scattered up the slope of a rocky hill. At the top, and almost part of the village, a cluster of windmills completes the scene which so charmingly epitomises La Mancha. The mills, many rebuilt, still work for their living and new vanes were being installed while I was there, in readiness for the imminent harvest from the vast fields of grain which stretch away to the horizon. There are wonderful views from here and it is the gathering place for the villagers' evening stroll.

For devotees of Cervantes, a detour to the nearby village of El Toboso will enable them to visit the house of Dulcinea, the damsel of whom Don Quixote dreamed. It is furnished in keeping with period and region, and

A meadow near Manzanares in the spring.

contains a large collection of Cervantes' work, including over thirty different language publications of *Don Quixote de la Mancha*. Continue along the N 420 to Moto del Cuervo, where yet more mills decorate the hilltop, and from here along the same road to *Belmonte*.

The *castillo* of Belmonte is the most imposing in the region: much of its vast perimeter battlements remain and still partially surround the town. The heavily fortified castle was built in the 15th century and restored in the 19th century. Its now empty interior can be visited, and some beautiful Mudéjar ceilings may be seen, together with far-reaching views of the countryside from its walls. The collegiate church contains interesting altarpieces and 15th-century choir stalls.

Returning to Moto del Cuervo, continue back along the N 420 to Pedro Muñoz and then along the CR 122 to the town of Tomelloso. This is the heartland of the wine industry: vast areas of vines dominate the landscape, the endless rows of green vines contrast vividly with the red-brown soil. Tomelloso itself has been described by the Spanish writer, Victor de la Serna, as being built over a reservoir of wine. In the nearby town of Argamasilla de Alba you can visit the Cueva de Medrano, the small lodging house in which it is claimed Cervantes spent his time writing the first chapters of *Don Quixote*.

Make a detour along the valley of the Río Guardiana to the Lagunas de Ruidera. Here the landscape differs from the familiar fertile red soil patterned with vines and olive trees, for it is wild and rocky, with hillsides covered in shrubs and stunted trees. Lavender and rosemary scent the air; hawks trace lazy circles in the sky, rabbits run across your path and partridges flutter from every bush. At the point where the river runs free of the dam, the Embalse de Peñarroya, there is the 12th-century ruined castle of Peñarroya set high up above the lake and containing a small chapel in which an image of the Virgin of Peñarroya is still worshipped.

From Ruidera los Villares the road runs alongside the lakes of Ruidera. Contained in a rocky basin they descend in a series of shallow steps, emptying into each other by pouring over the edge like a tilted saucer, or in a network of tumbling streams across the separating terrain. Some of the lakes have been developed as summer resorts, with villas, small hotels and restaurants by the waterside together with small beaches. The road continues up to the source of the lakes, where it is quiet and remote, the turquoise water fringed with reed beds and the rocky hillsides dotted with gorse and pine trees.

From the head of the lakes, continue to the town of Ossa de Montiel where you can take the AB 640 to Villa Hermosa and then the C 415 to Villanueva de los Infantes, a spacious town with an elegant *plaza mayor* surrounded by classical arcades and façades of white stone. There are many lovely old buildings including the palace of Los Baillo, the convent of Los Dominicas de la Encarnación and the house of El Duque de San Fernando. Now take the C 415 towards Valdepeñas and after about 20km turn right on to the CR 644 to San Carlos del Valle. Here, in a quiet and outwardly nondescript small town, there is a surprisingly large and beautiful *plaza mayor*, lined with brick-built houses decorated by wooden balconies and overlooked by an imposing church. Continue north along the same road to Solana, where there is also an attractive *plaza mayor*, and then take the N 430 to Manzanares.

MANZANARES

THE PARADOR NACIONAL DE MANZANARES is a large modern hotel on the N 4, the Madrid/Bailen road, just to the south of the town and about 2km away from the centre. Essentially a stopping place for travellers, its proximity to Almagro makes it a useful alternative to the Parador there if the latter is fully booked. Its com-

fortable, spacious rooms are air-conditioned and there is a garden and a swimming pool.

The menu contains many regional dishes such as El Pisto Manchego, a dish of mixed vegetables cooked in olive oil and flavoured with garlic. Las Migas are coarse breadcrumbs sautéed in olive oil and garlic and often mixed with small pieces of ham, salt pork and sausage. They are sometimes included in the breakfast buffet and make a wonderful accompaniment to fried or scrambled eggs. Caldereta de Cordero a la Manchega is a casserole of neck of lamb with a wine-rich, glutinous sauce and El Guiso de Bodas is a hearty peasant-style chicken soup.

For those with a sweet tooth, try Leche Fritas, literally fried milk but in fact slices of a rich, stiff custard coated in batter, fried to a golden brown and then sprinkled with sugar – very naughty. The wine list includes Yuntero excellent red and white wines from the neighbouring town of Damiel which is also well-known for its wine.

Manzanares is an important wine centre whose wines, along with those of Valdepeñas, are allowed to be sold under its own name. The bustling town contains a delightful *plaza mayor* and a 14th-century church with an imposing Renaissance façade.

The town of Valdepeñas lies just 30km to the south and its name has become a genetic term for the wines of La Mancha. There are numerous *bodegas* (bars) and wine cellars to which visitors are welcomed. Throughout the region you will see large clay, aladdin-shaped pots, often used to decorate the entrance to farms and villas. These are the traditional vessels in which the wines of La Mancha were fermented. Today the wine is made on a much grander scale and in huge quantities but, rather charmingly I think, the enormous modern concrete containers holding 15,000 litres and more are still made in the same traditional shape.

ALMAGRO

ALMAGRO IS JUST OVER 30km to the south-west of Manzanares and, as a base for exploring the region, the Parador in Almagro is much to be preferred to the one at Manzanares. The Parador Nacional de Almagro is situated in the ancient convent of San Francisco, built in 1596. It is a vast pale-orange-bricked building with a maze of corridors and staircases which link together no less than sixteen courtyards and patios. The spacious, atmospheric interior includes a *bodega* (bar) furnished in rural style with flagstone floors and solid wooden tables and benches. Beautiful antique furniture decorate the public rooms. In one a lady from the town demonstrates the local craft of lace-making, which she also sells. There is also a swimming pool. The Parador is only a few minutes' walk from the *plaza mayor*.

The Plaza Mayor of Almagro.

A good selection of regional dishes and wines on the menu includes the local speciality Berenjenas de Almagro, egg plants in a spicy sauce. On the occasion I tried them they were served in a casserole with ham and shrimps. Puelos y Quebrantos is scrambled eggs served with *chorizo* (sausage) and brains, and another dish with which to start the meal is Judías Verdes Almagrenas, green beans cooked in a sauce. Mojete de Conejo Manchega is pieces of rabbit sautéed with garlic and white wine.

To finish you might try Tocinello de Cielo, a rich custard somewhere between a mousse and a flan. If you don't have a sweet tooth you could end with Queso Manchego, the cheese for which the region is famous. There is a good selection of local wines including Vino Albalí, red, white and *rosé* wines from Valdepeñas and an excellent full-bodied, deep-red wine, Vega Fría.

The *plaza mayor* of Almagro is quite outstanding, even for a region noted for its lovely squares. It is very large and long with a central paved area, and surrounded by houses with arcades, the upper floors of which have literally hundreds of small windows with uniform green frames. It almost seems unreal but for the local people who go about their business or stroll around it in the evening as if it were nothing special at all.

The town was the centre of the Order of Calatrava and there are numerous mansions and palaces with beautiful doorways decorated with crests. The 17th-century church of San Augustín beside the square contains paintings by Zurbaran. The Corral de Comedias is the town's most important sight, after the square, and is delightful. It is a tiny open-air theatre with decorated wooden balconies. Classical plays are still performed there in August on the feast of St Bartholomew.

THE ENVIRONS

THE REGIONAL TOWN OF Ciudad Real, less than 40km away along the C 415, was founded in the 13th century and retains some of its ancient buildings. The Puerta de Toledo, the town gate, is one of the most important examples of the region's Mudéjar architecture and the cathedral of Santa María del Prado, built in 1531, is also

worth a visit. So too is the church of San Pedro and the church of Santiago, the town's oldest building.

The town of Damiel, about 30km along the N 420 to the east has a 14th-century church, Santa María with a lovely Renaissance façade. The 16th-century church of San Pedro possesses a beautiful baroque retable, and the town has an attractive arcaded *plaza mayor*.

On the way to Damiel at the village of Carrión de Calatrava there is a small detour to the north to the ruined castle of Vieja Calatrava in an atmospheric setting beside the Río Guadiana and the nearby hermitage of La Encarnación. It is set amidst delightful and peaceful fields and vineyards. As I drove by I saw at least half a dozen pairs of Bee Eaters flitting from tree to tree with their iridescent turquoise and gold plumage flashing in the sunlight.

From Damiel a small road to the north leads to the Parque Nacional de las Tablas de Damiel, protected area of lakes, brooks and marshy terrain fringed with reeds, created by the confluence of the Ríos Guadiana and Ciguela. Signposted walks through this region allow you to observe a fascinating variety of plants and birdlife.

After returning to Almagro you can take the C 417 to Calzada de Calatrava where a few kms to the south-

The Castillo of Belmonte.

west is the ruined castle of Calatrava la Nueva, a vast construction with its imposing towers and walls intact, seemingly in defiance of neglect and the passage of time. By taking the C 410 southwards you will come to the village of Viso del Marqués, where the magnificent Renaissance palace was built in the 16th century by the Marqués de Santa Cruz.

From here it is only 6km to the Madrid/Bailén road. If you are continuing south to Andalucía a brief detour to the north is worth while to visit the sanctuary of NS de las Virtudes. It has a small, very pretty 16th-century chapel containing a beautiful gilded retable and small exquisite painted domed ceiling. Adjoining it is one of the oldest bullrings in Spain. Built in the 17th century it is square. Bullfights are still occasionally held there.

If you are continuing south it is less than two hours' drive to the paradors of Bailén or Úbeda (the tours for this region are described on pages 200–225). The parador of Córdoba is less than a further two hours' drive to the west (the tour for this region is described on pages 176–187).

TOUR 11 Begins in the province of Toledo and leads southwest into Extremadura to the provinces of Cáceres and Badajoz, providing a scenic route between Madrid and the western region of Andalucía and the Costa del Sol. Combined with tour No 10 (page 108) it can also be used to create a round trip. Extremadura is perhaps one of the least visited regions of Spain. It is certainly one of the most sparsely populated areas. The tour includes several historic towns, a magnificent monastery and numerous spectacular castles. The countryside is richly varied and there are a wealth of beautiful buildings. The paradors featured include two magnificent 15th-century castles, two convents and a medieval pilgrims' hospital.

— TOUR 11 —
MICHELIN MAP NO. 447
Oropesa
Trujillo — GUADALUPE
Mérida
Zafra

OROPESA
GUADALUPE
TRUJILLO
MÉRIDA–ZAFRA

OROPESA

THE ITINERARY BEGINS AT the Parador of Oropesa, about 150km from Madrid. The route, from the capital, is initially along the N 5 to Navalcarnero and Magueda. Here there is a 15th-century castle with round towers at each corner and Mudéjar archway. A detour can be made 12km north to Escalona; an old town whose magnificent 11th century fortress has extensive battlements and towers and is set on a hillside overlooking the Río Alberche. Some of the town walls and gateways survive and there are numerous arcaded houses lining the ancient streets and square. The 16th-century Convento de Immaculada Concepción has an especially fine Plateresque portal.

The N 5 continues westwards to the large, busy town of Talavera de la Reina, set at the confluence of the Ríos Tajo and Alberche. Famous for its ceramics, there is a museum, Ruíz de Luna, with an important collection of work and numerous churches and mansions in the old part of town. The 15th-century church of Santa María is in Gothic style and the churches of San Miguel and San Pedro are of Mudéjar design.

The Parador Virrey Toledo, is situated 33km further to the west on the edge of the town of Oropesa. This imposing 12th-century castle, which can be seen on its hilltop long before you arrive, has been the source of many battles – both feudal and with the Moors – because of its important strategic position. It was extensively rebuilt in the early 15th century by Don Garcia Álvarez de Toledo to whom it was given by King Enrique III.

It is a massive building surrounded by impregnable walls. The entrance to the castle is through a tunnel-like gateway into a large courtyard overlooked by a gallery, balconies and towers. Outside the castle a small square and a promenade are a popular place for the villagers to gather in the evening. There are sweeping views over the plain towards the distant Sierra de Gredos – a wonderful sight at sunset. The interior is full of medieval atmosphere with tiled floors, high wooden-beamed ceilings, large stone fireplaces and antique furniture.

Regional specialities on the menu included: Perdiz a la Oropesana, partridge stuffed with pâté and braised in a red wine sauce; and Salteado de Ternera Lagarterana, veal stew with mixed vegetables. A delicious sweet is Suspiros de Monja (literally 'nun's sighs'), light fluffy puffs of whisked egg-white, poached in a creamy cinnamon-flavoured egg custard. The house wine is from the vineyards which surround the castle.

Some of the old town walls have survived and the streets are lined with old houses and mansions. There are two 16th-century Renaissance churches, one with a fine Plateresque portal. A few kms to the west of Oropesa is the town of Lagartera, famous for its unusual embroidery, a local craft which dates back to the 16th century.

GUADALUPE

THE NEXT STAGE of the tour is south along the TO 701 to the Parador at Guadalupe a distance of 90km. This quiet country road at first runs through open countryside with gentle hillsides planted with wheatfields and dotted with oak trees. A few kms before reaching Puente de Arzobispo there is a small chapel, the Ermita NS de Bienvenida, which dates from the 16th century. Puente de Arzobispo is known for its ceramics, in fact rivalling Talavera de La Reina. Numerous shops line the main road. The town is named after the 14th century bridge over the Río Tajo, built by Archbishop don Pedro Tenorio.

Beyond Puente del Arzobispo the landscape becomes more hilly with views of the distant Sierra de Guadalupe. At Navalmoralejo there are the ruins of the Roman town of Vascos. The road climbs steadily into the mountains, which are covered in dense pine forests and carpeted with yellow broom and rock rose, to the Puerto de San Vicente. This marks the division between Castile and Extremadura and the scenery becomes stark and dramatic. You can see for miles over the mountainsides with no sign of farms, houses, or even other roads.

The Parador Nacional Zurbarán, in the centre of the medieval mountain village of Guadalupe, is adjacent to the huge monastery which dominates the surrounding countryside. The Parador occupies the old hospital of

San Juan Bautista founded in the 15th century to care for the pilgrims who came to pay homage to the Virgin of Guadalupe. It is named after the famous Spanish artist Zurbarán (1598–1664). An important collection of his work is kept in the monastery's vestry.

The public rooms are ranged around a lovely patio with Mudéjar arches. Moorish-style gardens, shaded by orange and lemon trees, surround a pool and a Mudéjar fountain. The bedrooms have balconies which overlook the garden and the monastery beyond. The interior has a wealth of wooden beams, stone arches, terracotta-tiled floors and comfortable traditonal furniture.

Local cuisine on the menu included: Bacalao Moncal, dried salts cod cooked in a casserole with spinach and potatoes and flavoured with garlic; and Cabrito Asado a la Serrana, kid cooked in the oven with garlic. A deliciously rich pudding is Puding de castañas, a thick creamy custard-like purée of chestnuts. Local wine included those from neighbouring Cañamero and Mentrida. I had a bottle of Castillo de Escalona, an excellent full-bodied red.

The village of Guadalupe is criss-crossed by a web of fascinating old streets, lined by ancient houses decorated with balconies and arcades supported on

The Castillo and Parador of Oropesa.

massive weathered wooden beams. The monastery was originally a small hermitage consecrated to NS de Guadalupe. When the Moors invaded in 711 the figure of the Virgin, reputed to have been carved by St Luke, was buried. It was not discovered again until the 13th century when a shepherd found it by chance. In spite of being buried for 600 years it was perfectly preserved. A spate of miracles soon made the Virgin, and Guadalupe, a principal place for pilgrimages.

The monastery is a monumental building containing an extraordinary collection of treasures. There is a magnificent Mudéjar cloister with horseshoe arches, a well and a beautiful Plateresque staircase. As well as paintings by Zurbarán there are many other works by great Spanish painters decorating the rooms as well as a museum of miniatures and embroideries. The monastery was endowed with many gifts of treasure from noblemen, explorers and the Conquistadores. Hernán Cortés spent his last days here before departing for his conquest of Mexico. Permission for Columbus' voyage by the Catholic Monarchs was first granted in Guadalupe and he named an island to honour it.

Nearby is the 15th-century hermitage of El Humilladero, the 16th-century palace of Granja de Valdefuentes and the 17th-century palace of Granja de Mirabel, built for the Catholic kings.

An interesting round trip can be made from the Parador into the countryside to the south. From Guadalupe the route leads south-west through attractive mountain scenery to the wine town of Cañamero. A few kms further a small road leads south-east across flat, open countryside to Valdecaballeros on the banks of the Embalse de García de Sola. The road skirts the lake which is fringed by pine trees and surrounded by rugged mountains. At Herrera del Duque there is a 16th-century Gothic church, a ruined Renaissance convent and the remains of a hilltop castle. The route leads north across a flat open landscape to Castilblanco and then to the edge of the Embalse de Cijara, designated as a National reserve. The road returns towards Guadalupe joining the C 401 just below the Puerto de San Vicente.

TRUJILLO

THE NEXT STAGE of the tour is west to the Parador at Trujillo, a distance of abut 80km. Returning to Cañamero the route continues along the C 401 to Logrosán, with a 14th-century church, a 15th-century hermitage and the ruins of a castle. The road continues along a broad green valley covered by wheatfields and meadows and shaded by oak trees. At Zorita the C 524 leads north-west to Trujillo.

The Parador Nacional de Trujillo, located in the 16th-century convent of Santa Clara, overlooks a small square and is only a few minutes' walk from the *plaza mayor*. In front is a small courtyard with a well. By the door is a small revolving cubby hole where the nuns would place their home-made sweets to be sold .to passers-by. Although most of the bedrooms are situated in a modern extension at the rear, the nuns cells in the original building have also been converted into bedrooms. The public rooms open on to a charming cloister with an ancient stone well set in the centre of the patio. There is also a patio in the modern wing with a small swimming pool in its centre.

The restaurant is in the refectory, a long room with a high arched ceiling decorated by a large mural of blue azulejos on one wall. Among the regional specialities represented on the menu was: Caldereta de Cordero, small pieces of lamb on the bone, casseroled with onions, peppers and ham in a wine rich sauce and flavoured with garlic; Patatas y Judías a la Extremena, potatoes and green beans cooked in a casserole with

The Monastery of Guadalupe with the parador in the foreground.

Trujillo seen from outside the city walls.

onions, tomatoes and peppers and flavoured with garlic and parsley; and Ternera a la Extremena, veal cutlets cooked in a sauce with onions, garlic, peppers and *chorizo*. The regional wines on the list included those from nearby Montánchez and Almendralejo.

Trujillo is set on a rocky hill overlooking a wild heathland, rimmed by distant mountains. Parts of the fortified walls have survived and above the town is a massive Arab fortress with towers and gateways. The hub of the town is the *plaza mayor*, a delightful, irregular square surrounded by old mansions and arcades. In one corner is a statue honouring Francisco Pizarro, the conqueror of Perú. Many other Conquistadores also came from the town and its surroundings. The Gothic church of Santa María was built on the site of a mosque and contains a beautiful painted retablo by Francisco Gallego.

Overlooking the *plaza mayor* is the Palacio de Marqués de la Conquista, built by Hernando Pizarro, the son-in-law of the Conquistador. It has a lovely Plateresque façade and is richly decorated with coats of arms, statues and window grilles. The Palacio de los Orellana-Pizarro also has a beautiful Plateresque façade and a patio in the same style. Numerous other fine buildings are dotted throughout the town, making it a pleasure to explore. A walk along the battlements in the evening is one of the best ways of capturing the atmosphere of the place. From here you can look down onto the ancient rooftops and into the huge untidy storks' nests which adorn every building.

The provincial capital of Cáceres is only 47km to the west of Trujillo. This too is an exceptionally beautiful city and merits an extended visit. Within surrounding walls are a wealth of exquisite building, towering above the narrow streets like medieval skyscrapers of golden stone. The entrance into the old city is by the Plaza del General Mola, a lively square buzzing with the chatter of the students of the University of Extremadura, who tend to dominate the city. The Parador, or the tourist office in the square in Cáceres, will provide a map and a guide to the buildings.

MÉRIDA

FROM TRUJILLO the next stage of the tour is south-west to the Parador at Mérida, a direct journey of 90km. The route is along the CC 800 to Montánchez. This old hilltop town is famed for its hams and sausages made

A street in Guadalupe.

The Castillo of Medellín.

from the velvety brown pigs which forage beneath the oak trees. Montánchez is also known for its wines from the vineyards which cover the surrounding hillsides. There are the remains of a large Moorish fortress above the town. The road continues south-west along the CC 801 to join the N 630 where the route continues south to Mérida.

The Parador Nacional Vía de la Plata is situated in a 15th-century convent which faces on to a quiet square. It is a short walk from the centre of the town. The Baroque building contains elements of much older origin Among its many uses in the past it has been a jail and is believed to occupy the site of a Roman temple. There is a small, pretty patio with columns decorated with Moorish inscriptions. The beautiful lounge was once the convent chapel.

The menu includes a variety of Extremaduran dishes: Cordero Asado a la Pobre, lamb baked with potatoes and garlic, and Gaspacho Extrameño, a soup made by combining olive oil, egg yolks, garlic, bread-crumbs, wine vinegar and water to make a thick creamy liquid and served chilled. A delicious pudding is Tarta del Convento, flaky pastry layered with cream, quince jelly and chocolate. Local wines are from Montánchez, Cilleros and Ceclavin. I had a bottle of Fuente Vieja, a dry fruity rose from Villafranca de los Barros.

Mérida is set beside the Río Guadiana and was once the capital of the Roman province of Lusitania. Today it is largely a modern town but possesses the most extensive Roman remains in Spain. There is a superb Roman bridge, over 2,500ft long spanning the Guadiana with 60 arches. Nearby, beside the Plaza de España, is a massive Moorish alcázar built on the site of a Roman castle. There are also the remains of two aqueducts and the Circus Maximus which could contain 25,000 spectators.

The pride of Mérida is however, the Roman theatre. Dating from C. 20 BC it is one of the best preserved Roman buildings anywhere in the world. It is extremely impressive with a colonnaded stage and a façade containing more than 30 marble columns with Corinthian capitals. The terraced auditorium can seat over 5,000 spectators, even the entrance passages are all intact. Nearby is the amphitheatre which could seat

15,000 people. It is quite remarkable complex and still used today for theatre and concert performances.

ZAFRA

THE NEXT STAGE of the tour is south to the Parador at Zafra, a direct journey of only 60km so I have outlined a roundabout route which explores some of the places of interest between. From Mérida the route is first along the N 5 north-east towards Miajadas. After 24km the N 430 and then the C 520 lead south-east to Medellín set beside the broad Río Guadiana. This town was the birthplace of Hernán Cortés, the conqueror of Mexico, and there is a statue of him in the main square. The town is dominated by an impressive castle on the high-domed hill. Nearby is a 17th-century Gothic church where the Conquistador was baptised. There are a number of old mansions in the town and a stone bench marks the site of Cortés' birthplace.

The road continues to Don Benito, where there are two 16th-century churches, several old mansions and an arcaded *ayuntamiento*. The route leads south-west from here to Alange where there is another Moorish castle set on a hill and very well-preserved Roman baths contained in two round chambers with high-domed roofs. The C 423 continues south-west to Almendralejo through countryside patterned with vineyards and olive groves. The town, an important wine centre, has a 16th-century Renaissance church and the 18th-century Palacio del Marques de Monsalud, which houses an important collection of Roman antiquities.

The route leads south-west along the C 423 through gentle vine-covered hillsides to Villalba de los Barros, where there is a Mudéjar castle and a 16th-century church. Beyond, at Santa Marta, a quiet country road leads south through vine-covered hills to Salvatierra de los Barros. Here too there are the imposing remains of a 13th-century castle. Returning to the main road, passing the hilltop castle of Feria, another small road continues north-east to Fuente del Maestre whose 15th-century Gothic church has a fine Mudéjar tower and an imposing granite portal. Nearby is the 13th-century monastery of San Pedro with a Baroque chapel and a Mudéjar gallery. The road continues to Villafranca de los Barros, where the 16th-century church of Santa María del Valle has a fine Gothic portal.

A goatherd near Mérida.

The Roman Theatre at Mérida.

The BA 613 leads east through peaceful rural scenery to Ribera del Fresno, where there are a number of old mansions. Further on, the town of Hornachos is dramatically situated below a steep rocky mountain overlooking a wide fertile valley. There are the ruins of an Arab castle and a Gothic church with Mudéjar additions. A small road leads south-west from here to Zafra.

The Parador Nacional Hernán Cortés is located in the 15th-century fortified palace where Hernán Cortés lived before he departed for Mexico. It is square with round towers at each corner and semi-circular towers between. At the rear is the keep which overlooks a garden and swimming pool. In the centre is a magnificent two-storey Renaissance patio with galleries supported by Ionic and Doric columns, constructed in white marble and, reputedly, designed by Juan de Herrera, the architect of the Escorial. It is quite stunning. There is also a lovely chapel with an octagonal Gothic cupola. The *sala dorada* (golden room), situated in the main tower has a beautiful painted ceiling.

Regional dishes on the menu include: Menestra de Alcegas a la Extremeña, a dish of sautéed potatoes, greens and onions; and Berenjenas a la Extremeña, eggplants coated in flour and then fried in olive oil. Local wines on the list included Viña de los Barros and Castell de Zafra, a full-bodied red.

The Parador is only a few minutes' walk to the main square of Zafra, the Plaza Grande. Adjoining is the Plaza Chica, an enchanting small square surrounded by arcaded whitewashed houses with balconies brimming with flowers. Zafra is known as Sevilla la Chica, little Seville, for the resemblance of its character to the Andalucian towns further to the south. The 14th-century collegiate church of NS de la Candelaria has a retablo decorated with nine paintings by Zurbarán. The convent of Santa Clara, founded in the 15th century by Don Gómez Suárez de Figueroa, contains the tomb of Don Lorenzo Suárez de Figueroa who built the castle. The 16th-century hospital of Santiago has a fine Gothic portal and lovely patio.

An interesting excursion can be made into the countryside to the south of Zafra. The N 435 and the C 4311 lead south-west of the town to Burguillos de Cerro where a Knight Templar's castle is set on a hill

The Plaza Chica at Zafra. Overleaf: Aiguablava.

above the village. There is also a church with an 18th-century Baroque tower. 20km further is Jerez de los Caballeros. The name stems from the Knights Templars who took the town from the Moors in 1229. They were later defeated by Ferdinand IV's army who had them beheaded in a tower now called Torre Sangrienta, the bleeding tower. Parts of the town walls and the fortress remain, together with two of the gates. The most remarkable building in the town is the massive 17th-century church of San Bartolomé which soars above the narrow streets surrounding it. Its ornate Baroque façade and lofty towers are studded with polychrome azulejos and glazed decorations. It is a quite remarkable sight.

Adjacent to the castle is the 16th-century Baroque church of Santa María, founded in the 7th century and the oldest in Extremadura. In the town centre is the 16th-century Baroque church of San Miguel with a massive and ornately decorated tower. The church of Santa Catalina also has a fine Baroque tower.

The N 435 leads south-east to Fregenal de la Sierra. Above the town is an impressive 13th-century castle and there are two churches and several old mansions. The route continues south-east along the C 434 to Segura de León, a quite delightful old town built on a hill and threaded by impossibly steep narrow streets. It has a well-preserved 13th-century castle and a fine Gothic church.

The route leads north-east from here along the C 437 to Fuente de Cantos, famous as the birthplace of Francisco de Zurbarán. It has a 16th-century church, NS de la Granada, with a Baroque retablo, and the convent of NS del Carmen which has a fine Baroque altar. There is also an 18th-century hermitage, NS de la Hermosa, with a 13th-century image of the Virgin.

A small road leads due east to Llerena. Here there's an elegant and spacious *plaza mayor* surrounded by classical arcaded buildings overlooked by the imposing church of NS de la Granada. Its tower is reminiscent of the Giralda in Sevilla and its façade is decorated by graceful arcaded galleries.

The Parador at Zafra is about 40km north-west along the N 432. The nearest alternative parador to Llerena is at Córdoba, 155km (page 182).

PART THREE

Eastern Spain

ZARAGOZA

13

12

BARCELONA

14

TERUEL

ALBACETE

15

OUR 12   Explores the coastal region and hinterland of Cataluña in the north-east corner of Spain in the provinces of Gerona and Barcelona, a proudly partisan region where local customs, traditions and language are jealously guarded. Indeed, as in the Basque provinces, the regional language of Catalán is used extensively in road signs, place-names and in menus. Fortunately place-names are not greatly altered: Gerona becomes Girona in Catalán, for example, and Lérida changes to Lleida. Menus, however, are a different matter. Conejo con Caracoles (rabbit cooked with snails) becomes Conill amb Caragols. Fortunately most restaurants also give the Castilian Spanish version of the menu and often in English, French and German as well.

—TOUR 12—
MICHELIN MAP NO. 43

Aiguablava

Cardona   Vich

BARCELONA

AIGUABLAVA
VICH
CARDONA

The area covered by this tour is bordered in the north by the Pyrenees and to the west by the valley of the Río Segre. To the south is Barcelona and the Mediterranean forms the western limit. This part of Spain's coastline is known as the Costa Brava, the wild coast. It is aptly named, a region of wild and rugged beauty. Massive ochre cliffs descend steeply into a sea of such intense and translucent blue that it makes you catch your breath. The headlands are covered in pine trees and the coastline itself is so tortuously indented that many coves and beaches are accessible only by boat. Immediately inland however the landscape is surprisingly soft and green. It is also very fertile. Fields of wheat scattered with poppies mingle with vineyards and meadows. Further west the landscape changes again and there are rugged mountains, wide, fast flowing rivers and remote lakes.

It is also a region rich in architectural treasures. Imposing cathedrals, pretty Romanesque churches, medieval mansion, arcaded plazas and some of the most delightful and unspoiled villages in Spain remain to be discovered. In addition the three paradors which are featured are all quite spectacularly situated.

AIGUABLAVA

THE PARADOR NATIONAL DE AIGUABLAVA is the starting point. It is about three hours' driving time from Barcelona airport, about 60km from Girona airport and approx 100km from the French/Spanish border. The most direct route is to take Exit 6 from the Autopista A 7 and follow the C 255 to Palafrugel. From here take the road to Begur and on reaching the village the Parador is signposted.

Situated on a small pine-covered headland called the Punta d'Esmuts, plunging cliffs almost surround the building which overlooks a beautiful small sandy beach and a ravine-like rocky cove. The Parador is a long, low, modern, building in white. The most dominant features are the large balconies which provide each bedroom with magnificent sea views. A garden, with a swimming pool, leads to small pathways which enable you to walk down through the pine trees to the beach of Aiguablava and the rocks below. The interior is light and airy with huge glass windows. The furnishing are modern and it is decorated with contemporary prints and paintings.

The menu contains many Catalán dishes: Conill con Caragols, casserole of rabbit with snails; Sopa de Bacalao, soup made with salt cod; and Mero a la Esencia de Nueces, sea bass served with a rich sauce made with pine nuts and cheese. Fresas con Pimienta Negra is an unusual and delicious dessert made by combining lightly mashed strawberries with sugar, orange juice, Grenadine, Pastis and masses of freshly ground black pepper. It is served with ice cream or whipped cream. The Catalán wines are also well represented. The house wine comes from Peralada and there are wines from the Penedes vineyards. I tried a Sangre de Toro from Miguel Torres in Penedés, an excellent full-bodied red.

There are numerous small beaches and villages quite close to the Parador which can provide several excursions. A small road, providing spectacular views, climbs the headland beyond Aiguablava to Tamariu, a fishing village which has become a charming small resort. It has a crescent of coarse yellow sand bordered by rocky pine-clad headlands. Small beach-front cafés and bars make it a very agreeable place to pass the time. From here you can follow the road to Palafrugell with the Gothic church of Santa María and the remains of ancient walls.

A few km further on is the wooded headland of Cap Roig. With lovely views of the bay of Calella, a castle and a botanic garden. Beyond is the fishing town of Palamós on a wide bay overlooked by the Sierra de Gabarras. Although now a busy resort it still has the atmosphere of a working fishing port. A few kms to the west is the medieval town of Calonge with old town walls and a 12th-century castle.

Further south the town of San Feliú also has a busy fishing port with a lively and attractive seafront. It too is a resort but the character of the town has survived far better than those further to the south, like Tossá del Mar, which have been swamped by the worst excesses of the developers.

The medieval town of Begur, only a few kms to the

north of the Parador, is built on a steep domed hill encircled by fortified walls. It dates from the 11th century and was an important part of the coastal defences. From the village there is access to a number of delightful small beaches, like Sa Riera and Aiguafreda for example. They are reached by narrow roads which wind round the steep pine-covered headlands. Sa Tuna is a particularly attractive small cove with a cluster of fishermen's cottages and colourful boats pulled up on to the shingle beach.

Close by is the picturesque old village of Pals with a beautiful old 9th-century tower and a 15th-century church. The village is a maze of narrow, rough-cobbled streets lined with shops, art galleries, small bars and restaurants. A few kms to the west is another ancient village, Peratallada. It too has a tangle of fascinating old streets, narrow alleys and small squares clustered with flowers. There is also a lovely church and an 11th-century castle.

The northern part of the Costa Brava can also be explored from the Parador of Aiguablava. I have suggested a route which follows the coast quite closely and then returns along the Autopista A7 enabling the trip to be made comfortably in a day's drive.

A view from the gardens of the parador at Aiguablava. Overleaf: Cadaqués.

From the Parador you can make your way back to Pals and then continue along the same road across the wide flat plain of Ampurias to Torroella de Montgri, an ancient town partially surrounded by battlements, towers and gateways, with a 16th-century church, a 14th-century *ayuntamiento* and the Casa Solterra, a mansion with a lovely courtyard. On a jagged spur of rock high above the town is the 13th-century castle built for King James of Cataluña.

The route continues through countryside cultivated with fields of wheat, fruit, vegetables and vineyards towards La Escala. A brief detour to the west leads to the crumbling medieval town of Verges. Here too are the remains of walls, ancient houses, an arcaded square and lots of atmosphere.

La Escala, once a fishing village, is now a large busy resort. On its northern outskirts however is the excavated site of Ampurias, the ancient Greek settlement of Emporion and the ruins of a Roman town. There are many foundations, mosaic floors and columns to be

seen. It is in a lovely setting dotted with pine trees and close to the sea. The site is closed on Mondays and in the middle of the day.

The route continues across the coastal plain to San Pedro Pescador on the banks of the Río Fluvia. A brief detour to the west leads to San Miguel de Fluvia where there is an 11th-century church once part of a Benedictine monastery. Further on at Castello d'Empurias is a 13th-century church and a restored market hall of the same period. From here the road continues to Rosas, a large resort on a wide curving bay backed by mountains.

Just to the west of the town a road strikes inland and crosses the mountains towards Cadaqués. It is a very scenic route and as the road curves around the steep terraced mountainsides there are fine views over the Bay of Rosas. Cadaqués is an attractive fishing village in a lovely setting, huddling below the Sierra de Rosas on the shores of a deep sheltered bay. The 16th-century church looks down on the village rooftops. There are small bars and cafés along a seafront promenade shaded by plane trees, and small sardine fishing boats are pulled up on the beach.

On the edge of the town a small road curves up around the headland to Cala Port Lligat, a small attractive bay, almost enclosed by its rocky headlands and a small island. Salvador Dalí, the Catalonian painter, had a house built overlooking the bay and lived there for many years.

Another small road continues to the very top of Cabo Creus, a savagely beautiful place, windswept and treeless with brush and lichen covering the ragged, pitted rocks. This is where the mighty Pyrenees finally dwindle down to meet the Mediterranean.

From Cadaqués you can continue along the coast to Puerto de la Selva, another attractive fishing town in a similar setting to Cadaqués on the opposite side of the peninsula. The road continues close to the sea towards Llanca. A short distance from the town a small road to the left leads right up into the mountains to San Pedro de Roda, a partially ruined Benedictine monastery with a 9th-century church which contains one of the earliest examples of Romanesque barrel vaulting.

At Llanca you can take the C 252 directly to join the Autopista A 7 at Figueras for your return to Aiguablava. If you have time however there is an impressive scenic road which continues close to the sea, snaking round the steep terraced hillsides with spectacular views, to the French border just beyond Port Bou.

Between Llanca and Figueras, just north of the C 252, is the picturesque old wine town of Peralada whose imposing 14th-century castle contains a wine museum. The Monastery of Santo Domingo has a beautiful Romanesque cloister.

Figueras is a lovely old town with cobbled streets, ancient houses, small shady squares and interesting shops. There is a 14th-century church, San Pedro, and the castle of San Fernando. The town also contains the Salvador Dalí Museum, housed in a converted theatre built in 1836. This alone warrants an extended visit. The displays create a complete entertainment with three-dimensional models, vast paintings, set pieces and fascinating examples of visual trickery. It manages to shock, mystify and amuse in rapid succession.

The journey back to Aiguablava can be made most easily by taking the Autopista A7 to Exit 6 at Gerona and then following the C 255 to Palafrugell where the road to Begur can be joined.

The provincial capital of Gerona is also worth an extended visit. Built alongside the Río Onar with ancient houses lining its banks, there is a 14th-century cathedral with a beautiful cloister, a 17th-century *ayuntamiento*, the 14th-century church of San Feliú and the Casa Carles which houses the Museo Diocesano, containing religious paintings and relics. Gerona is an excellent place to shop and there are many good bars and restaurants. It could be combined with Figueras as a separate day's excursion – the journey between them is very swift on the Autopista.

VICH

THE NEXT STAGE of the itinerary is to the Parador at Vich. To begin return to Gerona where the C 150 leads north-west to Banyoles, an old town with narrow streets, ancient houses and an attractive arcaded square where there is a colourful market on Wednesdays. The Monasterio de San Esteban was built in the early part of the 19th century and the archaeological museum in the Casa de Pía Almoina dates from the 14th. On the outskirts of the town is a lovely lake surrounded by grassy tree-shaded banks.

The route continues northward through a broad valley cultivated with fields of wheat and market gardens to Besalu. This is a gem of a town on a hill overlooking the Río Fluvia. Its centre is a fascinating web of narrow cobbled streets with old arcaded houses and three lovely churches. The most beautiful building in Besalú however is its 14th-century bridge, which zigzags across the river. It has defensive towers, fortified gateways and elegant arches.

The route continues westwards to the village of Castelfollit de la Roca, dramatically sited on a sheer-sided outcrop of rock. The village houses are strung out along its edge and a small church at the end looks like the prow of a huge beached ship. Beyond at Olot the C 150 branches right towards Ripoll.

It is well worth making a short detour from Olot along the road towards Banyoles to visit the delightful small fortified town of Santa Pau. You enter through a tunnel-like gateway into a square surrounded by ancient arcaded stone houses and overlooked by a lovely 15th-century church.

From Olot the road runs high along the side of a beautiful broad green valley. At the Collado de Coubet you have the choice of detouring to the right to visit the 12th-century Monastery of Sant Joan de les Abadesses. Alternatively you can continue to Ripoll via Valfogona with its tall square-towered castle.

At Ripoll the route joins the N 152. In spite of its rather ugly industrial outskirts Ripoll is an interesting old town, containing the 6th-century Benedictine Abbey of Santa María, extensively restored since its partial destruction by an earthquake in the 15th century and a fire in the 19th century.

From Ripoll the road follows the course of the Río Ter through a steep rocky valley to Vich, an ancient town built on the site of an Iberian settlement. The cathedral, rebuilt in the 18th century, retains a massive tower and cloister from the 12th century. The interior is dramatic, the walls almost completely covered in huge paintings of sepia and sombre reds – the work of Jose Maria Sert. They represent the third version: the first he rejected and the second did not survive the Civil War. In the chapel is an exquisite 15th-century alabaster retablo carved in minute detail. Other buildings of interest are the episcopal museum, adjacent to the cathedral, and a restored 3rd-century Roman temple undiscovered until 1882.

The Parador Nacional de Vich, 14km from the city, is situated in the mountain region of Guillera in an isolated spot high on a hillside overlooking the beautiful Pantano de Sau. It can be reached by taking the C 153 towards Olot for 5km; it is then signposted along a road to the right which leads into the mountains. The modern building has been designed in the style of a Masía, a traditional Catalán farmhouse, with the bedroom terraces enclosed in typical high-arched stone windows. These have wonderful views over the lake and mountains. There is a magnificent galleried entrance hall with an outer enclosed courtyard filled with flowers.

The restaurant is illuminated by rows of enormous wrought-iron candelabra and an adjoining terrace overlooks the lake. Catalán cuisine is well represented on the menu: Butifarra con Judías Blancas, Catalán sausage cooked with large white beans; Pato con Judías a la Catalana, pieces of duck cooked with white beans, carrots and onions; and Suquet de Pescado, a delicious combination of small pieces of mixed fish and potatoes poached with white wine, garlic, tomatoes and basil. The house wine is from the Priorato vineyards. There is a good selection of Catalán wines. I had a Castillo de Perelada, a dry but fruity rosé from Ampurdán.

A round trip which can be made comfortably in a day's drive from the Parador is to return to the main road, the C 153, and continue towards Olot. Just before you reach this road you will pass the hamlet of Tabernoles with a small very pretty 11th-century church. The road towards Olot winds through attractive scenic countryside with densely wooded mountainsides and dramatic rocky outcrops. It is scantily populated with just the occasional small village and ancient *masia* to be seen along the way.

Some 30km along this road a turning to the right leads to what is, for me, one of the most captivating villages in Spain, Rupit, situated in a small, steep-sided rocky valley, almost ravine-like in places. The floor of the valley is lush and green and chequered with neat kitchen gardens. The village of small rough-grey stone houses with red-tiled roof clings to a precipitous rock in the centre of the valley through which a small river rushes.

Beyond Rupit the road breasts a pass from which there are stupendous views into the valley far below. It has a quite startling effect since you are, until then, unaware of being so high. The route descends into the valley to the village of San Esteve d'en Bas where there is an attractive Romanesque church.

The road continues through a wooded green valley to St Feliu de Pallerols and Amer where there is a Romanesque church and a 16th-century square surrounded by old arcaded houses. From here you pass through a fertile valley bordered by wooded mountain to Angles, a picturesque old town of crumbling sepia stone houses, and then to Santa Coloma de Farnes.

A delightful detour can be made from here to the 12th-century fortress of Farnes. It is in a beautiful setting, built on a jagged spur of rock and surrounded by peaceful woods a few kms to the west of the town and reached along a rough dirt road.

The road between Santa Coloma de Farnes and St Hilari is very beautiful, running high along the side of a deep narrow valley, bordered by steep rocky moun-

The village of Rupit.

The Castillo and Parador of Cardona.

tainsides covered in trees, bracken, gorse and scattered with wild flowers. From here the road descends in series of steep tight bends to a quiet valley where it follows the course of a small river back to Vich.

CARDONA

THE NEXT PART OF THE TOUR is west to the Parador at Cardona. It begins by taking the road towards Balsareny. At first the road climbs through a densely wooded valley and then along a high ridge with sweeping views over the countryside to the north and south.

About 20km from Vich a road to the south leads to the village of L'Estany, whose 12th-century Monastery of Santa María is a quite beautiful building possessing a lovely Romanesque cloister with finely carved capitals.

The road descends from the ridge into a valley to the town of Balsareny. A large square fortress stands on a conical hill just outside the town in a commanding position overlooking the valley. The road continues to the small industrial town of Suria where it turns north-

wards on the C 1410 along the valley of the Río Cardoner to Cardona.

Cardona is one of those towns which more than fulfils the expectations most people have of Spain. You can almost hear the *Concerto of Aranjuez* being played as it comes into view – a considerable distance away. The fortress and church, built of a sepia-coloured stone, are set high above the valley on a mountainous brown rock, ringed by battlements – to theatrical effect. The 9th-century castle contains a tower from the 2nd century. Within the walls is the church of San Vincente built in the first part of the 11th century and containing the tombs of the Duques de Cardona.

Inside the Parador Nacional Duques de Cardona, situated within the castle, there is a warren of stone passages, corridors and staircases illuminated by small high windows. A courtyard encloses the remains of an ancient cloister. The medieval atmosphere is sustained in the *bodegón* (bar), which is in a dungeon-like stone chamber. The restaurant is in a vast hall with a decorative plaster ceiling supported by wooden beams and massive stone arches.

During my visit the menu contained some interesting Catalán dishes. Starters included El Caldo de Olla de Pages, a strongly flavoured meat broth; and La Escaliba Catalonia, a cold salad of cooked vegetables

which included asparagus, peppers, cauliflower and carrots. Main dishes included: La Cazuela de Bacalao con Peras y Piñones, a casserole of salt cod, pears and pine nuts; and Parrillada de Carnes Catalana, a mixed grill which included rabbit, chicken, pork and *butifara* (Catalan sausage). I chose a bottle of Blanc de Baldus, a crisp, fruity, slightly petulant white wine from Penedes.

In addition to the castle Cardona is famous for a curious natural phenomenon which you may visit – the Montaña de Sal, quite literally, a mountain of rock salt which soars up on the other side of the valley opposite the castle.

The old city of Solsona, 20km to the north-west has a lovely 13th-century Gothic cathedral, the remains of walls and the ruins of a 12th-century castle. There are atmospheric streets lined with old houses and an 18th-century palace containing the Museo Diocesano.

A simple excursion can be made from Cardona to the Monasterio de Montserrat. Leaving Cardona to the south you return to Suria and continue along the C 1410 to Manresa. Its fine Gothic church, Santa María, is on a ridge overlooking the Río Cardona. There are also two medieval bridges spanning the river. From Manresa the C 241 continues south towards Montserrat – a quiet scenic road passing through green, hilly countryside planted with vineyards and wheatfields.

You can see the extraordinary serrated rocky ridge of Montserrat many miles away. The road climbs the mountain in a series of wide sweeping curves that seem to go on forever. The 9th-century Benedictine monastery is in a remarkable setting over 2,000ft up in the Sierra de Montserrat and dominated by towering pinnacles of limestone rock.

The journey back to Cardona can be made by taking the road from Monistrol to Terrassa, whence a small road leads northwards to Navarcles through a wild mountainous region called the Parc Natural de Sant Lorenc del Munt characterised by its formations of pinkish rock and densely wooded with pine and oak trees, and rosemary, thyme and wild flowers carpeting the ground. In the midst of this countryside is the small 11th-century Romanesque church of San Lorenc. From Navarcles the return to Cardona can be made by following the road to Manresa and Suria.

The nearest alternative Parador to Cardona is at Seo de Urgell, 93km (page 142).

The Sierra de Montserrat.

OUR 13 Takes you into the eastern Pyrenees in the provinces of Lérida and Huesca. The area covered by the tour reaches from the French border in the north to the beginning of the Aragenese lowlands in the south. The western limit is the valley of the Río Gallego and the Sierra del Cadí forms the eastern border. The tour includes some of the most magnificent scenery in Spain with snow-capped mountain peaks, green valleys, wild white-water rivers and remote villages. The distances are not great as the crow flies but winding mountain roads will make your journeys take much longer than you might think.

— TOUR 13 —
MICHELIN MAP NOS. 43 & 42

SEO DE URGELL
VIELLA
ARTIES
BIELSA

LA SEO DE URGELL

THE ROUTE BEGINS in the Parador Nacional de la Seo de Urgell. The nearest airport is at Barcelona, a drive of about four hours. The closest alternative Parador is at Cardona (page 140). La Seo de Urgell is about 60km from the French border passing through Andorra.

The Parador is a modern building in the old part of town close to the cathedral. It was built on the site of the 14th-century church of Santo Domingo and the old cloister has been preserved as an enormous lounge covered by a glass roof. It is a striking room, comfortably furnished with luxuriant plants hung from the ceiling and walls. There is also a large indoor swimming pool.

The restaurant offers a variety of Catalán specialities. I had Olleta a lo Serrano to start my meal, a substantial vegetable soup with carrots, onions, potatoes, cabbage, turnips and tomatoes; Conejo Quisado con Setas del País, rabbit cooked with wild mountain mushrooms, made a delicious main course. A good selection of regional wines were on the list.

The city has been the seat of bishops since the 9th century. The 12th-century cathedral of Santa María, a rather severe building in granite, has a fine cloister with four galleries. Nearby is the attractive small Romanesque church of San Miguel. The grandiose 19th-century episcopal palace is also quite close to the Parador. Around the cathedral are a number of ancient arcaded streets and old houses with wrought-iron balconies, notably the Carrer del Canonges and the Casa del Pegri.

In addition to the tours I have suggested La Seo de Urgell is ideally placed to explore Andorra. The border is only 10km away and you can make a round trip by crossing into France and returning into Spain over the Col de Puymorens to Puigcerdá.

The Parador makes a good base from which to explore the countryside along the valley of the Río Segre eastwards towards Bellver de Cerdanya. The route follows the main road, the C 1313, incorporating the huge mountains of the Sierra de Cadí to the south. There are a succession of small mountain villages along this road which can be seen from the main road high up on the mountainsides, such as Arsequel, a village of stone houses with red tiled roofs, high on a rocky spur with a dramatic backdrop of the peaks of the Cadí. To leave the main road and drive up to these small villages is the best way of seeing the superb scenery and capturing the atmosphere of this region.

Just beyond Arseguel another small road to the south leads high up into the mountains with simply spectacular views. The road is signposted to Bar and El Querforadat. It is an unsurfaced road but quite wide and good for most of the way. Toloriú is beautiful. Set high up on steep slopes it is quite isolated and the only sound is from the bells of the cows which graze the flower-strewn meadows above the village.

The road winds onwards around the indented mountainside to El Querforadat. This is perhaps the most lovely and remote of all the villages in the Cadí. Its tiny rough-stone houses cling to a precipitous rock which hangs out over the mountainside. The last 100m of this road is perhaps a little teeth-clenching as it narrows to a single track and appears to be attached to the mountainside by a dry stone wall. You could park and walk the last part if your nerve fails you. It will take you about an hour to make this detour without allowing for stops, but it would make a wonderful place to take a picnic lunch.

Another scenic detour is to the winter resort of Lles 10km further along the main road. The road to the village leads north through meadows and woods and as you climb there are stunning views of the Sierra de Cadí to the south. Lles is an attractive mountain village which is also a ski resort, although on a very modest scale. Another road continues round the mountainside and along another small valley to the village of Aransa.

The main road continues to Bellver de Cerdanya where there is a ruined castle and 13th-century walls. You can then either return directly to La Seo de Urgell along the same route or continue to Puigcerdá and return through France and Andorra. This however would be a long day's drive and if you want to linger in the mountains and explore the villages it would be best as a separate excursion.

Another excursion can be made into the mountains to the south of La Seo de Urgell along the C 1313. On the outskirts of the town is the fortress of Castelliutat

and beyond this the road passes through the Garganta de Organya, a narrow rocky defile with cliffs soaring to 2,000 ft. Just before reaching the town of Coll de Nargo, with its attractive 11th-century church, a road to the east leads towards St Lorenc de Morunys. The road winds high around the steep rocky slopes of the Sierra de Oden with sweeping views of rugged mountains ridges. It continues for about 40km until at the Puerto de Comte it descends to St Lorenc lying sheltered in a deep green valley, with a fine Gothic church.

From here a small road leads northwards towards the village of Coma at the head of a narrow valley. Beyond the village the road climbs up out of the valley to the Collado de Port with breathtaking aerial views of the valley. From the top of the pass the road descends into another small hidden valley to the village of Tuxent. It is a pretty cluster of brown-stone houses covering a knoll in the centre of the valley and surrounded by meadows and mountains.

A narrow unsurfaced road continues high into the sourthern slopes of the mountains in the shelter of the 8,000ft peak of Cadí. It is a world apart. Blissfully quiet and very isolated, the tiny hamlets dotted over the mountainsides farm steep pastures and tiny terraced wheatfields. There is little sign of 20th-century life. Cornellana and Fornels are singularly pretty villages,

The village of Fornells in the Sierra del Cadí.

their neat brown-stone houses decorated with wooden balconies and draped with flowers. This road continues along an unsurfaced but quite adequate road, eventually descending to La Seo de Urgell. Although it appears to be a relatively small distance on the map you should allow at least three hours for the journey from San Lorenc back to La Seo de Urgell.

VIELLA

THE NEXT STAGE of this this tour is to the Parador at Viella. Leaving La Seo de Urgell you need to return along the C 1313 to Col de Nargo whence a quite road leads westward across the Sierra de Carreu to Tremp, an attractive hilly route with constant views of the distant mountains. The village of Isona has a 12th-century church with a fine portal, and further on, Conques has the remains of a castle. Tremp is situated in a broad cultivated valley with fields of wheat, fruit, vegetables and vineyards.

From here the C 1311 continues westwards and joins the N 230 after about 25km. At this junction the route

The Plaza Mayor of Ainsa.

continues northwards along the valley of the Río Noguera to El Pont de Suert, at the head of the Embalse de Escales. It has a huge trout farm and is known for its rug-making industry. Viella is only about 40km to the north of this point along the N 230.

There is, however, a small detour which can be made into the National Park of Aigues Tortes. A short distance beyond Pont de Suert a road to the east follows the valley of the Río Noguera de Tor and leads to Caldes de Boi where there is a small spa. The valley is notable for a collection of fine Romanesque churches. The villages of Barruera and Erill la Val have especially fine examples. Along a small road to the east of Erill is Tahull, a village high in the mountains, with perhaps the most beautiful of all the churches in this region: the 12th-century church of San Clemente has an elegant six-storey bell tower decorated with multiple windows. A rough track beyond Erill leads deep into the mountains providing spectacular views; but a four-wheel-drive vehicle is necessary for those who don't wish to walk.

fireplaces create a cosy hunting lodge atmosphere.

The Parador is close to the French border, and the restaurant is very popular with French visitors who make weekend trips into Spain. The menu reflects this French influence: Magret en Salsa de Roquefort, is breast of duck cooked with blue cheese; and Surtido de Pates del Valle are a selection of pâtés from the region. I chose Cabrito a las Hervas del Monte, kid grilled with wild mountain thyme and garlic, followed by Guiso del Pirineo, a selection of mountain cheeses.

Viella is a lively town with access to ski slopes nearby. It makes an excellent centre for exploring the Val de Arán. In the old part of town is the 13th-century church of San Miguel with a large octagonal tower. It contains a carving of Christ called the Cristo del Mig Arán which is considered to be one of the finest examples of early Romanesque art. There are also a number of lovely 17th-century mansions.

The Desfiladero de Collegats.

Landrover taxis can be hired in some of the villages.

The road to Viella follows the course of the Río Noguera and passes under the mountains through a 5km-long tunnel. The Parador Nacional Valle de Arán, located close to the road a few kms beyond the tunnel exit, is high on the mountainside overlooking the valley and the town of Viella, 2km further on. It has an exceptionally beautiful setting. The most striking feature of the Parador is a huge, round tower-like room with a conical grey slate roof, housing a two-storey lounge enclosed by an almost circular window commanding 360° views along three valleys. Central open

The town is the capital of the region. The Val de Arán has been part of Spain for many centuries but was isolated from the rest of the country until earlier this century when the pass of Bonaigua was built. Consequently the valley has a strong individual character with a language of its own quite different from both Catalán and Castilian Spanish.

ARTIÉS

THE PARADOR NACIONAL DON GASPER DE PORTOLA is situated in the village of Artiés only 9km away along the Val de Arán. Unlike Viella, Artiés is a quiet village in a completely rural setting with few signs of tourism. It is located where the valley of the Río Valarties meets the Val de Arán. The community of grey-stone houses is surrounded by peaceful meadows and overlooked by the imposing Pico Montarto. The cows are led through the village streets to pasture each day to the accompaniment of a carillon of bells. There is a 13th-century church and close to the village are Roman baths fed by hot sulphur springs.

The Parador, named after a famous 18th-century military character who founded the Mission of San Diego during his exploration of California, is on the edge of the village close to the road which passes through the valley. It is a modern building constructed in the local style with a steeply pitched grey-slate roof. The bedrooms have memorable mountain views. The lounge is an attractive two-storied room with a gallery and open stone fireplaces. Adjacent to the parador is an *hostería* which is only open during the winter months and contains a 17th-century chapel and a medieval tower.

The restaurant is in a large L-shaped room with a pine floor, ceiling and furniture which creates an agreeably rustic atmosphere. I had Olla Aranesa as a starter, a substantial soup of mixed vegetables, chick peas, pasta, *chorizo* and salt pork. To follow I had Perdiz a la Salsa de Higos, a deliciously rich dish of partridge served in a sauce of figs. The wine list included a good selection of regional wines including an excellent dry rose from Bodegas Raimat of Lerida.

Since the two paradors of Viella and Artiés are so close to each other you can consider them as alternative bases for the tours which follow.

The Val de Arán is one of the most beautiful mountain valleys and you do not have to travel very far to enjoy it to the full. One of the pleasures of exploring this region is that you are able to drive along small forest roads which penetrate high into the mountain valleys. Most are unsurfaced but quite easy to drive,

In the valley of the Río Torán.

giving you an opportunity to see a remote landscape which could otherwise only be reached by an arduous climb.

From the village of Artiés one of these roads follows the course of the Río Valarties along a valley where the meadow grass is knee-deep and a carpet of wild flowers creates a pointillist dapple of colour. From the head of the valley, walkers can continue to the Pico Montarto and to a ring of lakes called Colomes.

A few kms to the east of Artiés is Salardu, the capital of the upper Aran with a 13th-century church containing the 12th-century Cristo de Salardú. To the south of Salardú a small road leads along the valley of the Río d'Aiguamoix into a small valley of exeptional beauty. The river runs fast over boulders with swirling white water and small cascades. Trees line its banks, enclosing it in a tunnel of foliage and, beyond, there are meadows through which small brooks ripple.

Beyond the village of Tredos, where there is a 12th-century church, a road leads north to the ski slopes of Baqueira Beret. As it climbs to the plain of Beret there are wonderful views along the valley of Arán towards the pass of Bonaigua. You can see the road begin its serpent-like ascent of the mountain. The plain is a peaceful spot in summer with a small river meandering through the moist springy turf. From this point walkers can visit the deserted mountain village of Montgarri which has a Romanesque monastery.

The pass of Bonaigua is a worthy excursion in its own right and can be used to create a longish round trip, enabling you to visit another valley which leads into the National Park of Aigues Mortes. From the summit of the pass the road descends towards Esterri de Aneu, passing the mountain village of Sorp to the left. Just after passing Valencia de Aneau a tiny winding road to the right leads up the mountainside to Son del Pino, a village of ancient stone houses with vast views of the valley.

The road skirts the Embalse de la Torrasa and just beyond a road to the west follows the Río Mauricio to the small mountain resort of Espot, a base from which excursions into the Aigues Tortes can be made. Four-wheel-drive taxis are for hire which makes it possible to drive across the mountains to Caldas de Bohí.

Beyond the town a good road continues much higher up into the mountains to the lake of San Mauricio. The landscape is dominated by the peaks of Los Encantats – evocatively named 'enchanted mountains' whose bare conical peaks of grey, snow capped rock look like a child's drawing of mountains – quite unreal. The countryside here is enchanting with a vigorous river rushing over boulders and winding between grassy banks overhung by trees. It's a wonderful place to take a picnic or go walking.

The route continues along the valley of the fast-flowing white-water Río Noguera Palleresa to Lavorsi and

Rialp. Here the valley opens out and the river calms down a little. At Sort there are the remains of a ruined castle. Beyond, at the pretty riverside village of Gerri, a fine 12th-century Romanesque church is picturesquely sited on the far bank of the river. A few kms past Gerri the road enters a dramatic gorge, the Desfiladero de Collegats, where monumental cliffs tower above, rising sheer from the river bed for hundreds of feet.

At Pobla de Segur the route follows the C 144 westward to Pont de Suert. This road too is a continual source of pleasure as it winds through quiet, unspoiled countryside, passing the attractive village of Sarrocca de Bellera which teeters on a rock jutting out from the mountainside. A little further along the valley is Perbes another charming village of small stone houses. The road climbs out of the valley to a more rugged, rocky landscape, covered in a blaze of yellow broom. The road descends again into another peaceful valley. This

The road meets the opening of a valley through which the Río Joeu runs and then continues along this high into the mountains. The slopes are densely wooded and the riverbed is so steep in places that it is almost like a waterfall. Overlooking the valley is the dramatic jagged mountain of Aneto.

The return from this road leads to the village of Es Bordes. A short distance to the south at the village of Arros a road leads into the valley of the Río Varrados. This too is spectacularly beautiful. Turning northwards again the road leads to Bosost where there is a ruined castle and a 12th-century church. Just beyond Les a road to the west leads to Bausen, a primitive hamlet of ancient stone farms and houses high up on the tree-covered mountainside. It has the appearance and atmosphere of a medieval community.

A short distance beyond, a road to the east leads along the valley of the Río Torán. A fork to the left weaves tortuously around the mountainside to Caneján, an attractive village located high above the valley with quite awesome views. The road continues, however, much higher into the mountains beyond the curious old hilltop village of San Joan de Torán. Here, among towering peaks, deep forests, meadows and rushing rivers, is another quite unforgettable place.

BIELSA

THE NEXT STAGE of this tour is to the Parador at Bielsa, a distance of about 200km. The route is initially to the south of Viella along the N 230. Just beyond Villaler it turns to the west along the C 144, passing through a quiet green valley. It then climbs steadily towards the Col de Espina with distant views of the Pyrenean peaks to the north. The wooded mountainsides give way to open heathland and the road continues higher to the Col de Fadas. The route descends into a wide green, fertile valley to Castejon de Sos where the road joins the C 139.

You can make a short detour to the north along the valley of the Río Esera to Benasque in a steep valley at the foot of the Sierra de Maladeta. The town has a 13th-century Romanesque church and the Palacio de los Condes de Ribagorza, as well as some old houses along its narrow streets. It is the centre for climbs to the Pic d'Aneto and the Pic de Posets, the two highest mountains in the Pyrenees.

Continuing south from Castejon de Sos the road passes through the Congosto de Ventamillo, a spectacular gorge where steep jagged cliffs overhang the road. The route continues high along the side of a steep mountain slope and then descends into a rocky

leads to Pobla de Segur from where you can follow the N 230 back to Viella.

The road north of Viella leads to the French border along the valley of the Río Garona, which becomes the Garonne in France. There are some lovely detours to be made from this road. The first of these is a small road from Viella to the village of Gausac whence the road climbs high up along the mountainside running parallel to the valley through a beautiful pine forest.

The Romanesque church of Gerri.

valley. Beyond, it heads westwards along the C 140 and crosses a rugged mountain range over the Collado de Fordada.

The road descends gently into a wide fertile valley, planted with wheatfields and vineyards, to Ainsa, an ancient town set on a low hill beside the Río Ara. Once the capital of the medieval kingdom of Sobrabe, it is surrounded by fortified walls and there are the ruins of a castle, which has a lovely courtyard and a tall tower. There is a broad cobbled *plaza mayor* surrounded by old houses with arcades and balconies and overlooked by 12th-century church. Around the square are a maze of steep narrow streets lined by warm brown stone buildings.

The road to Bielsa continues to the north along the valley of the Río Cinca. At Escalona a road leads to the west along a small green valley. This is a detour not to be missed. As you progress through the valley it begins to narrow. Quite suddenly you realise you have entered a canyon. Sheer jagged cliffs soar upwards for hundreds of feet and a clear, ice-blue river crashes over boulders beside the road. As you penetrate deeper into the gorge the cliffs become higher and steeper. At one point it feels as if you are entering a funnel with the cliffs converging above you. The canyon continues for more than 10km, then opens out on to a quite remarkable landscape of red rock mountainsides covered in yellow broom. To the north the Río Añisclo cuts its way through the mountains, forming another dramatic gorge towards the Pico de Añisclo. This wild, wonderful region is the National Park of Ordesa and Monte Perdido.

Returning to the main road, the C 138, the route continues along the valley which becomes progressively narrower while the mountains soar majestically above it for thousands of feet. Bielsa is an old town, damaged during the Civil War. It retains a 16th-century *ayuntamiento* and some old arcaded houses.

The Parador Nacional Monte Perdido lies 11km to the west at the head of the Valle de Pineta. A semi-circular wall of rock rises up from the valley floor and enfolds the Parador. Looming higher still is the massive snow-capped peak of Monte Perdido. The building is in the style of a hunting lodge built from solid blocks of granite with a grey slate roof. Inside it is warm and welcoming with pine floors and ceilings and decorated with hunters' trophies and oil paintings of animals and flowers. The views from its windows are

The village of Torla with Monte Perdido in the background.

stunning. A large sun terrace adjoins the restaurant and, a footpath below leads down through a meadow to a small wooden bridge which crosses the river.

The menu included some suitably hunter-like dishes: Receo de Binefar, a hearty soup with beans, potatoes, onions and salt pork; Codornices con Pimientos al Horno, quails baked with green peppers; and Caldereta de Cordero, a rich lamb stew with peppers, onions, mushrooms and tomatoes. I chose a bottle of Lalanne, a soft, fruity red wine from Bodegas Somontano de Sobrabe.

Some breathtaking views of the valley can be had by taking a small road to the north about 7km back towards Bielsa. It climbs high up on to the mountainside to the village of Espierba and beyond. Although very steep, the slopes are covered with green pastures and dotted with small stone cottages and barns.

To the north of Bielsa the road passes through a tunnel under a monumental wall of rock, the Circo de Barrossa, into France. About 1km before the tunnel a small road climbs westward into the mountains to the village of Parzán and far beyond. Although unsurfaced and narrow, it is passable for many miles. Here, isolated shepherds' huts and green meadows are to be found in the highest and most remote places just below the savage rocky peaks. A shepherd showed me where the ground had been disturbed by wild boar feeding and pointed out a flock of wild sheep high up on a distant ridge.

A memorable excursion can be made from the Parador to the National Park of Ordesa along the road back to Ainsa and then following the C 138 west to Boltana. The route follows a steep rocky valley beside the Río Ara. Just beyond Broto, attractively set beside the river, a road to the east leads to Torla, an ancient small town with medieval houses and an old church set on a rocky outcrop. The massive range of Monte Perdido creates an imposing backdrop. As the road enters the Valley de Ordesa; a broad river, shaded by trees, flows across the wide valley floor. You are, seemingly, surrounded by sheer mountainsides which rise to a dizzy height with trees clinging obstinately to the slopes. Above, massive peaks of bare rock seem to reach up to the sky. It is a place of magnificent natural beauty.

From Ordesa you can return to the Parador at Bielsa by the same route. The nearest alternative parador is at Sos del Rey Católico, 240km to the west (page 65).

*T*OUR 14   *Begins on the Costa del Azahar, the orange blossom coast of the province of Castellón, where millions of orange and lemon trees pattern the plains; continues northwards into the southern region of the province of Tarragona where the broad Río Ebro finally makes its exit into the Mediterranean. The route then delves eastwards into the province of Teruel to a mountain region of severe and epic beauty, the Maestrazgo. Here small villages are almost completely isolated from the 20th-century way of life. Within the rocky and often barren landscape there are hidden valleys where green meadows and wheatfields are rimmed by dry stone walls and wildflowers grow in vivid profusion. The tour continues south to Teruel, a city with a wealth of Mudéjar architecture.*

The four Paradors which are featured include two dramatically sited hilltop castles, one an ancient fortified palace. Another is set beside the blue waters of the Mediterranean and the fourth overlooks the historic city of Teruel.

— TOUR 14 —
MICHELIN MAP NOS. 43 & 445

Alcañiz
Tortosa
Benicarló
TERUEL

BENICARLÓ
TORTOSA
ALCAÑIZ
TERUEL

BENICARLÓ

THE PARADOR NACIONAL COSTA DEL AZAHAR, the starting point of this itinerary, is situated on the edge of Benicarló on the seafront. This town is on the N 340 between Tarragona and Valencia, only a short distance from the Autopista A 7 which connects Alicante with the French border. The nearest airport is at Valencia, 140km away. The nearest alternative Parador is at El Saler, 153km (page 172).

The Parador is a two-storey building in the form of a large open-sided square. The spacious airy bedrooms open on to private sun terraces which face a wide lawn shaded by palm trees. In the centre is an enormous swimming pool. Just beyond is the sea. The restaurant and lounge open on to a broad shaded terrace, furnished with comfortable wicker chairs and tables: a perfect spot in which to enjoy a drink after a few laps of the pool.

The menu includes dishes like Pucherete del Maestrazgo, a comforting country soup of rice, haricot beans, cabbage, onion, salt pork and *chorizo*. A similarly rustic dish is Lentejas Estofados de Manitas de Cerdo, lentils cooked with pig's trotters. Arroz Abanda is a creamy rice dish in which the rice is cooked in a strongly flavoured fish broth seasoned with paprika and saffron and garnished with prawns. It is rather like a *paella* without the pieces of meat and fish. A potent garlic mayonnaise is served with it for you to stir in. Gambas con Salsa Romesco, large prawns served with a typical spicy sauce of the region, is made with peppers, tomatoes, almonds, garlic, olive oil and wine vinegar. I had a bottle of Castillo de Liria, a crisp dry white wine from Valencia. The wine list also included, unusually, Vega Sicilia, the renowned and expensive red wine from the Valladolid region.

Benicarló is an attractive but unexceptional town with a 16th-century Baroque church with an octagonal tower and a dome of blue azuleos and some interesting old streets. It also has a busy and important fishing fleet which plies a region rich in crustacea known as the Triángulo de Langosta, the lobster triangle.

The Parador is set at the northern extremity of a particularly fine long beach of good sand. At the southern curve of the beach is a massive dome of rock, jutting out into the sea like a small peninsula. Upon this the fortified town of Peniscola, creates a most striking sight. Walls encircle a labyrinth of steep cobbled streets and there are imposing tunnel-like gateways through which you enter. The castle was built by the Templars and looks down over the brilliant blue water of the Mediterranean which laps around it. The town is almost like an island with only a small spit of land linking it to the mainland. It was the refuge of Pope Don Pedro de Luna when he fled from Avignon.

The coastal plain is flat but a short distance inland the countryside becomes quite hilly and mountains rise in the distance. The land is very fertile and is heavily cultivated with olive and almond trees, vineyards and fields of vegetables. As you travel south however the agriculture is dominated by vast orange and lemon groves with dense green foliage studded with millions of brilliant orange and yellow fruits.

The main road, N 340, runs parallel to the coast, but some distance inland. Access to the sea is by roads which lead to the coastal towns and adjacent beaches. Most of these are not very attractive, many being extensively and tastelessly developed. Oropesa, just to the north of Castellón de la Plana, is however an interesting and appealing old town set on a hill overlooking the sea and ringed by castle walls. There are also two good beaches here, Playa de Morro de Gos and Playa de la Concha. Oropesa makes a good alternative to Benicarló or Peñíscola for a day on the beach but, in general, it is not a coastline which offers rewarding sightseeing.

Just a little to the south of Oropesa a small road climbs high into the pine-covered mountains to the Desierto de las Palmas. Here you will come across an 18th-century monastery and will be able to enjoy beautiful views of the plain of Castellón, as well as of the shimmering blue sea beyond.

TORTOSA

The fishing port of Vinaròs.

THE NEXT STAGE OF THE TOUR is to the Parador at Tortosa. An interesting and scenic route can be made by, first, taking the N 340 north to Vinaròs, a busy fishing town with a lively and colourful harbour. I spent some time watching the boats bobbing around in the harbour, waiting for a place by the quayside to unload their catch. The skippers wheeled and manoeuvred their large, brightly painted boats around with the casual abandon of dodgem cars at a fairground. Most of the boats had lines draped from the rigging from which filleted anchovies were hung to dry in the sun like strange miniature washing. A frenetic fish auction takes place in the market house on the dockside.

From Vinaròs the route continues westwards along the N 232, signposted to Zaragoza. Initially the road is quite straight across flat, open country planted largely with almond and olive trees. The village of Traiguera has an atmospheric old quarter and is also known for its pottery. The landscape soon takes on a more rugged and mountainous character. San Mateo, a few kms to the south along the C 238, is an important town of the lower Maestrazgo with many old buildings and known for its wine. There is a fine *ayuntamiento*, an arcaded *plaza mayor* and a 13th-century parish church. A short distance further along the N 232 a road to the south leads to the old town of Cati. Set amidst wild rocky countryside patterned with ancient dry stone walls, its narrow streets contain many medieval houses, some with seignorial crests, and there is an arcaded *lonja*, or market house.

Continuing to the west along the N 232, the road follows the course of a dry riverbed bordered by steep sandy banks. Fig trees line the road and the dusty hillsides are covered with broom and gorse bushes. It is a severe and inhospitable landscape, sparsely populated. The road climbs progressively towards the Puerto de Querol in a series of sweeping hairpin bends. This pass is sometimes closed in the winter because of snow. Here the countryside becomes thickly wooded with oak and pine trees covering the steep mountainsides. From the summit of the pass the road crosses a plateau where wheatfields are planted in small terraces bordered by dry stone walls.

Soon you approach Morella. The first glimpse is almost startling. The old houses are tightly packed on terraces around the steep sides of a large domed hill. Above there is a circular wall of rock, crowned by castle walls and towers. The town retains a strong medieval atmosphere with ancient stone houses decorated with wooden balconies. Its steep narrow streets and alleys are entered through fortified gateways. There is a beautiful Gothic church, Santa María la Mayor and outside the town are the remains of a 15th century aqueduct.

From Morella the route continues northwards on the N 232 along a scenic road which climbs through steep mountainsides to the Puerto de Torre Miro, an open moorland landscape with few trees. Beyond, Monroyo, strikingly set below a dramatic rocky outcrop, overlooks a broad fertile valley planted with vineyards, wheatfields, and almond and olive groves.

The route now heads north-east along the TE 302 through a wide valley bordered by rocky pine-clad mountainsides. A brief detour to the south can be made to the picturesquely sited old town of Penarroya de Tastavines. Some 20kms further is Valderrobres beside the Río Matarrana. An ancient bridge crosses the river and the town is entered through a fortified gateway. Looming high above the village houses is the massive 14th-century castle of the Knights of Calatrava. There is also the lovely Gothic church of Santa María and a fine 16th-century *ayuntamiento*. The town is a fascinating tangle of narrow cobbled streets, alleyways, steps and small squares.

A short distance beyond Valderrobres a road leads off into a quiet fertile valley to the small village of Beceite, surrounded by small market gardens and vineyards and overlooked by the imposingly rugged mountain range of the Puertos de Beseit.

At Horta de San Juan there is a porticoed plaza said to be the inspiration for one of Picasso's first cubist paintings. There are many old buildings including an

Peñíscola.

ayuntamiento, the convent of Sant Salvador d'Horta and the church of Sant Joan Baptista. The scenery here is most impressive with plunging vine-cloaked valleys and the soaring mountain peaks of the Salto de Sutorras. This is the region of the Terra Alta, known for its strongly alcoholic wines.

Beyond Horta de San Juan the road joins the N 230 which leads south along the valley of the Río Ebro to Tortosa, an ancient city whose history dates back to Iberian and Roman times. The 14th-century cathedral was not completed until the beginning of the 18th century. Other buildings of interest include the 14th-century Episcopal Palace, with a lovely courtyard and gallery, and a *lonja*, a covered market hall, from the same period. The town is built along the river bank and a sculptured memorial has been created from the one remaining pile of the bridge which was destroyed during the Civil War.

Above the town on a hilltop crowned by extensive walls is the remains of the citadel of La Zuda. Within is the Parador Nacional Castillo de la Zuda, the site of an

Vineyards of the Terra Alta near Horta de San Joan.

Iberian settlement, then a Roman acropolis and finally a Moorish fortress. Remains of columns from Roman times are scattered within the grounds and there is a swimming pool which is very welcome during the summer months. There are superb views from the castle walls of the old city rooftops, the Río Ebro and the mountains beyond.

The Parador building is a modern construction using traditional methods with huge blocks of granite. The bedrooms have large wooden balconies with fine views. The restaurant has a high-beamed ceiling and retains some of the original large windows and fireplaces. The menu features Catalan cuisine including some specialities from the nearby Ebro Delta: Ancas de Rana Fritas, fried frogs legs; and Angulas en Suc, baby eels cooked in a garlicky sauce, brought to the table in a small earthenware crock and eaten with a wooden fork. There is an excellent selection of regional wines on the list including some from the Priorato region south of Tarragona. I had a bottle of Gandesa Sec Blanco, a strong dry white wine from the Terra Alta.

A fascinating excursion can be made easily from the Parador to the Ebro Delta, an almost tree-less marshy region as flat as the sea which surrounds it. From Tortosa the C 235 leads to a junction with the N 340. One

road on to the delta leads from a short distance to the north of this junction and follows the northern bank of the river through the villages of Jesus Y María and La Cava to Ríomar. From here it is possible to cross the Ebro on one of the typical barges to the Island of Buda.

A little to the south along the N 340 another road leads on to the Delta following the southern bank of the river. Extensive rice fields are criss-crossed by narrow paths which lead to small island-like farmhouses. It is said that it is possible to experience mirages in this region equal to those in a desert. The road continues to the edge of the delta where there is an enormously long beach, the Playa de los Eucaliptus, whence another road returns to the fishing town of San Carlos de la Rápita. Here there is a busy harbour and fish market and a long sandy beach just outside the town. The return to Tortosa can be made by returning north along the N 340 to the same junction with the C 235.

ALCAÑIZ

THE NEXT STAGE OF THE TOUR is to the Parador at Alcañiz. A very attractive route along the valley of the Ebro can be followed by taking the T 301 northwards along the

Castellote.

east bank of the river from Tortosa. It is a very fertile valley planted with small market gardens and huge orchards of apricot, peach, orange and lemon trees. The road soon climbs out of the valley along a rocky pine-clad mountainside. There are dramatic views of the valley and the Río Ebro far below from this small, quiet road.

Further north the road descends again and continues along the, now, broad open valley of the Ebro. Just beyond Rasquera a small road leads down to the river bank where you can cross the river by driving your car on to a small chain-operated ferry. It is simply a large platform supported on two hulls. It is a pleasant spot for a picnic lunch. The ferry crosses to the village of Miravet, set below a large rock from which a massive castle looks down over the river.

The alternative to the ferry is to continue for another 10km to the north and to cross the river at the twin towns of Mora la Nova and Mora de Ebre. A road follows the river south again to Miravete whence a quiet country road leads west to El Pinell de Brai, strikingly

The Mudéjar tower of San Martín in Teruel.

set on a jagged ridge of rock with many of the old houses rising sheer from its edge. Just outside the village is a wine co-operative with a striking modern mural of *azulejos*.

Beyond is a junction with the main road, the N 230. This leads northwards to Gandesa passing through a quite spectacular rocky defile called the Serra de Cavalls. Gandesa is an important wine town set among the extensive vineyards of the Terra Alta. It has a 13th-century Gothic church, an arcaded square and many old buildings.

At Gandesa the route continues to the west along the N 420, passing through Calaceite, an old town with a fine *ayuntamiento*, an arcaded plaza and a Baroque church. Nearby are the remains of an ancient Iberian settlement. This road provides an attractive scenic route along a high ridge with wonderful views of mountains and valleys covered in a sea of vines.

About 40km beyond is Alcañiz, a small town beside the Río Guadalupe with a most attractive *plaza mayor* overlooked by the massive early-18th-century Baroque church of Santa María la Mayor. Adjacent is a beautiful 16th-century *ayuntamiento* and a 14th-century galleried *lonja*.

On a hilltop above the town is the Castillo de los Calatravas, a 12th-century fortified palace visible for miles around. The location of the Parador Nacional La Concordia, it looks down over the old rooftops of the town to the river tumbling over a weir and the patterned plain reaching away beyond. In the distance the hazy blue ridges of the Maestrazgo can be seen.

The castle is a magnificent building, its imposing façade flanked by two huge square towers. There are Gothic wall paintings in the castle keep and a small cloister nearby contains the tombs of the Knights of Calatrava. There is also a partially destroyed alabaster tomb built for Juan de Lanuza, the Viceroy of Aragón, in the 16th century.

The Parador interior is satisfyingly atmospheric with a huge stone staircase, terracotta-tiled floors and walls decorated with heraldic flags and tiled murals. The restaurant occupies a long room with a high wooden ceiling and an impressive open-stone fireplace. It is illuminated by rows of huge wrought-iron candelabra and casement windows which provide superb views.

The menu offers dishes from the regional cuisine of Aragón, such as Pechugas de Pollo a la Aragonesa, chicken breasts cooked with red peppers, onion, tomatoes, ham and garlic; and Arroz Arogones, rabbit cooked with rice. I tried Muslos de Pollo Turolense, chicken legs cooked in a deliciously rich sauce of white wine, garlic, ham and almonds. The deserts included Dulces Tipicos de Alcañiz, pastries which included wickedly sweet honey turnovers and meringues made with ground almonds. The wine list included a good selection of regional wines. I had a bottle of Don Ramon, a good full-bodied red wine from Cariñena.

Alcañiz is an excellent base from which to make excursions into the Maestrazgo. A day's round trip can be made by taking the N 420 south across an open landscape planted with wheatfields to Calanda, a town known for its ceramics and its attractive arcaded plaza. From here a small road, the T 832, strikes off towards the mountains. It skirts the shores of the Embalse de Calanda towards Mas de la Mata. Here the landscape becomes more hilly with woods and meadows mingling with the wheatfields. The road then climbs into more rugged and mountainous countryside. It enters a narrow green valley, dominated by a massive striated mountain of red rock, and then passes through a tunnel to the village of Castellote, dramatically situated with the old houses strung out below a jagged rocky ridge. Above the town, and almost appearing to be moulded from the cliff, are the remains of a castle.

The road then climbs around the edge of a beautiful lake, the Embalse de Santolea. Its vivid turquoise water is enclosed by bare red rock cliffs. The Maestrazgo is a

Villarluengo.

landscape of boldly contrasting colours. There are rocks and soil of a deep reddish brown, wheatfields the colour of white gold, bright green vineyards and the deep dense green of the pine trees which cloak the mountainsides. There are few signs of human life between the small scattered villages. I drove for several hours along this road without seeing another car.

A few kms beyond the picturesque small village of Olocau del Rey the route turns back to the north-east towards La Mata de Morella. However, a brief detour can be made further south at this point to the enchanting village of Mirambel, encircled by walls with entrance gates, one of which is incorporated into a small tower-like house. There is a beautiful old church, and numerous elegant mansions lining its ancient cobbled streets. It is quiet and unspoilt.

Beyond La Mata de Morella the road leads through the broad fertile valley of the Río Cantavieja to Forcal. An appealing old town beside the Río Caldes and overlooked by jagged mountains, it has an attractive arcaded plaza, a lovely church and many old houses linked by narrow streets and alleys. A small road now leads north along the shallow rocky valley of the Río Bergantes to Ortells and Zorita del Maestrazgo. The latter is an ancient crumbling village of small houses

stacked up above each other like a house of playing cards. Their rough stone walls are decorated with small wooden balconies. Above sits a lovely old church with a tower and dome of blue azulejos.

A few kms beyond Zorita is the sanctuary of the Virgin La Balma set into a crevice in a massive wall of rock. The road continues through a dramatic canyon with startling views at every turn. At the end of the canyon is the village of Aiguaviva in a broad green valley planted with vineyards and wheatfields. The road returns to Mas de la Mata from where the same route can be followed back to Alcañiz.

TERUEL

THE FINAL STAGE OF THIS TOUR is south-west to the Parador at Teruel. The route I have suggested leads through more of the magnificent Maestrazgo countryside. The first leg of the journey is along the N 420 to Las Mata de los Olmos. A few kms beyond, the TE 821 turns southwards to the picturesque village of Ejulve.

A few kms further south the road enters a steep rocky valley and begins to climb towards the Puerto de Villarluengo. There is a spectacular towering peak of ridged rock, called the Órganos de Montoro, which dominates this valley. A short distance beyond, a small road to the right leads through a huge chasm in the rocks to the village of Ritarque in a peaceful, hidden, green valley through which a small river cascades over boulders and overlooked by two massive mountain peaks. Nearby is the Hostal de las Truchas, an isolated riverside hotel which would make a wonderful base from which to explore this region more fully. The countryside here is simply magnificent – wild, rocky and uninhabited – one of the most beautiful places I have seen anywhere.

The beautiful town of Villarluengo is just on the other side of the pass in a magnificent setting high on a terraced hillside overlooking a rocky valley. It contains a warren of narrow streets with ancient houses and a lovely 18th-century church. Like most villages in this region, it is completely untouched by tourism. Further along this road is another strikingly situated village, Cañada de Benatanduz. The road continues to the Puerto de Cuerto Pelado where the scenery has an almost Alpine quality with springy green turf strewn with wild flowers and dotted with pine trees, gorse and yellow broom.

At this point there is a junction with another road, the TE 800, leading westwards to Teruel, the capital of the province and the seat of a bishop. The city was founded by the Iberians and destroyed by the Romans in 218. After the conquest of the Moors in 1171 they were allowed to remain until the last mosque was closed early in the 16th century. Because of this the city became the focal point of Mudéjar art, a blend of Moorish and Christian architectural styles.

Among the many fine examples of this style to be seen in the city are the Cathedral and the 12th-century churches of San Salvador and San Martín, both with enormous, intricately decorated towers. The city is also famous for its tragic lovers, Isabel de Segura and Juan Diego Martínez de Marcilla, who, in the 13th century, were prevented from marrying by family prejudices and who died of grief. They have been the subject of much poetry and prose and their remains are preserved in the church of San Pedro. There is also a 16th-century aqueduct, a 16th-century Episcopal palace and the remains of the medieval city walls.

The Parador Nacional de Teruel, 2km to the north of the city on the road to Zaragoza, the N 234, is set on a quiet wooded hillside overlooking the city whose Mudéjar towers can be seen rising above the houses. It

Linares de Mora.

is a modern building constructed of stone in traditional style. The ground floor has tall French windows framed by pointed stone arches. There is a grand octagonal entrance hall with marble columns and a large stone staircase. Adjoining the bar and restaurant is a spacious conservatory furnished with cane chairs and tables. Marble floors, high ceilings and simple white decor create a cool, peaceful, elegant atmosphere.

Local dishes on the menu included: Sopa de Teruel en Pelico, garlic soup thickened with bread and enriched with egg; and Crema Fría de Pepino y Mariscos, a delicately flavoured chilled soup of shellfish and cucumber. I had Cazuela de Trigueros y Almejas Marinera, a delicious combination of slender fronds of wild asparagus cooked in a casserole with clams. The house wine is from the vineyards of Cariñena.

Teruel is a good base from which to make an enjoyable excursion into the Maestrazgo, taking the N 234 south-east to La Puebla de Valverde. From here the C 232 leads to Mora de Rubielos, an attractive old town with a massive 13th-century castle dwarfing the small community over which it presides. Adjacent is a 15th-century Gothic church. The road continues through rocky pine-clad mountainsides to the nearby and confusingly named village of Rubielos de Mora. It is particularly delightful, enclosed within medieval walls with entrance gates and threaded by narrow cobbled streets. There is a lovely 16th-century *ayuntamiento* with a charming arcaded patio and 17th-century church; and a 17th-century convent with a beautiful cloister is now a hotel.

From here the route continues to the north-east along the TE 811 through a deep green valley, climbing steadily along the mountainside and quite suddenly revealing the spectacularly sited village of Linares de Mora. Its small red-roofed houses with crumbling stone walls and wooden balconies seem to jostle for position on the hillside. The ruins of a castle and an old church are poised on a ridge of rock above them. The road continues to climb the mountainside beyond the village to the Puerto de Linares. The views from here are simply astonishing. The tiny village seems almost to be suspended above the valley. The surrounding hillsides are ridged and patterned by dry stone walls and terraced fields.

From the top of the pass the road continues along a high plateau, carpeted by meadows and fields of wheat. In the distance is a rim of hazy pine-clad mountainsides. The curious village of Puertomingalvo is like a ghost town and well worth a small detour. Encircled by walls with entrance gates, there is a castle perched on a rock at one end. Its quiet narrow streets are lined with ancient houses.

The road continues through the village of Mosqueruela to La Iglesuela del Cid, another fascinating old town with a 16th-century church and 16th-century arcaded *ayuntamiento*. The T 800 now leads north-west to Cantavieja. This too is a gem: an old walled town with a beautiful arcaded plaza overlooked by an imposing 17th-century church. The road continues to the Puerto Dé de Cuarto Pelado where the same route is followed from the previous itinerary to Allepuz.

The TE 802 now leads along a lovely valley through the Sierra de Gúdar to Alcala de la Selva. This too is an exceptionally beautiful and unspoilt old town in a picturesque setting overlooking a steep narrow valley, with a castle set on a rock, atmospheric streets, a pretty church and square. From Mora de Rubielos, 20km further south, you can return to Teruel along the outward route.

Another interesting excursion can be made to Albarracín only 40km from the Parador at Teruel and worthy of at least a few hours' exploration. It is reached by taking the N 234 north towards Zaragoza for a few kms and then the TE 901 westwards along the valley of Guadalviar. Albarracín is set at the head of this valley at a point where steep red cliffs form a semicircular wall of rock. The pinkish brown village houses are tiered up the mountainside almost appearing to be sculpted from it. Along one side of the rock a vast castle wall extends like a spine of stone. Inside the village there is a jumble of steep, narrow streets and alleys with steps and small squares. It has retained a strong medieval atmosphere. There is a 13th-century cathedral, El Salvador, and the parish church of Santa María which is of Mozarabic origin, although its present form dates from the 16th century. The Episcopal Palace has an imposing Baroque façade. For the energetic, a path leads up to the castle walls from where there are stunning views.

Beyond Albarracín a road leads into the Sierra de los Montes Universales to Orihuela del Tremedal. Here, among deep pine forests is the birthplace of the Río Tajo and dozens of springs which feed many other of Spain's rivers.

An appealing route back to the Parador can be made by taking the TE 900 from Albarracín to Bezas, a quiet country road which runs along a rocky mountainside covered in pine trees. In some places the mountain has been eroded into weird and wonderful shapes creating a quite surrealist landscape. It would make an ideal place to take a picnic lunch.

The airport at Valencia is about 150km from Teruel. The nearest alternative paradors are Santa María de Huerta, 170km (page 104), El Saler, 170km (page 172) and Alarcón, 220km (page 164). The latter can be used to join Tour No. 15 to complete a round trip back to Valencia.

A medieval gateway in Albarracín.

OUR 15 Begins in the province of Cuenca and leads south to the province of Albacete and the plains of La Mancha, then turning east to the provinces of Alicante and Valencia and exploring the fishing towns and resorts of the Costa Blanca. The countryside through which it leads ranges from the vast wheatfields and vineyards of the plains to the little-known mountain range of the Sierra de Alcaraz, the Valencian huertas and the marshy flatlands and lagoon of La Albufera. It is a region of impressive castles and hill-top towns as well as white fishing villages and palm-fringed beaches. The four Paradors which link the tour include one of the most beautiful and atmospheric castles in the Parador network and a beach-side modern hotel which has one of the loveliest golf courses in Spain on its doorstep.

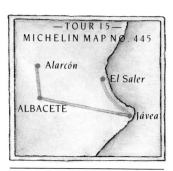

— TOUR 15 —
MICHELIN MAP NO. 445

Alarcón
El Saler
ALBACETE
Jávea

ALARCÓN
ALBECETE
JÁVEA
EL SALER

ALARCÓN

THE STARTING POINT of the tour is the Parador Nacional Marqués de Villena, situated in a small village set on a rocky, island-like, promontory in a loop of a gorge where the Río Júcar emerges from the Embalse de Alarcón. It is a short distance from the main road, the N 111, which links Valencia with Madrid. The nearest airport is at Valencia, about 160km distant. The nearest alternative Paradors are at Teruel (page 161), Chinchón (page 108) and Manzanares (page 117).

The Parador occupies one of the loveliest castles in the region and was built during the early part of the Moorish occupation. The village itself is encircled by extensive walls and guarded by towers and fortified gateways. Indeed the approach to the village is along a narrow ridge between two towers which gives the impression that you are crossing a drawbridge. The castle played an important role in the final overthrow of the Moors. The Parador is named after one of the castle's more notable owners, Juan Pacheco the Marqués de Villena. He was a powerful friend of Henry IV of Castile who gave him the castle along with many other properties throughout Spain.

The restaurant occupies one of the castle's great halls with massive rough stone walls. The local Manchegan cuisine is represented on the menu with dishes such as Morteruelo, a highly spiced dish of chopped pigs' liver fried with breadcrumbs; Tortilla Guisada, an omelette made with potatoes and onions and served in a sauce flavoured with paprika and garlic; and Queso Manchego con Mostillo, the local ewes' milk cheese served with a slice of a delicious jelly-like preserve, similar to *membrillo* but made from grapes instead of quinces. Local wines include those of Valdepeñas, Utiel and Jumilla. I sampled the Castillo de Almansa, which is a good red

wine from the vineyards of Yecla.

The village of Alarcón is a peaceful and unspoiled place with an almost deserted atmosphere. There is an arcaded *ayuntamiento* in the plaza and many ancient houses decorated with escutchions along its quiet cobbled streets. There are several old churches: Santa María has an attractive façade with a portal decorated by sculptures and pillars.

The Parador is a convenient base from which to visit the town of Cuenca about 80km to the north. An attractive and quiet route, which avoids the main road and leads through pleasant rolling farmland, is to take the N 111 east towards Motilla del Palancer and after a few kms turn north on to the CU 721 and then the CU 714 to Olmedilla de Alarcón and Valeria. Here there is a ruined castle and the remains of a Roman town. Beyond Valeria the road joins the N230 a few kms south of Cuenca.

Set on a rocky V-shaped promontory, created by the junction of the gorges of the Río Júcar and the Río Huéscar, it is an attractive old town with a lovely plaza mayor. Here café tables spill on to the street and it's a charming place to relax a while with a drink or meal. Overlooking the plaza is the cathedral, a most imposing building with a monumental facade. It contains many treasures including paintings by El Greco, Flemish tapestries and a magnificent 16th-century screen.

The town is famed for just two buildings, the Casas Colgados, the hanging houses. These houses quite literally hang over the edge of the 600ft cliffs which tower above the Huéscar gorge and are occupied by a restaurant and an art gallery. A flimsy suspension bridge spans the gorge, enabling you to walk out and obtain a dizzy view of the already vertiginous houses. Way below a small road runs alongside the river with lovely views of the hanging houses, and the small rocky valley, to Palomera where there are some attractive riverside spots, perfect for a picnic. In the gorge of the Río Júcar is the prettily situated church of San Miguel in which concerts of religious music take place.

From Cuenca a round trip can be made into the Sierra de Valdecabras, a rocky, pine-clad mountain range. A natural curiosity can be visited along this route called the Ciudad Encantada, the enchanted city. A series of paths lead off into the pine forests to a region where the rocks have been eroded into strange and exotic shapes. One, for example, is like a monumental mushroom 100ft high and others look like the hulls of huge beached galleons. The return from Cuenca to Alarcón can be made more swiftly by taking the N 320 back to Motilla del Palancar.

ALBACETE

The Castillo and Parador of Alarcón.

THE NEXT STAGE of the tour is south to the Parador of Albacete. I have suggested a slightly circuitous route, first visiting the town of Villanueva de la Jara, 17km to the south of Motilla del Palancar on the N 320, with a lovely 16th-century church, an arcaded plaza mayor as well as the remains of medieval walls. The CU 804 then leads westwards across a land as flat as an expanse of water and planted with vineyards, wheatfields and olive trees. San Clemente is a most attractive old town with numerous medieval buildings to admire including an arcaded *plaza mayor* and an elegant porticoed *ayuntamiento*.

About 20km to the south-west, after crossing the N 301, is Villarobledo, a town known for its excellent wine and also a centre for Manchegan cheese and saffron. It too has a fine 18th-century *ayuntamiento* and an interesting church of the same period. Upon returning to the N 301, Albacete is some 70km to the east along a road which runs as straight as a plumb-line across the plains. The red soil is patterned by endless rows of green vines and golden wheatfields.

Albacete is a largely modern town at a busy cross-roads, founded in the time of the Moors. It is now the main centre for saffron and is also known for the manufacture of knives and daggers, Puñales and Navajas, which have rather evil-looking spring-loaded blades. The only notable old building which remains is the 16th-century cathedral of San Juan Bautista. There are excellent shops, bars and restaurants however.

The Parador Nacional La Mancha is situated a few kms to the south-east of the town along the N 430. It is set like an island amidst the flat and seemingly endless plain which surrounds it. The low modern building makes full use of space. It is in the form of a vast square with additional wings. In the centre is a garden shaded by trees. There is a spacious bar and café popular with the local people, especially at the weekends. An outdoor swimming pool is nearby in the garden. Long cool corridors link the spacious bedrooms and terracotta tiles and mellow wooden furniture and fittings help to create a pleasingly rustic atmosphere enhanced by the use of antique farming equipment as decor.

The restaurant with its high, sloping beamed ceilings also enjoys local popularity. Regional handicrafts decorate the walls. There are two rooms, one offering à la carte meals and the other a lavish buffet of both hot and cold dishes from which you serve yourself. The local speciality here is Gazpacho Manchego. The name is misleading since it is not served cold and it contains meat: it is a rich and substantial soup made from pieces of rabbit, flavoured with garlic, onions and mushrooms and thickened by the addition of pieces of a special local, unleavened bread, like pitta. It is most unusual, delicious and very filling, calling for a very light main course. I, mistakenly, ordered Paletilla de Cabrito al Romero to follow, kid braised in a rich sauce and flavoured with rosemary. I chose a bottle of Estola, a strong, dry white wine from Villarobledo.

Strangely the most enjoyable excursion to make from the Parador is in mountain countryside, although scarcely a molehill is visible from the building. It is to the Sierra de Alcarez 100km or so to the south-west of Albacete. You can continue beyond the Parador along the small road which leads from the main road. This joins the N 301 where the route leads south for a few kms before branching to the right along a small country road to Pozohondo.

From here a road leads west to Peñas de San Pedro, where there are the remains of a hilltop castle. The route now turns south again along the C 3211 to Ayna. At first the countryside is as flat as only La Mancha can be, but as you travel further south it becomes more undulating with the promise of distant hills and mountains. At Villarejo a small road leads eastwards to the small town of Lietor, on the edge of a steep rocky hillside and overlooking a luscious green valley through which a small river runs. Beyond Lietor the road joins another, the C 3211, which leads north towards Ayna through a rugged, dramatic landscape. Initially it runs high along the side of a deep valley bordered by pine-covered mountainsides and then descends to follow the Río Mundo through a steep narrow canyon.

Ayna is in a spectacular setting high on the mountainside with dizzy views down into the plunging rocky valley. The road continues to climb high above the village with increasingly awesome panoramas. On

The cathedral of Cuenca.

The Castillo of Chinchilla de Monte Aragón.

reaching the summit the road passes through relatively flat countryside, planted with olive and almond trees, towards Bogarra.

Quite suddenly the landscape opens out and a broad deep valley is revealed far below – a startling sight. The reddish soil is planted with thousands of olive and almond trees creating a vivid pattern. The road descends into the valley and follows it to Bogarra, attractively set at its head. The road follows a series of small valleys through gently sloping mountainsides. It is hard to believe that you are only an hour or so away from the unrelieved flatness of the La Mancha plains.

Beyond Paterna de Madera the road joins the C 415 where the route continues north-west to Alcaraz. It is a historic town, originally an Iberian settlement with a wealth of ancient buildings, built from the pinkish brown stone characteristic of the region and dominated by the remains of a Moorish fortress. It retains a strong medieval atmosphere within its narrow-stepped streets and alleyways. There is an attractive arcaded *plaza mayor* overlooked by a fine 16th-century *ayuntamiento* and the beautiful 15th-century church of La Trinidad. Other interesting buildings include two *lonjas*, a 16th-century clock tower, the 16th-century church of San Miguel and the remains of a medieval aqueduct. From Alcaraz the return to Albacete can be made by following the N 322 to the north-east, a distance of about 80km.

JÁVEA

THE NEXT STAGE of the tour is to the Parador at Jávea. The route is eastwards towards the coast following the N 340 towards Almansa. Chinchilla de Monte Aragón is a delightful old town set on an isolated ridge overlooking the plains. A web of steep narrow streets radiate from the *plaza mayor* where there is an 18th century *ayuntamiento* and the 15th-century church of Santa María del Salvador with a beautiful façade and tower. Nearby is the 14th-century monastery of Santo Domingo. A massive castle crowns the top of the hill which can be reached by a rough track. There are superb views from here of the vast La Mancha plain.

Almansa is dominated by a very picturesque castle set on a steep conical outcrop of rock. The town, largely modern in appearance, also possesses a fine Gothic church, Santa María a la Asunción, and a 16th-century convent. Beyond Almansa the route continues along the N 330 to Villena, where there is another impressive castle and the 15th-century Gothic church of Santiago. From here the route turns eastwards along the A 210, through a landscape which becomes progressively more mountainous, to Biar. Its small houses are grouped below a castle mounted precariously on a pine-covered rocky bluff. Just beyond is the hilltop town of Castella, with the remains of a castle.

The road continues to a junction with the N 340 where the route proceeds northwards for a few kms towards Alcoy. Just before reaching the town a small road, the C 3313, leads east into the mountains to Benasau. The mountainsides here are covered in pines and layered by small terraces planted with peach, apricot, almond and olive trees. Beyond Benasau the road climbs steadily along the side of a steep valley with the landscape becoming impressively rugged. A few kms past Confrides a small road leads to the village of Abdet from where there are magnificent views of the mountain landscape.

The road continues to Guadalest, a curious village built on an enormous pinnacle of rock high on the side of a valley. A small church teeters on the very edge of the cliff. The village, little more than a single street and a few houses, is entered through a tunnel in the rock. It is a very popular excursion from places like Benidorm so it is best to plan your visit early or late in the day when the tour coaches have departed.

The road now descends from the mountains through Callosa de Ensarriá and Altea la Vieja to join the N 332 coast road. Here the route is north to Calpe, an attractive scenic drive, following the coast closely along rocky red-brown mountainsides which slope down into a deep blue sea. The hillsides here are heavily developed and peppered with villas and apartment blocks. Calpe is distinguished by a towering pinnacle of rock, the Peñon de Ifach, which juts out into the sea. Below this is the harbour where brightly painted fishing boats lie alongside yachts and motor boats.

A small road follows the coastline from Calpe to the resort of Moraira, from where it crosses the headland to Jávea. The town overlooks a glorious wide sandy bay from a hill about 1km inland. There are the remains of old city walls and many ancient towers dot the mountainsides around it. Narrow streets within the old town indicate its Moorish past and there is a fine Gothic church.

The Parador Nacional Costa Blanca is at the northern extremity of the long curve of sand, one of the finest on

The Sierra de Alcaraz near Ayna.

the Costa Blanca. To the north is the Cabo de San Antonio and to the south the Cabo San Martín and Cabo de la Nao. The Parador is a modern building in the Spanish Mediterranean style with the bedrooms opening on to large sun balconies with sweeping views of the bay. They are thoughtfully provided with canvas sun awnings. The public rooms all face the bay and open on to a wide terrace scattered with comfortable garden furniture. Beyond, a wide lawn and gardens, shaded by tall palm trees, sweep down to the water's edge where a small jetty completes an ideal setting for an after-dinner stroll.

The menu has a good selection of rice dishes, a speciality of the Valencia region, as well as excellent sea food: Arroz Empedrado, rice with salt cod and haricot beans; Paella de Pato, paella made only with rice, vegetables and pieces of duck; Arroz con Costra, rice with mixed meats and chick peas and Dorada a la Sal, sea bream baked in salt, a delicious local method of cooking fish: coarse sea salt is heaped over the whole fish and baked until it forms a hard crust; when broken

The bay of Jávea seen from the Cabo de San Antonio.

open the fish inside is succulent and moist and not at all salty. Among the regional wines on the list Castillo de Murviedra is an excellent red from Valencia.

An interesting excursion can be made along a small road which continues beyond the southern end of the beach to Cabo San Martín and Cabo de la Nao. There are several small rocky coves and wonderful views of the impossibly blue sea from the steep pine-clad cliffs. The road continues to Playa de la Granadella, a small, pretty cove enclosed by steep headlands.

To the north of Jávea a road climbs over the headland to Denia. Almost at the top of this hill a narrow road to the right leads out on to Cabo de San Antonio, from where there are breathtaking views of the bay and mountains beyond. You can watch the toylike fishing boats far below making their way back to the harbour which nestles under the headland. Denia is an attractive resort town with a castle, a busy fishing port and a lively fish market.

EL SALER

THE FINAL STAGE of the tour is to the Parador at El Saler, about 80km further north along the coast. I have suggested an indirect scenic route which leads first into

The Castillo of Almansa.

the mountains north of Guadalest and then along the coastal plain. From Jávea the route follows the N 332 to Benisa, an old town with stepped streets, small squares and a magnificent twin-towered Gothic church known as La Catedral de la Marina, the cathedral of the sea. It is set on a steep hill and surrounded by terraced vineyards with superb views towards the sea.

The route continues to Altea, a pleasantly situated resort dominated by a church with a large dome of blue azuleos. From here a road leads west into the mountains to the picturesque old town of Polop. A web of old streets surrounds a castle and there are some fascinating shops to explore. The route continues north to Callosa de Ensarriá, and then along the C 3318. The road follows a rocky valley filled with oleander bushes and climbs up to the village of Taberna. There are wonderful views from this road across the *huertas*, patterned with rows of orange and lemon trees, to the shimmering blue sea beyond. The road continues around the side of a towering mountain, a landscape of monumental proportions. The road ascends to the Col de Rates from here the views surpass any seen so far on this journey.

The route continues through delightful scenery to Pego and then westwards through the Vall de Gallinera. This too is strikingly beautiful. Steep-sided and narrow the dry river bed on the valley floor traces a pink and purple ribbon of oleander blooms along its course. Beyond is the picturesque village of Planes, surrounded by cherry orchards with a castle set above the old brown tiled houses. There are also the remains of a medieval aqueduct.

A short distance beyond, the road joins the N 340 where the route heads northwards to Albaida. The C 320 leads back to the coast to Gandía. There is a very long golden sand beach here backed by a promenade and dotted with *merenderos* (beach bars), sun shades and games areas. North of Gandía there are small market gardens scattered among the vast orchards of orange and lemon trees which carpet the Valencian plain. Continuing north along the N 332 you can see in the distance the massive rock of Cullera, crowned by a castle, below which the town spreads out beside the mouth of the Río Júcar, whence a road follows the coastline quite closely through a sequence of small beach resorts which become progressively less developed.

Here on the coastal plain the orange and lemon plantations give way to small market gardens often enclosed

The lagoon of La Albufera near El Saler.

behind tall cane fences to protect them from the winter winds. The long sandy beach which runs along this part of the coast is backed by pine forests.

A few kms south of El Saler, the Parador Nacional Luis Vives is hidden among the pines between the long sandy beach of Dehesa and the lagoon of Al Albufera. A long low white building, its large bedroom balconies are framed by elegant arches. From these are lovely views over the pine trees and one of the best golf courses in Spain. A small footpath leads over sand dunes to a massive sandy beach which extends in both directions for many kms. It is one of the few places along this coast where there is no sign of development. The Parador interior is cool, spacious and elegant.

The first-floor restaurant has panoramic views of the dunes and sea beyond and there is an intimate bar and comfortable lounge on the ground floor. Extensive rice fields in the marshy region which surrounds the lagoon are the reason why Valencia is the home of *paella*. Paella Valenciana is the name given to the dish with which most people are familiar, a mixture of saffron-flavoured rice with pieces of chicken, fish and shellfish. The traditional Paella Valenciana, however, is made with snails, green beans and chicken or rabbit

and contains no fish. Another dish related to *paella* is Fideua, made in a similar way, but noodles are used instead or rice. Arroz Negra, black rice, is so called because it is made with squid and their ink sacks give the rice a dark colour. The wine list has a good selection from Valencia.

For those interested in the regional rice dishes it is worth taking a trip to the village of El Palmer, a short distance from the Parador on the edge of the lagoon. This curious village is almost surrounded by the rice fields and there are many excellent restaurants here, each with their own definitive version of *paella*, Arroz Abanda and Fideua as well as with excellent seafood.

The provincial capital of Valencia is only a short drive from the Parador. It is a large modern city with broad avenues, spacious parks, shaded squares and a lively and cosmopolitan atmosphere. However, it also has a well preserved, and quite compact, old quarter, centred around the cathedral. This was started in the 13th century but not completed until the 16th century. As a consequence it reflects three different architectural

The Cathedral of Valencia. Overleaf: The village of Casares.

styles in its three portals, one Romanesque, another Gothic and the third Baroque. Its octagonal Gothic tower is a distinctive landmark. It contains many treasures including paintings by Goya and, legend has it, the chalice used by Christ at the last supper. This gem-studded agate vessel is carried through the streets of Valencia in a solemn procession on Maundy Thursday.

Adjacent to the cathedral, and linked by an archway, is the Baroque church of NS de los Desamparados. There are many other churches and mansions within the city. A particularly beautiful building is the Palacio del Marqués de Dos Aguas, a soaring flight of Baroque fancy with its entire façade intricately decorated with sculptures and an elaborate portal carved from alabaster. It houses Spain's most important museum of ceramics.

For those interested in ceramics the neighbouring town of Manises, near the airport, is the home of Spain's leading school of ceramics. The famous Lladró brothers attended here and the Lladró factory and shop is to be found in a suburb of the city called Tabernas Blanques. Valencia also possesses a fascinating botanical garden – one of the best in Europe.

About half an hour's drive north of Valencia along the Autopista A 7 is Sagunto. Founded by the Iberians, the present town is set below a mountainous ridge of rock, over 2000ft long, which rises up abruptly from the plain. Surmounting the ridge are the remains of a Roman city. Massive castle walls encircle the mountain top with numerous gates, towers and squares. From the highest part, the Plaza Ciudadela, there are superb views looking down over the walls to the plain below and the sea beyond. Set just below the castle walls are the extensive remains of a theatre founded by the Greeks and later enlarged and improved by the Romans. The old town, on the slopes below the castle, is also interesting and atmospheric. There are two churches, 14th-century Santa María and 13th-century San Salvador.

To return to the Parador, follow the Autopista A 7 back to Valencia where you take the southern part of the city's ring road to join a brief section of the Autopista south to El Saler. The nearest alternative Parador to El Saler is at Benicarló, 150km north (page 152).

PART FOUR

Southern Spain

SEVILLA

CADIZ

GIBRALTAR

16

17

19 18 · MURCIA

· GRANADA

OUR 16 Explores the provinces of Málaga, Córdoba and Sevilla in the central region of Andalucía. Bordered in the north by the Sierra Morena, the natural barrier which almost isolates this part of Spain from the rest of the country, the southern limit is the Costa del Sol. The eastern extremity is the maritime city of Málaga and to the west is the delta of the great Andalusian river, the Guadalquivir. Andalucía is the region of Spain whose characteristics most colour the visitor's expectation of the country. It is a land of white hilltop villages threaded by narrow Moorish streets, mountains covered by silvery-green olive trees, shimmering heat and the deep-blue Mediterranean sea.

The itinerary begins in the city of Málaga, heads north through the mountains to Antequera and Córdoba and then follows the course of the Río Guadalquivir to the historic hilltop town of Carmona.

—TOUR 16—
MICHELIN MAP NO. 446

CÓRDOBA
Carmona
SEVILLA
Antequera
MÁLAGA

MÁLAGA
ANTEQUERA
CÓRDOBA
CARMONA

MÁLAGA

MÁLAGA IS A BUSY CITY and seaport with the unmistakable atmosphere of the Mediterranean. Founded in Phoenician times it gained its importance after its capture by the Moors in the 8th century. Its most notable building is the cathedral begun in the early 16th century. It has a most imposing façade with three portals flanked by two large towers. Among the many fine features in the interior are superb carved 17th-century choir stalls and a gilded statue of the Virgin which was carried during the wars against the Moors. The church of NS de la Victoria occupies the site upon which Ferdinand and Isabella were encamped during the seige of Málaga.

Set up on a hill above the cathedral is the Alcazaba, the Moorish fortress, surrounded by beautiful terraced gardens which cascade with flowers. It now contains an archaeological museum. Nearby are the remains of a Roman theatre. Other buildings of interest include the 15th-century church of Santiago el Mayor, the 17th-century church of Santo Cristo, and the 18th-century Episcopal Palace with a magnificent Baroque façade.

On the eastern edge of the town, on a high wooded hill overlooking the port, is the Castillo de Gibralfaro, so-called because it had a beacon in one of its towers to guide ships. During the seige of Málaga, at the time of the reconquest, it took the Spanish forces 40 days to overcome the stronghold.

The Parador Nacional de Gibralfaro, adjacent to the castle and surrounded by pine and eucalyptus trees, occupies the site of an old hostelry, parts of which have been retained in the modern building. It has been constructed in traditional style of large blocks of stone and tall elegant arches. The bedrooms are particularly large

and have furnished balconies from where there are superb views of the city and the sea. The Parador has a delightfully peaceful, cool and slightly remote atmosphere in spite of its proximity to the city. It is a popular place for a drink or a meal with the Malagueños.

The restaurant offers an aperitif to diners called Trajinero, which is a sweetish Oloroso-type wine made from grapes grown on the hillsides around the city. I chose Ajo Blanco Malagueño to start my meal. It is a delicious and unusual chilled soup – an interesting alternative to the more familiar gazpacho. It is made by combining ground almonds, breadcrumbs, garlic, wine vinegar, olive oil and water, garnished with small green grapes. Of the bewildering choice of seafood in this region *chipirones* and *chanquetes* are frequently seen on local menus. The former are tiny squid fried quickly with garlic until golden. The latter are minute anchovies often prepared in a similar way but also sometimes combined into an omelette.

ANTEQUERA

THE NEXT STAGE OF THE ITINERARY is north to the Parador at Antequera, a distance of only 50km and I have suggested an indirect route which leads through the valley of the Río Guadalhorce and then through the Sierra de Alcaparrín to the Embalse del Guadalteba-Guadalhorce. From the centre of Málaga you should follow the signs to Campanillas. This road, the MA 402, leads across the fertile plain of the Río Guadalhorce to Cártama, where there is a ruined Moorish castle.

This part of the journey is through vast plantations of orange and lemon trees. Beyond Pizarra the road continues through a progressively narrowing valley called the Valle de Sol, the valley of the sun. Álora is strikingly situated, the small white houses of the town are grouped together in the saddle of a ridge above which is a castle. Behind is an imposing backdrop of rugged mountains. The narrow streets and alleys of the town climb the hill upon which it is built at a dizzy angle.

The road begins to climb into the mountains beyond Alora and leads alongside a steep valley terraced with olive groves. The scene is dominated by a vast ridge of rock. This is the Garganta del Chorro. The Río Guadalhorce forces its way through a deep narrow crevasse and beside it a railway tunnel is bored like a massive mousehole into the rock face. Beyond, the road leads through a narrow gorge with steep cliffs to Bobastro. A few kms past this village, a small road leads to the

Antequera.

remains of a 9th-century Mozarabic sanctuary on rocky slopes covered by pine trees and clouds of yellow broom.

The little town of Ardales, overlooking the Embalse de Guadalhorce, is set in the midst of soft rounded hills dappled with beige, brown and green. The road continues, with constantly pleasing views of hillsides chequered by wheatfields, to Teba. This too is an attractive old town set on a spur of rock with a castle and the remains of battlements. The route continues, skirting the embalse, to Campillos, and then along the N 342 to the east. A few kms to the north of this road is the Laguna de la Fuente de Piedra, a limpid blue salt water lagoon, rich in bird life and surrounded by low olive-covered hills. 30km beyond Campillos along the N 342 a junction with the N 334 leads south to Antequera.

The town is attractively situated on the slopes of the Sierra de Chimenea and looks out over the plain of the Río Genil. Above the rooftops of the houses a Moorish castle commands superb views of the countryside. In the old part of the town is the church of El Carmen with a beautiful Baroque altarpiece and a Mudéjar ceiling. There is also the 16th-century hall church of Santa María la Mayor, and the 16th-century church of San Sebastián. Near the town there are three dolmen, of which the most impressive is the Cueva de Menga with a massive block of stone weighing nearly 200 tons forming its roof.

The Parador Nacional de Antequera, on the western edge of the town a few minutes' walk from its centre is a modern building set in a quiet location with lovely views over the plain. There is an attractive garden with a large pool shaded by palm trees. The rooms are spacious and airy with high, sloping ceilings.

The menu included Remon Antequerano, a local dish which is an unusual salad of salt cod, with orange, onion and garlic. I had Porra Antequerana to start my meal, a creamy gazpacho-like purée with ham, egg, tuna fish and tomato. From the good selection of seafood I chose Rape en Pimentón, monk fish cooked with paprika. A delicious sweet is Bienmesabe Antequerano, a tart filled with a mixture of honey and ground almonds.

A fascinating morning's excursion can be made from the Parador to El Torcal, a series of extraordinary

El Torcal.

ridged and striated silver-grey rocks to be found in the mountains 13km to the south of the town. They have been sculpted into strange abstract shapes, creating a quite bizarre landscape. Numerous small footpaths lead off into this curious region. It is reached along a road which climbs through a steep-sided green valley from where there are fine views of the old town.

A longer round trip can also be made from the Parador which explores the countryside and villages to the east of Antequera. The first place of interest is Archidona, reached by taking the N 342 to the east of Antequera. The road crosses a flat, fertile plain, patterned with olive groves and wheatfields and dotted with *cortijos* (farms). Archidona is set on a steep craggy mountain with a forest of small white houses clinging to its slopes. It has a charming old quarter with a pronounced Andalucían character. Here there is a very pretty, and most unusual, octagonal *plaza mayor*. There are also the remains of town walls and a sanctuary within the Moorish castle above the town.

A quiet road, the MA 214 leads north-east to Villanueva de Tapia through a virtual sea of olive trees, in peaceful countryside populated only by small isolated farms. Beyond is the picturesque town of Iznájar built on a mountainous rock overlooking the Embalse de Iznájar and threaded by steep narrow streets which rise precipitously to the small church at its summit. The road continues northwards along a very attractive scenic route, skirting the embalse to the old town of Rute, then leading north-east towards Priego de Cordoba, passing the strikingly situated village of Carcabuey, with a castle crowning the rocky crag upon which it is built. Priego de Córdoba is a very appealing old town with numerous Baroque churches as well as a castle and a *lonja*. The streets are lined with old houses which are festooned with flowers and decorated with ornamental grilles. There is also a beautiful 18th-century fountain, the Fuente del Rey, and from the town walls there is a wonderful view over the surrounding countryside.

From here the route back to the Parador can be made by returning along the C 336, past Carcabuey, to Cabra with the ruined castle of San Juan, formerly a mosque, and the 16th-century church of Santo Domingo. The C 327 then leads south to Lucena, a large lively town with the 15th-century church of San Mateo and a

ruined castle. At a junction, the road meets the N 331 which leads south to Antequera.

Landscape near Antequera.

CÓRDOBA

THE NEXT STAGE of the tour is north to the Parador at Córdoba. From Antequera the route is along the N 334 across a flat, undulating landscape covered by wheat-fields to Estepa, on a steep hill overlooking the plain and whose streets rise steeply towards the castle. The entire town seems to be built on a one-in-four hill with a tangle of narrow cobbled steps and alleys threading between the blindingly white houses. From the top, by the castle, there are staggering views over rooftops to the countryside beyond. Here too is the Convent of Santa Clara with a fine Renaissance portal, the Baroque churches of the Virgin de los Remedios and El Carmen and the Palacio de los Marqueses de Ceverales with an impressive Baroque façade. The town is also famous for its Pulvorones; sweet almond biscuits.

At Estepa the C 338 leads north-east to Puente Genil beside the Río Genil and then east towards Lucena. After 18km the CO 761 heads north to Moriles, a wine town amidst extensive vineyards. This is an important wine-growing region. Those produced with the Montilla/Moriles label are as highly regarded as the more well-known wines of Jerez further to the west. The CO 760 now leads to Aguilar, an attractive hilltop town surrounded by olive groves and vineyards with a broad octagonal plaza and a ruined Moorish castle. Of its several old churches the extravagantly decorated Baroque chapel of the Convento de Carmelitas Des-calzas is of special interest. Here, at the junction with the main road, the N 331, the route continues north to Montilla and then through rolling vineclad hillsides to Córdoba.

Córdoba is a mellow city on the banks of the broad Río Guadalquivir with a backdrop of the wooded Sierra de Córdoba. The Moorish capital during their occupa-tion of Spain, it retains a fine bridge and numerous buildings from this period along with a labyrinth of narrow shady streets.

Le Mezquita, the mosque, is one of the largest and most magnificent of those built by the Moors though-out their Empire and one of the finest buildings from

this period remaining in Spain. Started in the latter part of the 8th century, on its completion at the end of the 10th century, it was over 600ft long and 400ft wide with 19 aisles. It is surrounded by massive, buttressed walls and faces a square shaded by orange trees. After the capture of Córdoba in 1236 it became a Christian church and then a cathedral. The present building is a fascinating mixture of different architectural styles, resulting from 9 centuries of continual building. The interior has a quite mystical atmosphere with subdued daylight filtering through a forest of elegant columns and horseshoe arches.

You will need a guide book if you are to see all the city has to offer, but much pleasure can be derived from just strolling along its narrow, flower-laden streets and discovering it for yourself. It is particularly enchanting after dark when the mellow glow of street lanterns creates pools of yellow light and dark mysterious shadows.

Among its squares the charming Plaza del Potro (which contains an inn mentioned by Cervantes in *Don Quixote*), the Plazuela de los Dolores and the Plaza de la Corredera are particularly appealing. The latter was once used as a bullring and is now the setting for a lively and colourful street market. The Roman bridge is also lovely and one of the finest views of the city can be had by walking over it to the opposite bank.

The Parador Nacional La Arruzafa, in a quiet setting 3km to the north of the city centre on the slopes of the Sierra de Córdoba, occupies the site of the old Manor of Abderramán I who had the first palm trees in Europe planted in his garden. *Arrazufa* is Arabic for a garden of palm trees. From its hillside setting the modern Parador building commands extensive views of the city and the valley of the Guadalquivir. All the spacious bedrooms have large, furnished balconies with a beautiful outlook. A large sun terrace extends the full length of the hotel. Below this are attractive gardens with paths and steps leading to a large swimming pool surrounded by lawns. Beyond are tennis courts.

The restaurant offers a choice of à la carte meals or a grand buffet with a large selection of hot and cold dishes from which you serve yourself. Among the regional dishes on the menu during my stay was Salmorejo Cordobés, a chilled soup based on lean meat, garlic and olive oil; and Cazuela de Rabo a la Cordobesa, bull's tail braised in a wine-rich sauce with vegetables. Cazuela de Mollejas con Champiñón Jamón are sweetbreads cooked with mushrooms and ham.

From the Parador an enjoyable excursion can be made to the Medina Azahara, and into the wooded Sierra de Córdoba, by taking the C 431 to the west of the city. After 8km a road to the right leads to the Medina Azahar. Here on a hillside are the remains of the once beautiful palace and town of Caliph Abderramán III. Its construction, in the 10th century, was an epic venture employing many thousands of men, mules and camels for over 25 years. The complex included a mosque, baths, stables, gardens, lakes and accommodation for its large population. It was laid to waste in 1010 by Berber mercenaries and little remained. In 1944, however, the remains of the Royal apartments were discovered and these have now been extensively reconstructed and are the most impressive relic of the site. Nearby, high on the wooded slopes, is the 15th-century Monastery of San Jerónimo, built from the ruins of a Moorish castle and containing a particularly lovely Gothic cloister.

A small country road continues through beautiful woods high up into the mountains. There are extensive views over the Guadalquivir valley and the mountains beyond. You can see for miles and miles. It continues along the edge of the Sierra to Las Ermitas from where you can look down on to the city far below. It is a wonderful place to take a picnic lunch among the pine trees. At Santa María de Trassierra, a few kms to the west, a small chapel within the ruins of a castle was originally a mosque.

CARMONA

THE FINAL STAGE of this itinerary is westwards along the valley of the Guadalquivir to the Parador at Carmona. Leaving Córdoba along the C 431 leads to Almodóvar del Río, an attractive old hilltop town overlooking the river. At its summit is a most impressive castle with battlements and towers, around which steep narrow streets spread in a tangle. The road follows the river through fields of vegetables and orchards to Palma del Río. This too is an atmospheric old town with a castle and several interesting churches.

At Palma del Río a road to the south, the C 430, runs alongside the Río Genil to Ecija. This beautiful riverside town with shady squares, parks and fine old buildings is known as Ciudad de las Torres, the city of towers, and as you approach it across the plain at least a dozen lovely towers can be seen soaring above the rooftops. Many are decorated with colourful *azulejos*. It is also known, less attractively, as La Sartenilla de Andalucía (the frying pan of Andalucía) because of its searing summer heat.

There is a Moorish castle and a beautiful *plaza mayor* surrounded by arcaded houses and a fine *ayuntamiento*. Among its many churches the 16th-century Santiago el Mayor and the 18th-century Santa Cruz are of particular interest. The Palacio de los Marqueses de Peñaflor has a magnificent Baroque façade. There are also many

Córdoba seen from the Roman Bridge.

fine mansions to be seen along the Calle de los Caballeros. Many of the houses have beautiful patios.

The town of Osuna is about 30km to the south of Ecija along the C 430. This too is an atmospheric old town with numerous medieval mansions along its streets. The Calle Carrera and Calle San Pedro contain the best examples. At the highest point of the town is a 16th-century university and an imposing 16th-century Colegiata.

From Osuna the route continues westwards along the N 334 through quite flat countryside to La Puebla de Cazalla. Here the SE 701 leads north-west to Marchena, a rather faded and crumbling old town with considerable charm and character. Some 25km to the south is Morón de la Frontera, an ancient town with the remains of a huge Moorish fortress dominating the landscape from its hilltop setting.

From Marchena the C 339 leads to the north-west across an undulating plain to Carmona. Set high on a steep hill, it is visible from a great distance. Battlemented walls surround the town which is entered through imposing fortified gateways, the Puerta de Córdoba and the Puerta de Sevilla. Within stand three Moorish fortresses, the Alcazar de la Puerta de Córdoba, the Alcazar Puerta de Sevilla and the Alcazar de Puerta Marchena. One of the most prominent features of the town is the tower of the 17th-century church of San Pedro, a copy of the famous Giralda tower in Seville. The 15th-century Gothic church of Santa María la Mayor has a patio with horseshoe arches, a fine Plateresque retablo and 18th-century carved choir stalls. There is a lovely square, the Plaza de San Fernando, surrounded by Mudéjar houses and overlooked by an 18th-century *ayuntamiento*. Of the many other interesting buildings the churches of San Bartolomé, San Salvador and the Convent of La Concepción are outstanding.

On the western side of the town is a Roman necropolis. There are over 1,000 graves and several hundred burial chambers which have been excavated. They date from between the 2nd and 4th centuries and represent one of the most important archaeological sites in Spain.

The Parador Nacional Alcázar del Rey Don Pedro, within the remains of one of the Moorish fortresses, the Alcazar de Arriba is on the western edge of the town with fine views overlooking the fertile plain. It was used as a residence by King Don Pedro who converted it into a lavish palace. It was also used by the Catholic Kings during their final battles with the Moors in Granada. The castle was abandoned after an earthquake in 1504. It is only a few minutes' walk away from the centre of the town through a maze of narrow cobbled streets lined with white-washed houses.

An old house in Marchena.

The Puerto de Córdoba in Carmona.

The Parador is a modern construction in traditional style and contained within massive walls several metres thick. Long castle-like corridors link the rooms and there is a lovely terrace ranged along the sheer side of the hill with splendid views. There is a beautiful patio decorated with blue tiles and elegant arches surrounding a fountain. Below the Parador, on the hillside, is a magnificent blue-tiled swimming pool. The building is a most successful combination of medieval ambience and modern comfort.

The restaurant is situated in a vast room with a high-vaulted ceiling supported by stone arches and wooden beams. I chose a typical dish of the region to start my meal, Espinacas Estilo Carmona, a highly seasoned purée of spinach cooked with chick peas. To follow I had Lomo de Merluza a la Sevillana, pieces of hake cooked in a rich sauce of ground almonds, olive oil, lemon juice and garlic.

The city of Seville is less than 40km away along the N IV and the Parador makes a good base from which to visit the city for a day. For those who wish to avoid the traffic and parking problems of a busy city there is a good bus service from near Plaza San Fernando into the centre of Seville.

The Parador also makes a good base from which to make an excursion into the Sierra de Morena. From Carmona the route leads north-east along the C 432 to Lora del Río, where there is a ruined castle and an *ayuntamiento* with a Baroque façade. A quiet country road continues northwards to the attractively sited town of Constantina. It winds through hilly, open heathland which is dotted with oak and pine trees and carpeted with gorse, broom, wild flowers and herbs. In Constantina is the 18th-century church of Las Navas de la Concepción which contains a fine Baroque retablo. Beyond, towards Alanís, where there is a 14th-century church and the ruins of a castle, the landscape becomes more hilly and quite densely wooded.

From Alanís the route continues to the south, along the C 421, through a wild and remote landscape to Cazalla de la Sierra. The town church of Santa María de la Consolación is built in a blend of Mudéjar and Gothic styles. Just beyond, a small road leads westwards across an even more lonely and beautiful landscape to El Real de la Jarra. Here wild asparagus grows by the roadside and the hillsides are covered in clouds of yellow broom and a sea of rockrose. A few kms further on, the road crosses the very pretty valley of the Río Calla, the scene of a Romería at the end of April. There is also an idyllic spot for a picnic lunch on the banks of the small river. Beyond is the attractive old town of Olalla del Cala where narrow streets and ancient houses surround a hilltop castle and a 15th-century church.

From here a small road continues westwards to the enchanting village of Zufre, one of the prettiest white villages in Andalucía. It is ranged along the edge of a sheer cliff and its narrow cobbled streets and alleys are lined with immaculately white houses which literally cascade with floral colour. It is completely untouched by tourism and I felt that this was how the narrow streets of Córdoba and Sevilla must have looked centuries ago. There is a 16th-century Mudéjar church and *ayuntamiento*.

Beyond Zufre the road joins the N 433 where the route continues north-west to Aracena, an attractively-sited town crowned by a Moorish castle and an imposing 13th-century church. Nearby is the Gruta de las Maravillas, one of the largest stalactite caverns in Spain.

From here a road climbs into the highest parts of the Sierra Morena. It is surprisingly green and wooded; massive chestnut, walnut and oak trees cover the mountainsides and below them velvety brown pigs forage contentedly. This is the country of jamon serrano, mountain ham, and region where many would claim the best Spanish ham is produced. Jabugo is the village which gives its names to these hams, the huge curing factory almost dwarfs the small community. The route continues south from Jabugo and after a few kms a small road leads east back towards Aracena. There are superb views to the south along this road from a viewpoint called La Peña de Arias Montano, just above the pretty village of Alajar. Upon returning to Aracena the route back to the Parador is south along the N 630 to Seville and then the N 4 east to Carmona.

From Carmona you can continue to the Parador at Ayamonte, 165 km (page 188), to join Tour No 17) and complete a round trip back to Málaga. The nearest alternative Parador is at Zafra, 140km distant (page 128).

La Mezquita in Córdoba.

OUR 17 Centred in the western region of Andalucía in the provinces of Sevilla, Huelva, Cádiz and Málaga, it explores the coastal regions of the Costa del Sol and the Costa de la Luz as well as the Guadalquivir Delta and the mountain ranges of the Sierra de Ronda and the Sierra de Bermeja. The landscape is immensely varied since it ranges from the marshy lowlands of the Coto Doñana and the vine-covered sandy hills of Jerez to the vast beaches of Spain's Atlantic coast and almost alpine-like valleys hidden among the country's southernmost mountains. The itinerary also provides an interesting and scenic route from the Portuguese border to Málaga and, combined with Tour No 16 (page 176), can create a round trip. The Paradors which link the tour include one in an evocative hilltop village, another overlooking the finest and quietest, beach in southern Spain and a third in the atmospheric maritime city of Cádiz.

AYAMONTE – MAZAGÓN CÁDIZ – ARCOS DE LA FRONTERA TORREMOLINOS

AYAMONTE

AYAMONTE IS THE STARTING POINT of this route, although of course it can be followed in reverse, starting from Torremolinos. The nearest airport is at Sevilla, 150km. The closest alternative Parador is at Carmona, 165km (page 186). Ayamonte is the border town lying beside the broad estuary of the Río Guadiana which separates Spain and Portugal. On the opposite bank is the Portuguese town of Villa Real de Santo Antonio which is linked by car and passenger ferries. The town contains a number of interesting buildings. The church of NS de las Angustias dates from the 16th century. The convent church of San Francisco, with a superb panelled ceiling and Mudéjar tower, is also from this period and so too is the convent of Santa Clara. There is also a 15th-century palace in the plaza mayor with an attractive façade.

The more modern parts of the town are centred around the mouth of the river but the old town extends in a series of narrow streets to the summit of a hill. This was the site of the ancient castle and is now that of the Parador Nacional Costa de la Luz. It commands magnificent views over the river estuary, the sea and the Portuguese countryside beyond. The sunsets seen from the Parador are simply spectacular. It is a single-storey building, in a hilltop setting. There is a swimming pool and terrace adjoining the restaurant, all enjoying the same sweeping views. The interior is cool and welcoming with green foliage cascading down the walls of the tiled corridors and rooms.

The restaurant has an excellent selection of seafood on the menu. I chose Pez Espada Parador, a swordfish steak cooked with a delicious orange sauce. Arroz a la Ayamontina is a seafood *paella* and La Raya en Pimentón is ray cooked with paprika.

MAZAGÓN

THE NEXT PARADOR at Mazagón is only 85km away on the other side of the estuary of the Río Odiel beyond Huelva. Since it is set beside a superb beach it is a more attractive base for those wishing to spend some time by the sea which is the main attraction in this part of Spain. The landscape here is very flat and the coastal plain is heavily cultivated with vast fields of strawberries and citrus fruits. The stretch of coast between the estuaries of the Guadiana and the Odiel provides some excellent beaches. The most attractive region is between the village of El Rompido and the resort of Punta Umbría. This is reached by taking the N 431 to the east of Ayamonte to Lepe and Cartaya. A short distance further a small road leads south to El Rompido, an attractive small fishing community sheltered by a long bar of sand.

The road follows the coastline closely, and the long quiet beach is backed by sand dunes and pine trees. Access to the sea is possible in many places. Towards the large and heavily developed resort of Punta Umbría the beach becomes a vast and smooth expanse of fine golden sand.

The Odiel estuary is crossed at Huelva, a busy port at the junction of the Río Odiel and Río Tinto. Although a town of ancient origins few buildings survived an earthquake in 1755. Of these the most interesting are the 16th-century cathedral and the 16th-century church of San Pedro.

Beyond Huelva and its industrial suburbs, the C 422 leads south-east along the Paseo de los Piñones to La Punta del Sebo and then crosses the mouth of the Río Tinto. Here on a promontory is a monolithic monument to Christopher Columbus, a gift to the town from the United States of America, perhaps to thank them for discovering it. It was from the small town of Palos de la Frontera, a few kms up-river, from which Columbus sailed with his small fleet of three ships on 3 August 1492, returning on 15 March 1493. The water has now retreated far from the town and there is no longer a harbour. Nearby is the 15th-century Monasterio de la Rábida from where Columbus made the preparations for his voyage. It contains a small museum of relics associated with the expedition.

A few kms north of Palos is Moguer, a neat, orderly town with shady squares and blindingly white houses lining its streets. It has a splendid *ayuntamiento* decorated with arches and columns. There are two interest-

The coastline near El Rompido.

ing churches, NS de la Granada and the convent of La Esperanza with a fine Baroque retablo. On the northern edge of the town is the 14th century Mudéjar convent of Santa Clara.

Returning to the main road, the C 442, the route follows the coast eastwards to the resort of Mazagón through a forest of umbrella pines. The Parador Nacional Cristóbal Colón, hidden among the pine trees 6kms to the east of Mazagón is a low white building spread out in an L-shape over a broad expanse of lawn and garden shaded by pine and palm trees. The gardens reach down to the edge of a cliff below which a vast beach of firm yellow sand stretches away in both directions for several kms. Close to the cliff edge is a swimming pool. The bedrooms are large and airy and open on to spacious verandahs which over-look the garden. The Parador has a remote and peaceful atmosphere with only the rumble of the Atlantic surf breaking on the beach below to disturb the silence.

The restaurant is an attractive L-shaped room on the first floor with a pretty, tiled floor and a wooden-beamed ceiling. It opens on to a balcony overlooking the garden. Seafood is understandably a strong feature

on the menu. I had Sopa de Rape to start my meal, a delicately flavoured fish soup with monk fish, calamares, prawns, rice and tomato. Rape a la Andaluza is pieces of monk fish sautéed with paprika. I chose Solomillo a la Sevillana for my main course; fillet steak cooked with olives. An excellent local white wine is Viña Odiel from the Huelva vineyards.

The road continues close to the sea beyond the Parador to Matalascañas, a huge unattractive resort. For most of this distance the sea is hidden beyond pines and access to the beach is limited. Just before reaching Matalascañas a road to the north leads along the western edge of the Coto de Doñana to the village of El Rocío. This countryside is one of the most important nature reserves in Europe. Known as Las Marismas (the marshes) it is a flat, sandy terrain dotted with lakes, pools and waterways fringed by reeds. It is especially important to ornithologists since it is a resting place for birds making their migratory flights between Africa and Northern Europe. In addition, animals such as red and fallow deer, lynx, wild cat and wild boar are also found. It is possible to make trips into the national park by applying to the Park centre on the road between Las Matalascañas and El Rocío.

El Rocío is a small, curious town on the edge of the marshes. Little more than a collection of shanty-like

buildings lining dirt roads, it is dominated by the enormous white church of NS del Rocío, Our Lady of the Dew. It is the scene of one of the largest and most famous *romerías* (pilgrimages) in Spain which is held at Pentecost. People from all around, Sevilla, Huelva and Cádiz, make their way to the village on horseback, in decorated wagons and by the busload to commemorate a statue found here to which mysterious and miraculous powers are attributed.

The route continues north of El Rocío through the wine-growing towns of Almonte and Bollullos par del Condado to Palma del Condado where there is a 16th-century Plateresque church and an attractive *ayuntamiento*. Here the route joins the main road, the N 341. Before continuing eastwards it is worth making a brief detour to the west to Niebla, a Roman town and later the capital of a small kingdom. It is encircled by massive walls, punctuated by over 40 towers. Four of the original gateways have survived. The church of Santa María de la Gran dates from the 10th century and there are also the ruins of a 15th-century church.

From Palma del Condado the route follows the N 431 eastwards to Sevilla and then the N 4 south to Dos Hermanos, where you can join the Autopista A 4 and

century retablo. Among the other churches worth seeing is the monastery of Santo Domingo with a fine Gothic cloister. The town's medieval mansions include the Palacios of Duc de Monnpensier and the Duque de Medina de Sidonia.

The small port of Bonanza, a few kms to the north of the town has numerous small bars where you can drink Manzanilla and there are some good simple fish restaurants with plenty of local atmosphere. From Sanlúcar the road follows the coastline south to the pretty flower-decked town of Chipiona whose church of NS de la Regla has a 17th-century Gothic cloister.

Rota is a lively, rather chaotic American base, and further on, El Puerto de Santa María, an appealing old town with a busy port engaged mainly in wine exporting, has numerous *bodegas*, those of Osborne and Terry being particularly impressive. The 14th-century Moorish castle of San Marcos lies in the centre of the town and nearby is the 13th-century church of NS de los Milagros with an impressive Gothic façade and a beautiful Plateresque portal. There are many other churches and mansions to see and the town is well worth exploring.

CÁDIZ

THE ROUTE CONTINUES past the busy commercial port of Puerto Rea to Cádiz, a city built on a slender 9km long promontory whcih juts out into the Bay of Cádiz. The old part of the city is built on a rock at the very tip and is almost surrounded by water.

The Hotel Atlántico is the Parador of Cádiz and overlooks the sea. The gardens and pool in front of the hotel extend to a promenade which runs along the water's edge. It is a large modern building in the established style of Mediterranean hotels. The bedrooms are angled and staggered, giving the large balconies good views of the sea. The interior is spacious and luxurious with polished marble floors and elegant columns. The hotel is famous for its spectacular sunsets. Whenever travellers swop tales the question of the best place for a sunset is often mooted. Those seen from the hotel terrace are equal to the splendid displays on Kuta beach in Bali and on the Serengeti plain.

The restaurant shares this fine outlook. The menu is understandably centred on the superb seafood of the region. I chose Fritura Gaditana which was quite simply the best dish of mixed fried fish I have ever tasted. It contained tiny sole no more than 5in long, hake the size of a fish finger, miniscule anchovies, squid that would fit into a teaspoon and red mullet no longer than a small sardine. Urtas Asadas al Vinagre de Jerez is a type of sea bream, filleted, grilled and served with a light sauce flavoured with sherry vinegar. The wine list

continue to Exit 3. Here a road leads south-west to Lebrija, an attractive old town whose church of Santa María, once a mosque, has a tower reminiscent of the famous Giralda tower in Sevilla.

The road continues through low chalky hills ridged by the vines from which the wines of Jerez are made. Sanlúcar de Barrameda beside the estuary of the Río Guadalquivir where it flows into the Atlantic ocean, known for its Manzanilla wines, like the *fino* sherries but with a distinctive flavour attributed to the nearness of the sea. The church of NS de la O has a fine Mudéjar portal with *artesonado* (moulded) ceilings and an 18th-

The beach at Cádiz.

Vineyards near Jerez de la Frontera.

includes Castillo de San Diego, a crisp, fruity white wine made from the vines grown on the Albarizo soil around Jerez.

The city of Cádiz possesses many fine buildings. The New Cathedral, not completed until the early 19th century overlooks the sea and has a magnificent dome nearly 200ft high. The original 13th-century cathedral, the church of the Sagrario was reconstructed at the beginning of the 17th century in the Renaissance style. The 19th-century *ayuntamiento* is a massive building with an imposing and elaborately decorated façade. The 18th-century Baroque church of NS del Carmen contains a retablo by El Greco and a fine patio.

The old part of town is a warren of narrow tunnel-like streets and alleys. To stroll through these at night evokes a strong sense of the past. The cobbles glisten as if wet, lit only by small pools of yellow lamplight cast by hundreds of lanterns. As well as its historic buildings and busy city life, Cádiz also has superb sandy beaches which extend along the southern edge of the promontory for many kms.

An interesting circuit can be made from Cádiz along the coast towards Gibraltar and then inland through the Sierra de los Melones. The route is initially southwest along the N 4 which runs alongside the magni-

ficent sandy beaches of Victoria and Cortadura to San Fernando. Here there is a Roman bridge and an 18th-century *ayuntamiento*. At Chiclana de la Frontera, where there is a large 18th-century church, a road leads eastwards to the coast to Sancti Petri. The remains of a 13th-century castle can be seen on a small offshore island. From Chiclana the N 340 continues south to Conil de la Frontera, an old fishing town with a 16th-century church and the remains of a Moorish fortress.

Beyond is the white hilltop town of Vejer de la Frontera which has retained a strong Moorish atmosphere. It has a tangle of steep narrow streets lined by white-washed houses, a castle and an interesting Gothic church. From here a small road leads out to the Cabo de Trafalgar. Little more than a spit of sand marked by a lighthouse, it is the place where Nelson defeated the combined French and Spanish fleets. The road continues alongside a series of good sandy beaches to Barbate de Franco, a busy fishing port.

The route continues through peaceful countryside close to the sea to Zahara de los Atunes, a small fishing

village set on a large sandy beach on the edge of a small creek. Although unexceptional it has an agreeably relaxed and unhurried atmosphere. There are a number of excellent seafood restaurants with a tempting array of locally caught fish and shellfish. From here a road leads back to the N 340 whence the route continues south-east towards Tarifa. After 15kms a road to the right leads to the ruined Roman town of Bolonia.

Tarifa is a town of considerable atmosphere and character. It is entered through a fortified gateway and inside is a fascinating web of narrow streets and alleys. The town is set at the narrowest point of the Straits of Gibraltar and has a 10th-century Arab fortress built to defend its vital position. Superb views of the Straits can be seen from the ramparts. There is also the medieval Torre de Guzmán and a 16th-century Gothic church with a fine Baroque façade.

The landscape changes now from the flat coastal plain surrounding Cádiz and becomes progressively more interesting as the road continues towards Algeciras. It climbs around steeply indented mountainsides to the Puerto de Cabrito from where there are sweeping views to the sea. Beyond, at the Puerto del Bujeo, there are impressive views of the rock of Gibraltar rising up from the sea like a massive iceberg.

The route continues beyond Algeciras, an unattractive modern town, towards San Roque. A few kms before reaching the town the C 331 leads north to Almoraima, where there is a 17th-century convent in a peaceful wooded setting. Here a road leads to the left, winding up a steep and dramatic hill to Castellar de la Frontera. On its rocky crest is a castle and below a small Moorish village of ancient whitewashed houses. There are fine views over the craggy wooded hillsides and of the Embalse de Guadarranque from the village.

Beyond Almoraima the road begins to climb into the mountains to Jimena de la Frontera, an attractive hilltop village crowned by a ruined castle from where there are sweeping views over the surrounding landscape. The road continues high along the side of the precipitous valley of the Río Hozgarganta. It is a remote and wild region with only an occasional isolated farmhouse to be seen between the villages. Deep woods with gorse, rosemary and broom cover the hillsides. The road climbs to the Puerto de Galiz. Here the CA 511 descends into a green and pleasant valley to Alcalá de los Gazules. The village is set on a knoll on the side of the valley, its cluster of small white houses stacked like boxes on its slopes.

The road continues westwards for 24km to Medina-Sidonia, a picturesque old town set high on a hill. It was founded by the Phoenicians and has been home to Greeks, Romans, Visigoths and the Moors. It possesses a Gothic church with a particularly fine 16th-century Plateresque retablo. There is a gateway decorated with horseshoe arches, an interesting *ayuntamiento* and the remains of the Arab fortress. From here the return to Cádiz is made by following the C 346 back to Chiclana de la Frontera.

ARCOS DE LA FRONTERA

THE NEXT STAGE of the tour is north-west to the Parador at Arcos de la Frontera. The first part of the route is along the N 4 to Jerez de la Frontera. The town is of course famous for its wines which are grown on the white chalky hillsides known as *albarizas*. It is possible to visit a *bodega*, of which there are many, and have the process of sherry-making explained. The cellars of González Byass are to be found right in the centre of the town next to the remains of the 11th century Moorish Alcázar but there are many others to choose from. The town also contains some interesting buildings. There is a 17th-century church, San Salvador, and the 15th-century Gothic churches of San Miguel and Santiago; the 16th-century Renaissance Casa del Cabildo Viejo now houses a library and an archaeological museum. The Palacio de los Marqueses de Monatana has an impressive Baroque façade and a beautiful patio. The Casa de Bertemati, the Casa de Riquelme, the Casa del Marqués Domecq and the Palacio de los Marqueses de Campo Real are also notable.

Perhaps the most beautiful building is to be found on the outskirts of the town. This is La Cartuja de NS de la Defensión, 5km to the south of Jerez. The building, a 15th-century Carthusian monastery, abandoned in the 19th century and re-established in the middle of the present century, is entered through an imposing doorway which reveals an exquisitely decorated façade of golden stone. Not all of the building is open to the public but its exterior is exceptionally beautiful.

Leaving Jerez the N 342 leads eastwards to Arcos de la Frontera. The town is strikingly set on a precipitous crag overlooking the Río Guadalete. Sheer cliffs rise from its banks and vineyards, olive groves and orchards spread out beyond. The streets are so narrow they feel like tunnels as you drive through and so steep that walking down the rough cobbles needs considerable care. Blindingly white houses brim with flowers and the atmosphere is profoundly Andalusian. One of the narrowest and steepest streets leads into the Plaza de España. Here the 16th-century church of Santa María de la Asunción looks over the square with an impressive Plateresque façade and soaring bell tower. Nearby is the Gothic church of San Pedro, containing paintings by Zurbarán and Pacheco and a magnificent Gothic retablo. The western side of the square is dominated by an Arab fortress and to the south a balcony overlooks the river with sweeping views.

On the fourth side of the square is The Parador Nacional Casa del Corregidor. Formerly the mansion of González de Gamaza and today a comfortable hotel,

Left: A street in Arcos de la Frontera. Above: The church of Santa María de la Asunción in Arcos de la Frontera.

sitting right on the very edge of the cliff in a setting which makes it one of the most memorable of the Paradors. The bedrooms have balconies from which you can watch the sun go down. Long corridors connect the rooms with wooden-beamed ceilings, stone arches and terracotta-tiled floors. There is a small, charming patio filled with plants and set out with tables and chairs. Breakfast is served here. The restaurant opens on to a broad semi-circular terrace from where you can watch red kites wheeling around the cliff face.

Among the Andalusian specialities on the menu I tried Rape Sanlugueña, pieces of monkfish cooked in a sauce with peppers, asparagus and peas. The delicious fresh peas which were in season also featured in Guisantes con Jamón, in which they are cooked in a casserole with *serrano* ham and garlic. Cordero Quisado al Estilo de Arcos is small pieces of lamb on the bone cooked with potatoes, onions and carrots in a sauce flavoured with garlic and thyme. An excellent local wine on the list was Viñedos Regantío Viejo, a deep red made in the Arcos region from Cinsault and Cabernet Sauvignon grapes.

Arcos is a good base from which to explore some of the pueblos blancos (white towns) of the region. A day's round trip can be made by first taking the N 342 north-east through open rolling countryside to Bornos, an appealing old town attractively situated on the banks of the Embalse de Arcos. There is a large 16th-century convent and the streets are lined with old houses and mansions.

The road continues to Villamartín and Algodonales. The landscape becomes progressively more hilly as the contours of distant mountains draw nearer. A fiesta was in progress during my visit to Algodonales. I watched a solemn procession in which a statue of the Virgin was carried through the streets on the shoulders of a dozen or so brawny village maidens dressed in white gowns. A drum beat out time to their slow, swaying march. The statue was placed on a dais in front of the church. Throughout the day the villagers, family by family, brought large bunches of carnations and carefully arranged them in vases around the figure. Gradually the flowers formed a small mountain of brilliant colour.

The road leads further westwards through craggy hills to the Puerto Cabañas where a distant view of the

Olvera.

hilltop town of Olvera is dramatically revealed. Shimmering white houses are scattered on the slopes and above a church and a Moorish fortress appear almost to be sculpted from the rock.

A quiet country road leads through a small green valley to the south of Olvera and then passes through a gorge created by the Río Trejo to Setenil. It is a small, curious town built on and around an outcrop of tufa rock. Into this many homes have been tunnelled. Entire streets of cave dwellings with quite normal house fronts and small tiled roofs protruding from the rock have been built. There are also the remains of a castle and a 15th-century Gothic church. The 16th-century *ayuntamiento* has a fine *artesanado* (moulded) ceiling.

A road leads westwards from Setenil through a broad valley to Ronda, a town worthy of an extended visit. Its most famous sight is the deep cleft in the rock upon which it is built. A bridge crosses the ravine and houses are built along the sheer sides of the cliff. There is much more to see, however: the bullring dates from 1785 and has an extravagant Baroque façade. The collegiate church of Santa María la Mayor was formerly a mosque and has a wealth of interesting features in

Gothic, Moorish, Renaissance and Plateresque styles. The Casa del Rey Moro has delightful gardens from where steps descend to the bottom of the gorge. The 14th-century Mudéjar Casa del Gigante has a patio surrounded by elegant marble columns and an *artesanado* ceiling. There are also fascinating streets and alleys in which to wander and squares with pavement cafés where you can linger over a drink.

From Ronda the route continues north-west along the C 339. After about 15km a small road leads west along a dramatic valley bordered by soaring pinnacles of rock to Monteajaque. The road continues to the Cuevas de la Pileta where a cave nearly a mile long has been carved by an underground river. Here there are cave paintings of animals from the paleolithic age which are reminiscent of those at Altamira. Back on the main road the route continues north towards Algodonales along the side of a deep mountain valley. After about 15km a small road leads eastwards to the village of El Gastor. Nearby is a dolmen known as the Giant's Tomb. Continuing north along the main road for another 10km the route leads westwards along a quiet road to Zahara de la Sierra, strikingly set upon a steep ridge of rock – a very pretty village with an Arab castle and a 16th-century Baroque church. There are impressive views of the Sierra de Grazalema from the castle walls.

The road leads deeper into the mountains to the Puerto de las Palomas. The scenery around this pass is breathtaking – and as dramatic as any in the Alps. The road continues over the Puerto del Boyer to El Bosque and then through hilly farmland back to Arcos.

TORREMOLINOS

THE NEXT STAGE of the tour is south-east to the Parador at Torremolinos. From Arcos the route is first westwards along the C 344 to El Bosque and then south along the CA 524 to Ubrique. A large, lively town in an impressive mountain setting, Ubrique is well-known for its leather-work. There is also an interesting Gothic church here.

From here the route continues along the C 344 through the Sierra Ubrique to Grazalema, an isolated little town with a lovely Gothic church. Beyond, the road joins the C 339 where the route continues south-east to Ronda. A few kms south of Ronda the C 341 forks right through impressive mountain scenery, passing a sequence of attractive small villages. From a distance the clusters of brilliant white and red-roofed houses stud the green mountainsides like gemstones. Gaucín has an impressive Arab castle set high on a ridge above the town. It is possible, on a clear day, to see both Gibraltar and the Moroccan coast from the ramparts of the castle.

Here the MA 539 leads south-east through a remote and beautiful mountain landscape towards Estepona. A brief detour leads to Casares. It is one of the most picturesque and strikingly situated of the white hilltop towns, its small white houses clinging to the sides of a steep conical rock, the top of which is crowned by a castle. The road continues through Manilva, set among vineyards, to join the main coast road, the N 340, 11km west of Estepona.

The route now leads east along this road to Torremolinos through a succession of Costa del Sol holiday resorts, Estepona, San Pedro, Marbella, Fuengirola and Benalmádena Costa. Driving along this road offers little pleasure. It is fast, very busy and in the summer it can be quite dangerous. The scenery too is swamped by gross development. Towns like Estepona, San Pedro and Marbella still retain attractive old parts but they are places to stay for a seaside holiday more than sightseeing destinations.

The Parador Nacional del Golf is situated about 1km to the east of Torremolinos along a small road to the

A finca near Tolox.

right of the main road. It is clearly signposted. The approach is along an avenue lined with palm trees, oleander and bougainvillea. It is a long, low building of white brick built in regional style. The bedrooms have large sun terraces facing an enormous lawn, in the centre of which is a swimming pool. Beyond, low sand dunes border a long, quiet, sandy beach. The Parador is virtually surrounded by a splendid golf course. Leisure and relaxation are the essence of this Parador. The proximity of Málaga airport, however, makes it less than quiet on occasions.

Regional dishes on the menu include: Riñones a la Jerezana, lambs' kidneys cooked with onions, garlic, parsley and sherry; and Huevos a la Flamenca, eggs baked on a bed of sautéed mixed vegetables with *serrano* ham and *chorizo* sausage.

An interesting excursion can be made from the Parador into the Sierra de Mijas. From the main road the C 344 leads west through orange and lemon groves to Alhaurín el Grande. Here a road leads south over the Puerto de los Pescadores, with splendid views, to Mijas. This once remote Moorish village is now encroached upon by the Costa del Sol developments. Nevertheless it still has considerable charm. It possesses a 16th-century church, formerly a mosque, the remains of castle walls and an ancient rectangular bullring.

From Alhaurín el Grande the route continues to Coín. Here you have two choices. A full day trip can be made by continuing north-east through the valley of the Río Grande to the pretty hilltop village of Tolox. Continuing north to Alozaina, a road to the left leads through dramatic mountain scenery to the Puerto de las Abajes. Beyond is El Burgo, another delightful mountain village. The route continues with spectacular mountain views to the Puerto de Viento, where the road descends to Ronda. The return to the Parador can be made by taking the C 339 south to San Pedro where the N 340 leads back to Torremolinos.

The alternative, and shorter, journey from Coín is along the C 337 to Marbella. This leads over the Puerto de Ojén with stunning views of the coastline. A short detour can be made higher into the mountains to the Refujio de Juanar. Once a Parador, this charming mountain retreat is set in the midst of wooded mountains. It's hard to believe this peaceful and remote place is only a few kms from the hectic chaos of the Costa del Sol. About 1km beyond is a *mirador* with a breathtaking view of Marbella. Back on the main road the route descends to Marbella where the N 340 is joined.

The nearest alternative Parador to Torremolinos is at Málaga, 10km (page 176).

Gaucín.

*T*OUR 18 *Explores the eastern region of Andalucía, starting in the province of Málaga and then following the eastwards into Granada, Almería and Murcia before turning inland to the province of Jaen. The route explores an excitingly varied countryside. The most lovely of all Spain's southern coastal scenery is found to the east of Málaga and also some of its most barren. There are landscapes of desert-like hills, hidden green valleys and mountain ranges covered in dense pine forests – all within the space of a few hours' driving. Some of the most picturesquely sited villages in Spain are to be found on this trip, along with curious troglodyte villages and towns rich in magnificent architecture. The Paradors featured include two beside the sea, one in a unique mountain setting and another in a palace in the heart of a beautiful historic town.*

— TOUR 18 —
MICHELIN MAP NOS. 446 & 445

NERJA – MOJÁCAR –
PUERTO LUMBRERAS –
CAZORLA – ÚBEDA

NERJA

THE ITINERARY BEGINS at the Parador Nacional de Nerja, a short distance from the Málaga–Almería road, the N 340, and about 55km from Málaga. The nearest airport is at Málaga, about 1½ hours by car, and the nearest alternative Parador is also at Málaga (page 176).

The Parador is in an enviable setting on the eastern edge of the town of Nerja, built on a clifftop overlooking the splendid beach of Burriana – one of the loveliest on the Costa del Sol. The reception area of the Parador opens on to a beautiful garden cascading with tropical blooms and shaded by palm and lemon trees. Beyond is a swimming pool set in a wide green lawn which extends right to the edge of the cliff. From here there are superb views of the beach and the coastline beyond, which curves away for many miles with the lovely Sierra de Almijara creating an imposing backdrop. An elevator whisks you effortlessly down to beach level. The restaurant, bar and lounge are in a separate wing and open on to a paved sun-terrace which overlooks the sea.

The local cuisine includes excellent fish dishes like Fritura Malagueña, a mixture of fried fish which includes *calamares* (squid), *gambas* (prawns), *merluza* (hake), *lenguado* (sole), *boquerones* (anchovies) and *sardinas* (sardines). Another local speciality is Pollo con Ajillo, small pieces of chicken on the bone sautéed in olive oil until golden with whole cloves of garlic.

Nerja is set at the foothills of the Sierra de Almijara. The coastline here is the most beautiful of the Costa del Sol. The town is built on a cliff and a famous local landmark is the Balcón de Europa, a semi-circular terrace which juts out over the sea with superb views along the coast. Here in the evening people stroll or sit at the café tables which line the small square. Below is a pretty, sheltered beach dotted with fishing boats.

A fascinating excursion is to the nearby Cueva de Nerja, an impressive stalactite cavern which was not discovered until 1958 and is known as the Prehistoric Cathedral. It is over half a mile in length and contains paintings of animals. Numerous other finds from the Stone Age have also been made here and there is a small museum. The cavern is also used for concerts. Near the cavern is the attractive small village of Maro set between fertile green headlands. There is a secluded beach at the foot of the cliffs which can be reached by a small road zig-zagging down between fields of fruit and vegetables.

About 7km from Nerja is the charming Moorish village of Frigiliana, at the head of the small green valley of the Río Higuerón. Its small white houses are clustered around narrow, stepped and cobbled alleys which only people and donkeys can negotiate. It has an enchanting atmosphere and evokes an impression of a centuries-old way of life.

Nerja is also an ideal base from which to make an excursion along the coast to the west. A delightful scenic circuit can be made into the Sierra de Tejeda by following the N 340 towards Málaga and then taking the MA 137 north to Torrox, a little white town set in a valley filled with small market gardens. From here the road climbs higher into the mountains with increasingly impressive views. The region is known for its wines and the hillsides are covered with vineyards, olive groves and almond trees. Many of the fincas, small farms, have curious stone-edged 'beds' for drying the fat, sweet grapes. If you are visiting in the autumn a sprig or two of these freshly made raisins make a delicious accompaniment to the local wine. At this time too you will find small baskets of *higos* in the shops. These are juicy, just-dried figs – totally different from, and far superior to, the supermarket variety.

The road continues further into the mountains to the village of Cómpeta. This small town of white houses with red-tiled roofs is set in the middle of quite spectacular mountain scenery. From here the road winds back down towards the coast through the attractive villages of Sayalonga and Algarrobo to Algarrobo Costa from where you can return along the N 340 to the Parador.

MOJÁCAR

THE NEXT STAGE of the journey is eastwards along the coast to the Parador at Mojácar following the N 340 for much of the way. The first part of the journey is

A beach near Nerja. Overleaf: Terraced fields by the sea near Maro.

through magnificent coastal scenery. The road follows the steep and deeply indented mountainsides in a series of sweeping curves with superb views of the sea. A brief detour can be made along the old coast road around the headland of Cerro Gordo. This is sign-posted to the right just before entering the tunnel of Cerro Gordo, which carries the new wide road. The rocky headland is covered in vivid green pine trees and the views through these into the paintbox-blue water is nothing less than breathtaking. Just before reaching the resort of La Herradura another short loop of the old road leads around the beautiful villa-scattered headland of Punta de la Mona. From here are sweeping views of the long, curving beach of La Herradura.

Almuñécar is the next town, a heavily developed and unattractive resort which hides an old town in its midst with the remains of a castle. The road then follows the steep winding coastline until the town of Salobreña is suddenly revealed around a bend. This old Moorish town is set on a ridge about 1km inland in the midst of a vast plain planted with sugar cane. Its white

houses cover the rock like a snow-clad mountain peak and sparkle in the sunlight in brilliant contrast to the surrounding sea of green. Above the town is an impressive castle.

From Salobreña the road crosses the wide plain of Motril where fields of carnations mingle with plantations of tropical fruits and sugar cane. The coast is regained at Torrenueva, a large resort, and the road once again winds sinuously around steep mountainsides. Here they are arid and barren. However, extensive cultivation of vegetables and fruit is carried on under vast plastic greenhouses which shimmer in the distance like a mirage. Calahonda is an attractive fishing village which has become a relatively unspoilt, and undeveloped resort. So too has Castell de Ferro a few kms beyond.

The route continues through La Rábida to Adra, a large modern town with a busy fishing port. Beyond Adra you can make a detour into the Sierra de Gádor. This will add two hours or so to your journey to Mojácar but is a rewarding alternative to continuing along the N 340 between Adra and Almería.

At Puente del Río the C 331 leads north into arid brown mountains towards Berja. Shortly a broad green valley is suddenly revealed in the midst of which is Berja. Here the valley floor is planted with vineyards.

The Moorish town of Mojácar.

The vines grow 8ft high or more, supported on large trellises. These are desert grapes, fat, juicy and golden. Berja is a nice old town with a small arcaded market square.

The road continues northwards, climbing higher towards Lújar de Andarax, on a mountainside overlooking the fertile valley of the Río Andarax. Grape vines and fruit trees are planted extensively here. As well as desert grapes these vines also produce a wine for which the town is known. There is an arcaded *ayuntamiento* in the plaza and a fine old church.

The road now continues eastwards high along the side of the valley. A small detour can be made further north, and higher still, to the enchanting village of Ohanes, high in the steep mountain slopes with wonderful far-reaching views. The village is completely unspoilt, with a warren of steep cobbled streets and stepped alleys threading between the small whitewashed stone houses. This region was one of the last places where the Moors remained after their expulsion from Granada. Until only a decade or so ago it was commonplace for women of all ages to cover their faces when men were present in these remote communities.

The road continues beyond Ohanes back down the mountain with stunning views and then continues to follow the valley. As the road proceeds further east so the landscape becomes more arid. The valley is still green and fertile but beyond the landscape is brown and tree-less. There are two choices here: one is to continue along the valley rejoining the N 340 some 12km north of Almería where the route continues north-east to Tabernas. It is in this region that the most dramatic landscape of Almería may be seen. Here the bare red rock mountains are covered only with huge thickets of prickly pear cactus. It has been the location of many a 'paella' Western movie and just to the south of Tabernas is a replica Western town built as a film set and now used to stage gunfights for tourists to watch. Tabernas has an impressive Arab fortress and nearby is a futuristic solar-energy plant.

The longer alternative is to take a small road to the south beyond the village of Alcún. This leads over the Sierra de Gádor with breathtaking views and rejoins the coast at Aguadulce from where it is 10kms along the N 340 to Almería. There are two attractive mountain villages along this route which are worth a visit, Enix and Felix.

From Tabernas the road continues through similar scenery for about 30km or so to Sorbas, a strikingly situated town where the houses rise sheer from the side of the ridge on which it is built. About 20km beyond Sorbas a road leads south to Mojácar, a village built in the foothills of the Sierra Cabrera, 3km from the sea.

This too is a spectacularly sited town. Its brilliant white cube-shaped houses seem to trickle down the sides of the red-brown rock on which it is set, like a carelessly iced cake. It has been a settlement since the Bronze Age and has housed the Phoenicians and Romans in its time. Its present form, however, was created by the Moors with typically narrow streets, cobbled alleys and small squares. What was, not so long ago, a remote and undiscovered village is now a lively and atmospheric holiday town. The village has been extended to include several large holiday hotels, and numerous villages dot the surrounding mountainsides.

The Parador Nacional Reyes Católicos is situated beside the road which runs along the seashore between Garrucha and Carboneras. It is 2½km from Mojácar and just a few strides from the beach. It is a very large, low building which extends in several wings and provides most rooms with a sea view from their roomy balconies. Long, cool corridors connect the bedrooms with the restaurant, bar and lounges, and small furnished areas are scattered throughout. The public rooms open on to a large tiled sun terrace – grass does not grow very well in Almería. It is dotted liberally with straw parasols and sun-loungers and in the centre is a spacious pool.

Regional dishes on the menu include: Conejo con Gurullos, casserole of rabbit in a rich sauce, served with a small rice-shaped pasta; Merluza en Salsa de Almendras, fillets of hake, served in a creamy almond sauce; and Gazpacho Almeriense, the familiar Andalucían cold soup but with small pieces of fried bread added just before serving. I chose a regional wine from the list, Viña Amalia, a crisp dry white from the vineyards of Montilla-Moriles.

A day's excursion can be made easily from the Parador to the Cabo de Gata, a dramatic coastline of purple-tinged mountains which plunge precipitously into an intensely blue sea. First, however, it is worth making a brief detour to the north to Garrucha. This is an attractive fishing town 6km to the north of the Parador with a busy harbour and an atmospheric seafront lined with some excellent fish restaurants and small bars. There is also a 16th-century castle overlooking the sea.

Landscape near Tabernas.

The coastline near Carboneras.

The route to Cabo de Gata first returns to the Parador and then continues south along the coast road towards Carboneras. The first part of the journey runs close to the sea through a region of quite extensive development. Further south, however, the road begins to climb higher into the mountains with increasingly exciting views. There is little vegetation here apart from monumental cactus plants, which grow in some places like small forests. A few kms before reaching Carboneras the road climbs high around a steep headland revealing sensational views. From this point the road descends again to the sea and runs alongside a long, empty sandy beach. Carboneras is a large, modern-looking town but it has an appealing old quarter centred around the Castillo of San Antón. A busy market is held here on Thursdays.

The road now turns away from the sea. After a few kms a road to the left leads back to the coast through a parched landscape scattered with small white houses and farms. Here the attractive little fishing village and secluded resort of Agua Amarga, has a good beach and a quiet and intimate atmosphere. Joining the main road, the N 332, the route leads south-west towards Almería.

After a few kms a road leads north to Níjar, on a steep mountainside. It is an evocative old town with small squares and a maze of narrow streets. The centre of an active craft industry of ceramics, rugs and baskets made from esparto grass, Níjar is a good place to buy inexpensive and authentic gifts or souvenirs.

Back on the main road another small road leads south to San José, a fishing village and resort prettily situated in a small bay of crystal-clear water enclosed by steep domed headlands. Just before reaching San José, however, a road leads east to the villages of Los Escullos, with the remains of a castle, and Isleta del Moro. These are two tiny isolated fishing communities just with a few small bars and large unpopulated beaches.

A few kms beyond San José there is a fine long sandy beach backed by pine and eucalyptus trees. The road continues close to the sea towards the Cape, climbing steadily higher into the mountains. This section of the road is unsurfaced and a little rough in places but quite serviceable. All along this route there are small deserted coves and quiet beaches to scramble down to. The road continues to the lighthouse from where there are sweeping views down to the town of Cabo de Gata and the salt pans of Acosta.

Almería is a city well worth a visit but needing a separate trip to do it any justice. It has a massive 8th-

century reddish stone fort on a ridge, an imposing 16th-century cathedral and there are many interesting churches and mansions. From Almería the route back to the Parador is along the N 340 as before.

PUERTO LUMBRERAS

THE NEXT LEG of the tour is to the Parador at Puerto Lumbreras. It is a direct journey of only 62km and I have suggested an en-route excursion which takes you into the Sierra de los Filabres. From Mojácar you need first to return to Sorbas. A short distance to the west of the town a road leads north through open, undulating countryside to Uleila del Campo, attractively situated in the foothills of the Sierras. The road now begins to climb into the mountains, bare and rocky with little vegetation other than huge thickets of prickly pear cactus. Beyond, however, on the northern slopes there are plantations of almond and olive trees. It is a sparsely populated region with only the occasional isolated farmhouse to be seen.

The road now begins to descend to Cobdar, a village with narrow streets and little whitewashed houses, in a small fertile valley above which towers a monumental dome of red rock. Beyond, the road continues along the valley to Albánchez, an equally unspoilt village. The valley here is filled with fruit trees, almonds and fields of vegetables. From Albánchez the route turns westwards to Líjar along a dry riverbed filled with oleander bushes; a harsh and bleak landscape with a kind of gaunt beauty. Charcos is a small village of ancient, crumbling houses scattered down the mountain slope. At the attractively situated village of Alcudia de Monteagud the route leads northwards towards Macael. The road descends from here through a region dominated by vast quarries where the mountain is progressively blasted and hacked into manageable chunks. Below in the valley, the towns of Macael and Olula del Río seem almost entirely devoted to huge factories and workshops cutting and polishing the marble into all manner of shapes and sizes.

The route eastwards along the valley of the Río Almanzora joins the N 340 a few kms south of Huércal Overa where it heads south towards Vera. After about 10km a road leads eastwards to Cuevas de Almanzora. Near the town in the rocky hillsides are prehistoric dwellings, some still in use. The 16th-century castle belonged to the Duke of Alba. The road continues to the coast at Palomares, famous for nearly having been the scene of a major nuclear disaster in 1966 when the American air force accidentally dropped four atomic bombs – which didn't go off.

A road follows the coast with constant views of the sea to Águilas with an extraordinary coastline of bare red rock which simply plunges straight into a deep blue and very clear sea. Águilas is a large town with quite extensive development dominated by a massive domed headland upon which there are the remains of a castle. Beyond, the road continues to Cabo Cope where another sea fort is set beside the beach.

The route from Águilas is inland now along the C 3211 to Lorca, an ancient town on the slopes of a steep ridge upon which is an imposing castle. There are numerous churches, palaces and mansions including a 17th-century *ayuntamiento* and the 16th-century church of San Patricio. The town is also famous for its distinctive, and stylish, rugs as well as its spectacular Holy Week processions. It has now been designated a national monument.

The Parador Nacional de Puerto Lumbreras, on the eastern edge of the town, 18km south-west of Lorca beside the N 340 is quiet, comfortable and cooled by air-conditioning. The restaurant is an attractive semicircular rooms which looks on to a garden shaded by lemon trees. Beyond is a swimming pool. The interior is decorated with a variety of Lorca rugs used effectively as wall-hangings.

The local cuisine offered on the menu included: Ensalada de Pimientos Asados y Tomate, a refreshing salad of cooked peppers and chopped raw tomatoes; Costillos de Cabrito en Ajo Cabanil, succulent cutlets of kid cooked with garlic, paprika and wine vinegar; and Berenjenas a la Crema con Gambas y Jamón, aubergines cooked in a creamy white sauce with prawns and ham. The regional wines on the list are those of Castillo Jumilla.

CAZORLA

THE TOUR NOW CONTINUES north-west to the Parador at Cazorla. The first part of the journey is along the N342 through quiet, open countryside to Vélez Rubio, below a steep ridge with a massive and extravagantly decorated 18th-century church. Its ornate façade is flanked by two enormous Baroque towers and surmounted by a dome. A small road leads north, skirting the mountain, to Vélez Blanco, an atmospheric old town with an imposing castle high on a rock above the houses. Nearby are the Cuevas de los Letreros. In these caves the Neolithic painting of Indalo Man was discovered – a figure with outstretched arms holding a rainbow. The image is now used as a symbol for the region.

From Vélez Blanco the road passes through the Sierra de María, an attractive landscape of dry, ochre mountainsides dotted with pine and almond trees. Beyond, the road passes through a dense pine forest and then across a vast bleached plain of wheatfields, bordered by distant hazy ridges and dotted with occasional isolated farms.

The village of Jata at the opening of a shallow, green valley consists almost exclusively of troglodyte dwellings, tunnelled into the ridge of sandy stone which

borders it. Some are quite elaborate with tiled half-roofs projecting from the cliff face; others simply have a door and window opening directly into a cave. It is most peculiar to see chimney pots and even TV aerials rising straight out of the ground.

The road continues to Orca, where there are more troglodyte dwellings, many occupied. In the centre of this atmospheric old town is the 11th-century Alcazaba de las Siete Torres, the castle of the seven towers. Nearby is the 17th-century Palacio de los Marqueses de dos Fuentes and a lovely old church with a Mudéjar tower.

The road follows the course of a shallow green valley planted with maize, vegetables and sunflowers to Galera. Here the route continues north along the C 3329 to Huéscar, an appealing old town with a magnificent 16th century hall church around which are a web of picturesque tiled alleys called Las Santas.

The C 330 leads west across an exposed plain planted with wheatfields and almond trees, bordered by the imposing ridge of the Sierra de Marmolance. A bridge crosses a quite spectacular chasm hundreds of metres deep through which the Río Guardel flows fast and furious over the rocks. The road continues to the village of Castril, strikingly set between two towering peaks of rock. Upon one is a huge statue of Christ to which a footpath ascends to a *mirador*. Below is the Río Castril, a fast-running river known for its trout fishing.

Beyond, the route continues into the Sierra de Segura, a beautiful mountain range thickly covered in pine trees, to the Pantano de la Bolera, an expanse of water so intensely blue it looks as though it has been squeezed from a paint tube. At Pozo Alcón the route continues north-west along the C 323 climbing higher into the Sierras towards Tíscar. The views from this road are staggering: ridge after ridge recede hazily into the far distance.

Suddenly a bend in the road reveals the village of Tíscar. Its small houses are scattered down the steep mountainside beneath a jagged cockscomb of rock. Upon one a castle tower juts up like a pointing finger to the sky. It is an unforgettable sight. The road continues through a tunnel, climbing beyond the village to the Puerto de Tíscar from where there are sweeping views of the mountains beyond.

The distinctive candlewick pattern of millions of olive trees quite suddenly dominates the landscape – the unmistakable appearance of the province of Jaén. The road descends in a series of gentle curves to the valley where Quesada is set above it on a knoll. The town is the birthplace of the painter Rafael Zabaleta and a small museum is devoted to his work.

A view from the Sierra de Cazorla towards Quesada.

The route leads on north-east to Cazorla a picturesque town in a beautiful setting, cradled in an amphitheatre formed by the surrounding peaks of the Sierra de Cazorla. The small white houses of the old town spill down the mountain slope and above, on a ridge, is an Arab fortress. There are also the remains of a ruined Plateresque church. From the centre of Cazorla a road leads up into the Sierras passing the village of La Iruela, with the remains of a castle on a towering pinnacle of rock.

The road continues to climb higher towards the Puerto de las Palomas with sweeping views over the patterned plain below. The mountainsides are thickly covered with pine trees and carpeted with flowers, shrubs and aromatic herbs. From a *mirador* you can look down into a green valley far below where the youthful Río Guadalquivir is beginning its long journey to the sea. This region is one of Spain's richest wildlife reserves with large populations of animals like ibex, moufflon, wild boar, eagles and ospreys. There are also species of flowers and butterflies found nowhere else in the world.

The Parador Nacional El Adelantado, on a small road leading higher still into the mountains a few kms beyond the summit of the pass, is set on the edge of a rocky ravine 1400m above sea level and surrounded by pine forests. Beyond are the imposing ridges of the Sierra de Cazorla. It is hard to imagine a more peaceful and remote setting in which to stay. The silence at night was total except for the strident squealing of a wild boar somewhere in the forest. The Parador is built in the style of a traditional Andalusian *cortijo*, or manor house. There is a long sun terrace which extends along the first floor of the building and, below, another is enclosed behind large windows for the colder winter days. In front is a large natural lawn with sun-loungers scattered below the shady pines.

The restaurant and bar open on to the terrace, providing a memorable setting for a pre-dinner drink as the sun dips below the distant peaks. The menu offers appropriately hearty fare. I began with Olla Gitana, literally gipsy's stew pot, a knife-and-fork soup containing chunks of salt pork, *chorizo*, green beans, potatoes, chick peas, peppers and spinach, and followed this with Chuletas de Venado en Adobe, venison cutlets marinaded before grilling. Other delicious regional dishes were Tortilla de la Serrana, an omelette filled with finely chopped meat and ham and Trucha a la Cazorlena, trout sautéed with small pieces of serrano ham, salt pork and mushrooms.

The Parador is an excellent base for ramblers, with many signposted walks into the Sierras. Another, less energetic, possibility of exploring the more remote regions is in small groups by Landrover. Such trips are conducted by the park authorities and can be arranged by the Parador.

An enjoyable and varied round trip along the Embalse de Tranco begins by returning to the junction of the Parador road. The route continues to the left and quite soon after to the right – it is signposted to El Tranco – then along the shady valley of the Guadalquivir to Torre del Vinagre, where there is a museum explaining the region and its wildlife. There is also a botanical garden, and nearby a fish farm can be visited. The valley becomes progressively wider and the road begins to run quite close to the river with numerous spots where you can walk down through the trees to its banks.

At the opening of the lake, near Bujaraiza, is a wildlife park called the Parque Cinegético where many of the region's animals and birds can be observed. It is best to visit either early or late in the day when they come to feed. The road continues around the edge of the large, impressive lake to the dam itself at Tranco. Here the road climbs high above the lake with superb views to Cañada Morales where it follows a rich green valley dotted with small white farmhouses. There is soon a road junction with the C 3210. The route continues to the left but a brief detour to the right leads 4km to Hornos, a very pretty, unspoilt village set dramatically on a sheer spur of rock and overlooked by the remains of a castle. In the tiny square, by the church, a doorway leads through on to a balcony which overhangs the cliff. From here there are stunning views of the valley, the lake and the mountains beyond.

The route continues back along the C 3210 to Cortijos Nuevos where it follows a fork to the right. Soon another turning to the right leads across a fertile valley planted with wheatfields, vegetables, fruit and olive trees to Segura de la Sierra. You will see the town long before you reach it. The small white houses are tiered up a perfectly conical peak crowned with geometrical precision by a castle – like the fairy on a Christmas tree. Segura de la Sierra is completely encircled by crenellated walls and towers. Inside the fortified gateway is an enchanting web of stepped, tunnel-like alleys. There is an ancient *ayuntamiento*, Moorish baths, a medieval fountain and the house of a famous Spanish poet, Jorge Manrique.

From Segura the route continues north-west through Orcera and La Puerta de Segura to join the main road, the N 322, where it turns south-east towards Villacarillo. Just before reaching this town a small road leads to the right to a village which is as picturesque as its name promises, Iznatoraf.

At Villacarillo there is an 18th-century *ayuntamiento* and a church attributed to Vandelvira. An attractive

Above right: The Puerto de Tíscar. Right: The Castillo and old town of Cazorla.

— 210 —

scenic road leads south-east through Mogón and Santo Tomé back to Cazorla.

ÚBEDA

THE FINAL STAGE of the tour is to the Parador at Úbeda, a direct route of about 80km. The more circuitous journey I have suggested takes you first to the birthplace of the Río Guadalquivir and then through some of the wilder regions of Sierra de Segura.

After returning to the beginning of the Parador road a turn to the right leads shortly to Vadillo. A small road continues beyond through a park checkpoint and then alongside the Río Guadalquivir. Here it is no more than a small, mountain river. The valley begins to narrow and the road climbs higher into the mountains. It is thickly wooded and there are many delightful spots beside the river to take a picnic lunch or relax in the shade. The old bridge at Puente de las Herrerías is particularly attractive. From this point the road is unsurfaced and continues to climb high along the side of a narrowing rocky valley. The river is now no more than a trickle below over the boulder-strewn bed.

The birthplace of the river is a tiny wooded valley high in the mountains. A dribble of water seeps from a crevice in a large rock and moves almost imperceptibly from one small pool to another. It is hard to believe that this seemingly insignificant spring grows into a mighty river which moulds the character and appearance of the province of Andalucía, generates a livelihood for millions of people and has created the cities of Sevilla and Córdoba.

The road climbs steadily to the summit of the pass where the views to the south are simply sensational. Distant Quesada appears as if in an aerial photograph. From here the road descends gradually to meet a tarmac road and after 1km or so to the left it joins the main road from Quesada, the C 323. The route continues north-west through Peal de Becerro to Torreperogil, an attractive town set in the midst of vineyards. The table wines produced here are dry and strongly alcoholic – quite unusual in Andalucía. There is also an interesting church, Santa María, built in a mixture of Renaissance and Gothic styles.

Beyond Torreperogil the main road, the N 322, is joined and Úbeda is just 10km away to the west. However, a short detour can be made to the north to the atmospheric old hilltop town of Sabiote. Here there are cobbled streets, entrance gates, a castle palace, several old mansions and a fine old church.

Parador Nacional Condestable Davalos in the old part of Úbeda in the Plaza de Vázquez de Molina, is the

Part of the facade of the 18th century church of Velez Rubio.

Palacio de los Ortegas and at one time belonged to Don Fernando Ortega Salido, the Dean of Málaga. Built in the 16th century it was completely restored in the 17th century.

An imposing entrance and a stone staircase lead into a beautiful two-storey patio, shaded during the summer by a canvas awning. It is furnished with clusters of garden chairs and tables enhanced by palm trees in huge pots. It makes an evocative place for a pre-dinner drink. Another grand staircase, guarded by suits of armour, leads up to the bedrooms, some of which look out on to another small courtyard. The restaurant is an attractive L-shaped room decorated with arches.

From the local dishes on the menu I chose Ensalada de Perdiz as a starter, a delicious salad with slivers of marinated partridge combined with finely chopped onions, lettuce and diced tomatoes. Cabrito Guisado con Piñones is a casserole of kid with pine nuts. For those who like sweet things Natillas con Borrachuelos is a delicious concoction of a chilled creamy egg custard spiced with cinnamon and vanilla and served with small crispy fritters.

Next to the Parador is the Sacra Capilla del Salvador, an imposing church with an extravagantly decorated Renaissance façade, built by Andreas de Vandaelvira in the 16th century and containing a superb altar and choir stalls. On the other side of the Parador is the Palacio de las Cadenas, now the *ayuntamiento*, also built by Vandaelvira. Opposite this building is the 13th-century church of Santa María de los Reales Alcazares, built on the site of a mosque. Adjacent is the 16th-century Palacio del Marqués de Mancera. The town is filled with beautiful Renaissance buildings and, armed with a map from the Parador, wandering through its ancient streets will provide many hours of pleasure. Don't miss seeing the ornate Casa de las Torres, the Huerta de Granada, the 14th-century church of San Nicolás and the massive Hospital de Santiago.

Just 9km to the west along the N 321 is Baeza. This too is a town rich in architectural masterpieces. The 16th-century Gothic cathedral of Santa María has a beautiful wrought-iron pulpit and gallery as well as a cloister. Perhaps the most appealing corner of the town is the Plaza de los Leones, a beautiful square overlooked by the old abattoir, the Casa del Pópulo and the fortified gateways of the Arco del Pópulo and the Arco de Jaén. In its centre is the Fuente de los Leones, a romantically ornate fountain with four lions surrounding a female figure. Nearby is the 16th-century Arco de Baeza, and an attractively decorated *ayuntamiento* from the same period. Other fine buildings include the church of Santa Cruz and the nearby Seminario de San Felipe Neri, with a fine patio.

The nearest alternative Parador to Úbeda is at Bailén (page 214) where tour No 19 will provide a route back towards Málaga.

*T*OUR 19   *Based in the central region of Andalucía in the provinces of Jaén and Granada, the area covered is bordered in the north by the Sierra Morena and to the south by Las Alpujarras. To the east lies the Sierra de Cazorla and to the west the Sierra de Jabalcuz. The landscape ranges from the wide valley of the Río Guadalquivir to the stark mountain peaks of the Sierra Nevada. It is a region chequered by fields of ripening grain where shades of brown, ochre and white blend like shadows cast by clouds. There are vast hillsides patterned by millions of olive trees, deep green valleys and mountainsides terraced with almond trees and vineyards. Two great Andalusan cities are included, Jaén and Granada, the former dominated by a magnificent hilltop castle and the latter possessing one of Europe's architectural wonders, the Alhambra.*

The tour provides a scenic route connecting Andalucía and the coast with La Mancha and Madrid. It can also be used to create a round trip in conjunction with tour No. 18 (page 200). The paradors featured include one situated at over 8,000ft above sea level, one in a convent within the Alhambra and another in a dramatically sited castle.

—TOUR 19—
MICHELIN MAP NO. 446
Bailén
Jaén
GRANADA
Sierra Nevada

BAILÉN
JAÉN
GRANADA
SIERRA NEVADA

BAILÉN

THE PARADOR NACIONAL DE BAILÉN is beside the main road between Madrid and Andalucía, the N 4, which crosses the Sierra Morena through the Desfiladero de Despeñaperros. Nearby is the junction with the road to Granada, the N 323. It is a spacious and airy building in the motel style with air-conditioning, a shady garden and a swimming pool providing a welcome respite from the searing summer heat. The restaurant is a large room with a high, sloping ceiling and a polished marble floor.

The menu includes a selection of local dishes, such as Cazuela de Espárragos Jaenenses, a casserole of slender wild asparagus; and Gazpacho Andaluz, a perfect example of a dish suited to a region's climate – a refreshing chilled soup made by liquidising cucumbers, peppers, tomatoes and garlic with olive oil, wine vinegar and water, served with small dishes of croutons and a selection of its ingredients cut into small dice as a garnish.

JAÉN

THE NEXT STAGE of the tour is south to the Parador at Jaén, only 40km away. There are however two interesting short excursions which can be made en route from Bailén. The first is only a few kms along a small road to the north of Bailén through olive groves to the hilltop village of Baños de la Encina whose impressive 10th-century Arab fortress has massive walls, punctuated by a dozen or more large square towers. There is also a nice old church.

The second excursion is first along the N 4 to Andújar, on the banks of the Río Guadalquivir, with a Roman bridge and some interesting churches and old mansions. It is also noted for its ceramics. A quiet country road leads north towards Las Viñas through a region of steep, rounded hills covered with oak trees. Further to the north the countryside becomes more mountainous and craggy with large outcrops of rocks and pine trees. The Río Jándula, a wide river with grassy banks is crossed and a rough road runs alongside it for some distance with numerous shady picnic places under the pines. Stone benches and even some barbecue areas are provided. It is a beautiful spot for an alfresco lunch and the river is deep and clear enough to bathe in. The road winds sinuously round the boulder-strewn mountainsides to the remote sanctuary of the Virgen de la Cabeza, site of a heroic siege during the Spanish Civil War.

From Andujar the C 3219 leads south through olive-covered hillsides to Arjona and meets the N 324 at Pilar de Moya. Here the route continues eastwards to Torredonjimeno and then along the N 321 to Jaén.

A short detour to the south can be made from Torredonjimeno to Martos, at the foot of a large mountain. The town contains two fine churches, the 13th-century Santa María de la Villa and the 15th-century Santa Marta with a Gothic portal. There is also a medieval *ayuntamiento*, once a prison, and the ruins of the Moorish fortress of La Peña. The town is the largest olive-growing centre in Spain.

24km to the south of Martos is Alcaudete with an impressive castle above the town and the small Cathedral of Santa María with two Plateresque portals and the Mudejar church of San Pedro.

The Parador Nacional Castillo de Santa Catalina, high on a mountain beside the Alcázar de Santa Catalina overlooking Jaén, is 3.5 km from the city centre. The Alcázar was built by King Alhamar who was also responsible for the Alhambra in Granada.

The Parador is, however, a modern construction built in traditional style to create harmony with the historic castle. Indeed the interior gives an initial im-

Solera. Overleaf: The Castillo of Santa Catalina, Jaén.

pression of an authentic medieval castle. There are massive stone staircases, open fireplaces, galleries and corridors with flagstone floors. Heraldic flags, tapestries and huge wrought-iron candelabra decorate the walls and ceilings. The bedrooms have balconies with far-reaching views of the mountain ranges which surround Jaén. So too has a large terrace in front of the bar and restaurant. The latter is an enormously long room with high stone arches, next to another vast hall with a soaring vaulted roof.

A popular feature of the menu is Cena Jocosa, a tempting selection of regional dishes, different meats in sauces, for example, as well as various salads, vegetables and sweets. It includes Espinacas al Estilo de Jaén, a spicy, creamy puree of spinach, and La Piperana, a salad of finely chopped cucumber and tomato marinaded in a tangy dressing. The house wine, red and white, is from neighbouring Torreperogil.

The city of Jaén is an appealing mixture of old and new, built on the slopes of the Sierra de Jabalcuz, a rugged grey-green mountain range which creates a dramatic backdrop to the silvery-white buildings clustered below. The lower town, spread across the olive-patterned plain, is modern with broad avenues and shady parks and squares. However, on the slopes

of the Cerro de Santa Catalina, and extending up to the castle walls, is a tangle of narrow streets, an inheritance of Jaén's Moorish past. Indeed the city's name is derived from the Moorish word *geen* (caravan route), since it lies at vital crossroads linking Andalucía with Castilla-La Mancha.

The most notable building is undoubtedly the Cathedral, the work of Andrés de Vandelvira and considered by many to be his masterpiece. Built on the site of a former mosque, work commenced in the year 1500 but it was not completed until the end of the 18th-century thus combining Gothic, Renaissance and Baroque elements. Of impressive scale with a lavishly decorated main façade flanked by twin towers, among its many treasures is the relic of Santo Rostro which legend claims to be the veil used by Saint Veronica to wipe Christ's brow. There are richly carved 15th-century choir stalls and the museum contains many fine paintings.

Other historic buildings in the city include the 18th-century church of El Sagrario containing a statue of Christ which is carried in the Easter procession; the fortress-like 14th-century church of San Idelfonso, part of the city wall, has fine Gothic and Plateresque portals; the Gothic church of Santa Magdalena, the oldest

in the city occupying the site of a former mosque; the 17th-century monastery of Santo Domingo with a magnificent Renaissance façade by Vandalvira and a Plateresque cloister decorated by Corinthian columns. The 13th-century Monastery of Santa Clara has a cloister; the 16th-century Mudéjar chapel of San Andrés; the 17th-century *ayuntamiento*, near the cathedral, and the 15th-century Arco de San Lorenzo.

An interesting excursion can be made from the Parador into the countryside to the east of the city. From Jaén a country road leads south-east towards La Guardia de Jaén. It meanders through olive groves and wheatfields with striking views of the distant city and the towering mountain range above it. La Guardia is a jumble of small whitewashed houses spilled over a rocky hillside and surmounted by an 8th-century castle. There are the remains of a Dominican monastery and a church, both designed by Vandalvira. The route continues south along N 323 and then, after about 10km, to the east along the N 324 to Huelma.

This is a quiet scenic route winding through gentle hills with olive plantations and almond trees alternating with wheatfields and rocky uncultivated land. Far beyond is a constant vista of the lofty Sierras. After Huelma the route turns north along the C 325 towards Jódar and a few kms further on a road to the east leads to the village of Solera, on a steep hillside high above the valley floor. Its tiny white houses are clustered around a towering spike of rock upon which is a ruined castle, with the broad-patterned valley and distant mountains creating a dramatic perspective.

Upon returning to the main road the route proceeds north to Jódar through a peaceful valley scattered with fields of grain, almond and olive groves and the occasional small farmhouse. The roadside is lined by locust and pomegranate trees as well as wild grasses, cacti and tree-like thistles. At Jódar there are the remains of a massive fortress. There are two alternative routes back to the Parador. One is to continue to Úbeda and then follow the N 321 through Baeza back to Jaén. A more direct route is to return a few km south where the C 328 can be followed westwards to join the N 321 14km to the east of Jaén.

GRANADA

THE NEXT STAGE of the itinerary is south to Granada, direct journey of only 97km. I have outlined a route which offers an interesting and scenic alternative to the rather busy main road. The road which descends from the Parador joins the C 3221 and this leads south towards Valdepeñas de Jaén, winding around the lower slopes of the Sierra de Jabalcuz, with sweeping views, to the small thermal spa of Balneario de Jabalcuz. Beyond, the road begins to climb into the Sierra de la Pandera, a region of steep ridges of red rock bordering

a valley patterned by the ubiquitous olive groves. The route continues through a green fertile valley and then climbs up over the mountain and down again to Valdepeñas de Jaén, a town surrounded by fields of fruit, grain and vegetables.

The road climbs again, with enormous views, through rugged mountain scenery and over a remote and rocky pass; then descends through a small valley planted with vines and almond trees to Frailes, surrounded by large fields of sunflowers. The road continues to the attractive and lively town of Alcalá la Real. Set above it is the Fortaleza de la Mota, a huge 14th-century fortress. A Gothic church and several old towers are enclosed within the ramparts which encircle the steep sepia-toned hill upon which it is set.

The route leads south now along the N 432 through an open landscape of steep rounded hills. In the distance is the massive hazy ridge of the Sierra Nevada, snow covered for much of the year. At Puerto López a small road leads up into the mountains to a rocky valley. Here on a steep ridge is the strikingly situated Moorish fortress of La Mota, set above the small white town of Moclín. Just beyond is a *mirador* from where there are spectacular views of the village and castle and over the vast variegated plain which reaches away to the Sierra Nevada.

The road continues south through Tiena and Bucor to rejoin the main road at Pinos-Puente. Here there is an ancient fortified bridge over the Río Cubillas with a horseshoe arch and a gateway. A few kms along the N432 towards Granada a road leads south to Santa Fé. This curious old town is composed in a square and entered through four gates in its enclosing walls. It was built on the site of a Roman camp by King Ferdinand during the siege of Granada in 1491 and the Moorish surrender was signed here. The agreement between Christopher Columbus and Ferdinand and Isabella for their sponsorship of his voyage to America was made in the town. Santa Fé is also famed for its *piononos*, a creamy confection made from eggs, white wine and sugar. The city of Granada is just 10km or so to the east of Santa Fé along the N 342.

The Parador Nacional San Francisco is within the Alhambra precinct on a hill overlooking the city of Granada. You need only to follow the well-placed signs to the Alhambra to find it. The building was formerly a Franciscan convent founded by the Catholic Monarchs. It was built on the site of a mosque and palace founded in the 14th century. The convent retains some of the original Moorish construction. The bodies of Ferdinand and Isabella were laid to rest in the convent's crypt before they were taken to the Royal Chapel in the Cathedral of Granada.

It is surrounded by extensive and secluded gardens with an ornamental pool and shaded by trees. At the rear of the Parador there is a broad terrace from where

The Patio de los Leones in the Alhambra, Granada.

the old Moorish district of the Albaicín and the gipsy quarter of Sacromonte can be seen on the opposite hill. Lit by mellow lamplight in the evening it provides a romantic setting for a pre-dinner drink. The most distinctive feature of the Parador is its elegant two-storey patio. The mosaic-cobbled courtyard is dotted with plants and a fountain plays in the centre. The interior is furnished and decorated with antiques and local craftwork, creating a luxurious and welcoming atmosphere.

The restaurant is an attractive room which looks out on to a small courtyard filled with plants. The menu offers a number of local specialities of which the most renowned is Tortilla de Sacromonte, an omelette filled with a mixture of finely chopped calves brains, sweetbreads and liver. A delicately flavoured soup is Sopa de Picadillo, a chicken flavoured broth with chopped hard-boiled eggs and *serrano* ham added. Cordero a la Andalucía is a casserole of small pieces of lamb on the bone with potatoes and flavoured with garlic, paprika and herbs. An unusually flavoured fish dish is Lenguado al Hinojo y Jerez, fillets of sole cooked with sherry and fennel. For pudding there is an opportunity to try the Piononos de Santa Fé.

One of the great pleasures of the Parador San Francisco is that it is, quite literally, on the doorstep of both the Alhambra and the Palacio del Generalife – which means the architect's garden. They are the vast and extraordinarily beautiful gardens which cover the summit of the hill upon which the Moorish palace is built. The most photographed feature is the water garden, a long rectangular pool surrounded by trees and tropical blooms and along which rows of jets project a tunnel of silvery spray over the lake. It sounds just as delightful as it looks. At each end there is a pavilion where you can sit and contemplate the idyllic scene. The remainder of the gardens are equally beautiful. There are long avenues of trees and bushes, flower borders laid out with geometrical precision, and numerous pools and fountains shimmering and rippling in the sunlight.

I'm not sure if the current list of the seven wonders of the world includes the Alhambra – but if not it should. It is a magical place where you can easily become hypnotised by the sheer beauty of the buildings and decorations. A map and guide book are really essential as there is so much to see. The undoubted highlight is the Patio de los Leones the court of the lions, an exquisite courtyard surrounded by arcades supported by slender marble columns. At each end are pavilions of astounding beauty. The golden stone is minutely carved into the most intricate decoration. It is like a superb jewel on a massive scale.

Granada seen from the Mirador of San Cristóbal.

Granada has much more to offer than the Alhambra alone. Don't miss a visit to the Albaicín where a honeycombe of steep, narrow streets cover the hillside opposite the Alhambra. Here too is the hill of Sacromonte where the gipsy homes are carved into the rock and where *zambras* (parties), are held for tourists. From this region there are memorable views of the Alhambra and the massive snow-covered backdrop of the Sierra Nevada.

The cathedral of Santa María de la Encarnación, designed by Diego de Siloe in 1528, is one of the finest Renaissance churches in Spain, impressive both in scale and in the harmony and proportion of its architecture. The interior, nearly 400ft long, contains a wealth of art treasures, including gilded statues of the apostles, beautiful stained-glass windows and numerous tapestries and paintings.

Close to the cathedral is the Alcaicería a reconstruction of the Arab silk exchange which was damaged by fire in the middle of the 19th century. It now houses a market of regional crafts. The remains of the 16th-century Monasterio de la Cartuja is also worth visiting with a cloister and refactory preserved as well as a sacristy with elaborate Baroque decoration. The 14th-century Casa del Carbón, a fascinating example of a Moorish inn, has a courtyard surrounded by three-storey arcades.

If you would like to explore some of the countryside between Granada and the coast an interesting day's round trip can be made into the Sierra de Almíjara. The N 323 leads south of the city through the Puerto del Suspiro del Moro, the pass of the Moor's sigh. It is here that, legend has it, the defeated Moorish King Boabdil wept as he looked back towards the city. A quiet country road strikes off to the south-west through a region of rolling, wheat-covered hills, and shortly afterwards, the road begins to climb into pine-covered mountains.

Quite suddenly you arrive at the summit of a mountain pass from where a vast panorama of mountain peaks is revealed with the road hugging and curving round the steep slopes as it descends. Lower, towards the valley floor, a small road climbs up to the village of Lentejil high on the mountainside surrounded by meadows and trees.

Beyond the small villages of Ortiva and Jete the valley and hillsides are covered by thick jungle-like vegetation. It is called the Tropical Valley because of enormous plantations of avocados, bananas and custard apples which spread through the valley like a wide green river. The road joins the main coast road, the N 340 at Almuñecar and the route now heads west to Nerja (see page 200). Beyond, at the resort of Torre del Mar, the C 335 leads north again to Vélez Málaga where there is a ruined castle. From here the road climbs along the side of a fertile valley, planted with market gardens of olive and almond groves, into the Sierra de Tejeda.

About 20km beyond Vélez Málaga a fork to the right leads to Alhama de Granada, an attractive old town overlooking a steep rocky gorge created by the Río Alhama. Near the town is a thermal spring and there

are both Moorish and Roman baths. The route continues through peaceful olive- and almond-covered hillsides and fields of wheat through Cacín, Ventas de Huelma and Mala to rejoin the N 323 a few kms south of Granada.

SIERRA NEVADA

THE FINAL STAGE OF THE TOUR is to the Parador Nacional de Sierra Nevada, high on the slopes of the Pico Veleta above the ski resort of Sol y Nieve. It is only 25km from Granada but the unique location, nearly 8,000ft above sea level, makes it a fascinating place to stay for at least one night.

The road to the Parador runs, first, along a broad fertile valley which gradually narrows. It then begins to climb in a series of gentle sweeping curves. Soon the tree line is passed and the landscape takes on a grey, bleak appearance. The road continues to climb higher with landscape resembling an aerial-survey photograph. Wayside signs are passed, 1,000m above sea level, 1,500m, 2,000m – soon the road passes above the ski village of Sol y Nieve and the Parador comes into view.

The building is in the style of a mountain lodge with pine floors and ceilings and comfortable leather armchairs. A huge free-standing fireplace dominates the large galleried lounge which overlooks the first-floor restaurant. In front is a large terrace with awesome views of the valley and the massive stark grey peaks surrounding it.

There is usually a dish on the menu which features the famous mountain ham of Trevelez, a village on the other side of the mountains. I had it in the form of Habas con Jamón, casseroled with fresh young broad beans and flavoured with garlic. Gazpacho de Aguacates con Salmón Ahumado is a delicious chilled soup made from avocados and flavoured with pieces of smoked salmon; Salteado de Hongos con Mollejas is wild mountain mushrooms sauteéd with sweetbreads; and Chotos de Guijar en Salsa de Ajos, cutlets of young kid cooked in a garlic sauce.

An excursion from here not to be missed is to the Pico de Veleta. The road continues even higher beyond the Parador to the very summit – the highest road in Europe where the thin air makes itself felt. The twin peaks of Veleta and Mulhacén are the highest in Spain,

rising to over 3,400m. The panorama from the summit is memorable, receding ridges fade into distant haze like cardboard cutouts.

An exciting day's round trip can be made from the Parador. A small road crosses the Sierra Nevada just below the summit of the Mulhacén and descends into the beautiful mountain region of Las Alpujarras. I would hesitate to suggest this route however to a driver – or passenger – who felt anxious about mountain driving. Although not at all dangerous the first section of the road is rather daunting since it is unsurfaced, with an unguarded edge, and you can see the slender ribbon of road snaking round the steep mountainside for miles ahead. It is however a remarkable experience which you will not forget for a long while.

An alternative is to take the N 323 south of Granada and then the C 333 east to the attractive spa town of Lanjarón, known for its mineral water. The road continues to Orjiva where there is a 17th-century church and a castle which belonged to the Counts of Sastago.

The GR 421 leads north to Bubión and Capileira. It is to these towns which the mountain road descends from the summit. Capileira is set on the steep moun-

The mountain village of Juviles in the Alpujarras.

La Calahorra.

tainside and overlooks an immensely deep valley. The small flat-roofed houses, typical of the region, look almost like sugar cubes from a distance, dwarfed as they are by their enormous surroundings. The tiny village of Bubion is also pretty with several craft shops selling the distinctive cotton rugs of the Alpujarras which are woven on huge looms into fine ribbons of colour. From here the road skirts the mountain to the strikingly situated village of Busquístar overlooking a deep rocky valley.

The road now climbs along the side of another valley which leads high into the mountain. It is thickly wooded here, magnificent chestnut trees line the roadside and green meadows cover the slopes. The town of Trevelez soon comes into view. From a distance the cluster of brilliantly white houses look almost like an isolated snowdrift on the mountainside. It is the highest village in Spain, famed for its snow-cured hams and its legend of witches. The road returns along the other side of the valley to the picturesque village of Juviles and continues through Mecina Bombarón and Yegén, once the home of Gerald Brenan, towards the town of Ugíjar. The scenery all along this route is exceptional.

Just before reaching Ugíjar a road leads north to Laroles from where it begins to climb high alongside a huge valley with far-reaching views. It continues to the Puerto de la Ragua from where a gradual descent through pine woods leads to Lacalahorra. There is a dramatic view from the road of the small white town far below and its solid fortress set on a brown rocky hill. A vast bleached plain reaches away to the far horizon which is rimmed by hazy blue ridges.

Beyond Lacalahorra the road joins the N 324, where the route continues westwards to Guadix. It is a historic town, once an Iberian settlement and a Roman military camp, whose magnificent cathedral of sepia stone has a monumental Baroque façade. There is also a 15th-century Moorish Alcazaba and a *plaza mayor* which has been restored after being damaged during the Civil War. There are many troglodyte dwellings in the low rocky hills which border this region. The road continues to Purullena and through the Puerto de la Mora back to Granada. As the road descends to the city there is a superb viewpoint called the Mirador of San Cristóbal, where the classic view of Alhambra is seen with the distant Sierra Nevadas rising up in the background.

The nearest alternative Paradors to those of Granada and the Sierra Nevada are at Nerja (page 200) and Málaga (page 176).

AFTERWORD

*E*ach of the tours has been planned to include the main places of interest in the environs of each parador. The suggested routes between each parador are also intended to ensure that you miss nothing of outstanding interest in the region.

However, such a guide is necessarily selective, and if you have a special interest, for example Romanesque churches, there may well be some additional buildings or locations worthy of a visit which have not been included.

I have used a number of reference books in my research and two have been particularly helpful. Blue Guide: Spain, *published by* Ernest Benn Ltd *and* Spain: A Phaidon Cultural Guide, *published by Phaidon Press Ltd. Both contain a wealth of detailed information on places of historical interest.*

The Spanish National Tourist Office *produce a number of excellent booklets for each of the provinces and many of the cities. In most cases these are available from the relevant parador, so too are locally published guides and maps. For those wishing to book their holiday in advance, the tour operator, Mundi Color, can provide excellent advice and assistance on any tour included in this book.*

As the weather plays an important role in any holiday, here are a few points to remember when deciding on the best times to visit Spain. Needless to say the summer months tend to be very hot in most of the country and are more suited to lazing on beaches than touring. At this time too the paradors are at their busiest and advance booking is advizable for many of them.

However, the season for visiting Spain is considerably longer than many other European countries, and visits throughout the year can be most enjoyable. Andalucía, for example, enjoys a mild winter climate with plenty of sunshine, most of the rain in this region tends to fall in April and early May.

Spring arrives early in many parts of Spain. I travelled through the Maestrazgo in February and the valleys were filled with almond blossom, the first wild flowers were stippling the grass and hedgerows, and it was warm and sunny enough to wear summer clothes.

Summer can also end much later. I drove from Madrid through the Sierra de Gredos to Extremadura and Andalucía returning through La Mancha in November. The weather was wonderful and second crops of wheat and sunflowers, with wild flowers still freshly blooming, made the countryside look like spring again.

Northern Spain however, has a less favourable climate and rain, low cloud and mist are a potential hazard even in summer. I found the best times to visit regions like Galicia, Cantabria and Asturias are in the late spring, early summer and the autumn.

I hope you enjoy Spain as much as I have and, like me, want to visit it again and again.

ACKNOWLEDGEMENTS

I would like to thank Alan Walmsley of Mundi Color for his kind and efficient help with my travel arrangements, Anne Mapson of Fujimex for keeping me supplied with film and Julien Busselle for his help with sorting, mounting and printing the photographs.

Mundi Color: O.T.A. Travel Ltd., 276 Vauxhall Bridge Road, London SW1V 1BE. Tel no: 01-834 3492.

INDEX TO THE PARADORS

The Paradors appear in order of the tours and are situated in the town-centre unless otherwise stated. In addition to the five-star hotel ratings system, I have added my own points system based on a combination of the ambience of a particular Parador, its setting, its outlook and the interest of the building or its immediate surroundings. The point system is as follows:

1. A comfortable and convenient place to stay.
2. Staying there is recommended.
3. Worth a detour to stay there.
4. Exceptional – a real experience – worth planning a trip around.

NORTHERN SPAIN

TOUR ONE

GIL BLAS

A graceful manor house once the home of the local Barreda-Bracho family.
ADDRESS: Plaza de Ramón Pelayo, Santillana del Mar, Cantabria.
TELEPHONE: (942) 81 80 00.
CAPACITY: 52 beds. 24 double and 2 single rooms.
CATEGORY: Three stars.
AMENITIES: A bar, central heating, garage, garden and telephone.
AUTHOR'S POINTS: 4.
THE NEAREST PARADORS: Fuente Dé (101 km), Gijón (166 km), Argómaniz (209 km), Santo Domingo de la Calzada (218 km), Tordesillas (262 km), and Fuenterrabia (273 km).

MOLINO VIEJO

A modern building in the centre of the town beside a peaceful wooded park.
ADDRESS: Parque de Isabel la Católica, Gijón, Asturias.
TELEPHONE: (985) 37 05 11.
CAPACITY: 79 beds. 39 double rooms and 1 single room.
CATEGORY: Four stars.
AMENITIES: A bar, garage, garden, cider bar and telephone.
AUTHOR'S POINTS: 1.
THE NEAREST PARADORS: León (145 km), Santillana del Mar (166 km), Ribadeo (170 km), Fuente Dé (186 km), Benavente (215 km) and Cervera de Pisuerga (220 km).

RIBADEO

A modern parador built on a ledge overlooking the estuary.
ADDRESS: Amador Fernández, Ribadeo, Lugo.
TELEPHONE: (982) 11 08 25.
CAPACITY: 88 beds. 41 double and 6 single rooms.
CATEGORY: Three stars.
AMENITIES: A bar, central heating, garage, garden and telephone.
AUTHOR'S POINTS: 1.
THE NEAREST PARADORS: Villalba (74 km), El Ferrol (142 km), Gijón (170 km), Santiago de Compostela (194 km), Cambados (248 km) and Pontevedra (253 km).

EL FERROL

A parador with a sea-faring atmosphere of dark wood panelling, polished brass, and maps and charts on the walls.
ADDRESS: Almirante Vierna, El Ferrol, La Coruña.
TELEPHONE: (981) 35 67 20.
CAPACITY: 67 beds. 28 double and 11 single rooms.

Parador Gil Blas

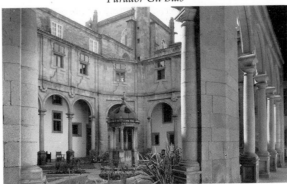

Parador Los Reyes Católicos

Parador Conde de Gondomar

CATEGORY: Three stars.
AUTHOR'S POINTS: 1.
AMENITIES: Air-conditioning, bar, garage, garden, Convention hall and telephone.
THE NEAREST PARADORS: Villalba (68 km), Santiago de Compostela (95 km), Ribadeo (142 km), Cambados (149 km), Pontevedra (154 km), Bayona (180 km) and Tuy (180 km).

TOUR TWO

LOS REYES CATÓLICOS

A unique and historical building, once a hospital founded in 1499 by Fernando and Isabel.
ADDRESS: Plaza de España 1, Santiago de Compostela, La Coruña.
TELEPHONE: (981) 58 22 00.
CAPACITY: 308 beds. 148 double and 6 single rooms and 3 suites.
CATEGORY: Five stars.
AMENITIES: Air-conditioning, bar, individual safes, central heating, garage, garden, shops, concert and exhibition hall, night-club, convention hall and telephone.
AUTHOR'S POINTS: 4.
THE NEAREST PARADORS: Cambados (54 km), Pontevedra (59 km), El Ferrol (95 km), Tuy (108 km), Bayona (114 km) and Villalba (120 km).

EL ALBARIÑO

A granite building in pazo style with a central courtyard and fountain.
ADDRESS: Paseo de Cervantes, Cambados, Pontevedra.
TELEPHONE: (986) 54 22 50.
CAPACITY: 114 beds. 51 double and 12 single rooms.
CATEGORY: Three stars.
AMENITIES: A bar, central heating, garden, Convention hall and telephone.
AUTHOR'S POINTS: 2.
THE NEAREST PARADORS: Pontevedra (25 km), Santiago de Compostela (54 km), Bayona (69 km), Tuy (74 km), El Ferrol (149 km), Villalba (174 km) and Ribadeo (248 km).

CASA DEL BARÓN

An 18th-century palace with a Baroque stone staircase.
ADDRESS: Calle Maceda, Pontevedra.
TELEPHONE: (986) 85 58 00.
CAPACITY: 91 beds. 44 double and 3 single rooms.
CATEGORY: Three stars.
AMENITIES: A bar, library, central heating, garden, Convention hall and telephone.
AUTHOR'S POINTS: 3.
THE NEAREST PARADORS: Cambados (25 km), Tuy (49 km), Bayona

Parador Condes de Villalba

(54 km), Santiago de Compostela (59 km), El Ferrol (154 km) and Verín (175 km).

CONDE DE GONDOMAR

Situated on a promontory surrounded by ancient fortifications.
ADDRESS: Carretera de Bayona, Bayona, Pontevedra.
TELEPHONE: (986) 35 50 00.
CAPACITY: 236 beds. 108 double and 20 single rooms.
CATEGORY: Four stars.
AMENITIES: A bar, central heating, yachting club, garage, seafood restaurant and tavern, swimming pool, beach, Convention halls, social halls, sauna, telephone and tennis.
AUTHOR'S POINTS: 4.
THE NEAREST PARADORS: Tuy (51 km), Pontevedra (54 km), Cambados (69 km) and Santiago de Compostela (113 km).

SAN TELMO

A modern building decorated in traditional pazo style.
ADDRESS: Tuy, Pontevedra.
TELEPHONE: (986) 60 03 09.
CAPACITY: 31 beds. 15 double and 1 single rooms.
CATEGORY: Three stars.

AMENITIES: A bar, central heating, garden, swimming pool and telephone.
AUTHOR'S POINTS: 1.
THE NEAREST PARADORS: Pontevedra (49 km), Bayona (51 km), Cambados (74 km) and Verín (178 km).

TOUR THREE

CONDES DE VILLALBA

An unusual octagonal tower with only six bedrooms.
ADDRESS: Valeriano Valdesuso, Villalba, Lugo.
TELEPHONES: (982) 51 00 11 and 51 00 90.
CAPACITY: 12 beds. 6 double rooms.
CATEGORY: Three stars.
AMENITIES: An elevator, bar, central heating, garden and telephone.
AUTHOR'S POINTS: 2.
THE NEAREST PARADORS: El Ferrol (68 km), Ribadeo (74 km), Santiago de Compostela (95 km), Villafranca del Bierzo (137 km), Pontevedra (170 km) and Cambados (174 km).

VILLAFRANCA DEL BIERZO

A modern two-storey building with spacious bedrooms.

ADDRESS: Avda. Calvo Sotelo, Villafranca del Bierzo, León.
TELEPHONE: (987) 54 01 75.
CAPACITY: 70 beds. 30 double and 10 single rooms.
CATEGORY: Three stars.
AMENITIES: Bar, central heating, garage, garden and telephone.
AUTHOR'S POINTS: 1.
THE NEAREST PARADORS: León (131 km), Villalba (137 km), Benavente (147 km), Ribadeo (189 km), El Ferrol (213 km), and Tordesillas (229 km).

HOTEL DE SAN MARCOS

This ancient convent has a magnificent hall with 16th-century coffered ceiling.
ADDRESS: Plaza de San Marcos, 7., León.
TELEPHONE: (987) 23 73 00.
CAPACITY: 520 beds. 246 double rooms, 10 doubles with sitting room and 2 suites.
CATEGORY: Five stars.
AMENITIES: Air-conditioning, central heating, private dining rooms, children's day-care centre, garden, hairdressers, banquet hall, night club, beauty parlour, Convention hall and telephone.
AUTHOR'S POINTS: 4.

THE NEAREST PARADORS: Benavente (70 km), Villafranca del Bierzo (131 km), Cervera de Pisuerga (133 km), Gijón (145 km) and Puebla de Sanabria (120 km).

FUENTES CARRIONAS

A large modern five-storey building with large balconies overlooking spectacular mountain scenery.
ADDRESS: Cervera de Pisuerga, Palencia.
TELEPHONE: (988) 87 00 75.
CAPACITY: 160 beds. 80 double rooms.
CATEGORY: Three stars.
AMENITIES: Air-conditioning, elevator, bar, central heating, garage, garden, Convention hall and telephone.
AUTHOR'S POINTS: 2.
THE NEAREST PARADORS: Fuente Dé (80 km), Santillana del Mar (112 km), Santo Domingo de la Calzada (179 km), Tordesillas (190 km), Benavente (203 km) and Gijón (220 km).

RIO DEVA

A low modern building, peaceful & remote, standing at the head of the valley.

Two views of the Parador de San Marcos

Parador Río Deva

Parador Santo Domingo de la Calzada

ADDRESS: *Parador Rio Deva, Fuente Dé, Cantabria.*
TELEPHONE: *(942) 73 00 01.*
CAPACITY: *150 beds. 72 double and 6 single rooms.*
CATEGORY: *Three stars.*
AMENITIES: *A bar, central heating, garage, Convention hall and telephone.*
AUTHOR'S POINTS: 4.
THE NEAREST PARADORS: *Cervera de Pisuerga (80 km), Santillana del Mar (101 km), León (175 km) and Gijón (186 km).*

TOUR FOUR

EL EMPERADOR

Once the palace of Carlos V, this is one of the most evocative paradors.
ADDRESS: *Plaza de Armas del Castillo, Fuenterrabia, Guipúzcoa.*
TELEPHONE: *(943) 64 21 40.*
CAPACITY: *30 beds. 14 double and 2 single rooms.*
CATEGORY: *Three stars.*
AMENITIES: *A bar, central heating, garden and telephone.*
AUTHOR'S POINTS: 4.
THE NEAREST PARADORS: *Argomaniz (129 km), Olite*

(156 km), Sos del Rey Católico (173 km), and Santillana del Mar (273 km).

ARGÓMANIZ

A solid stone building, two modern wings each side of a 17th-century palace.
ADDRESS: *Argómaniz, Alava.*
TELEPHONE: *(945) 28 22 00.*
CAPACITY: *108 beds. 54 double rooms.*
CATEGORY: *Three stars.*
AMENITIES: *A bar, central heating, Convention hall and telephone.*
AUTHOR'S POINTS: 2.
THE NEAREST PARADORS: *Santo Domingo de la Calzada (75 km), Olite (122 km), Fuenterrabia (129 km) and Calahorra (147 km).*

SANTO DOMINGO DE LA CALZADA

An old hospice, with huge stone arches and beautiful antique furniture.
ADDRESS: *Plaza del Santo, 3, Santo Domingo de la Calzada, La Rioja.*
TELEPHONE: *(941) 34 03 00.*
CAPACITY: *52 beds. 25 double and 2 single rooms.*

AMENITIES: *A bar, central heating, Convention hall and telephone.*
AUTHOR'S POINTS: 4
THE NEAREST PARADORS: *Argómaniz (75 km), Calahorra (95 km) and Soria (151 km).*

TOUR FIVE

MARCO FABIO QUINTILIANO

A contemporary building with a traditional ambience.
ADDRESS: *Era Alta, Calahorra, La Rioja.*
TELEPHONES: *(941) 13 03 58 and 13 03 62.*
CAPACITY: *120 beds. 57 double and 6 single rooms.*
CATEGORY: *Three stars.*
AMENITIES *Air-conditioning, elevator, bar, central heating, garage, Convention hall and telephone.*
AUTHOR'S POINTS: 1.
THE NEAREST PARADORS: *Olite (70 km), Santo Domingo de la Calzada (95 km), Soria (116 km) and Sos del Rey Católico (121 km).*

PRÍNCIPE DE VIANA

This parador forms part of a magnificent 15th-century castle with a complex of turrets, towers and battlements.
ADDRESS: *Plaza de San Francisco, Olite, Navarra.*
TELEPHONES: *(948) 74 00 00, 74 00 01, 74 01 50 and 74 02 01.*
CAPACITY: *77 beds, 38 double and 1 single rooms.*
CATEGORY: *Three stars.*
AMENITIES: *A bar, central heating, Convention hall and telephone.*
AUTHOR'S POINTS: 4
THE NEAREST PARADORS: *Sos del Rey Católico (51 km), Calahorra (70 km), Argómaniz (122 km), Santo Domingo de la Calzada (136 km), Soria (142 km) and Fuenterrabia (156 km).*

FERNANDO DE ARAGÓN

Built with local wood and stone this modern building blends in well with the older parts of the town.
ADDRESS: *Sos del Rey Católico, Zaragoza.*
TELEPHONE: *(948) 88 80 11.*
CAPACITY: *126 beds. 60 double and 6 single rooms.*
CATEGORY: *Three stars.*
AMENITIES: *Air-conditioning, elevator, bar, central heating, garage, garden, Convention hall and telephone.*
AUTHOR'S POINTS: 3.
THE NEAREST PARADORS: *Olite (51 km), Calahorra (121 km), Argómaniz (139 km), Fuenterrabia (173 km), Santo Domingo de la Calzada (192 km), Soria (193 km) and Vielsa (304 km).*

TOUR SIX

FERNANDO II DE LEON

A restored castle, with original 18th-century keep.
ADDRESS: *Benavente, Zamora.*
TELEPHONES: *(988) 63 03 00 and 63 03 04.*
CAPACITY: *83 beds. 39 double and 5 single rooms.*
CATEGORY: *Four stars.*
AMENITIES: *Air-conditioning, bar, garage, garden, Convention hall and telephone.*
AUTHOR'S POINTS: 2.
THE NEAREST PARADORS: *Zamora (65 km), León (70 km), Tordesillas (82 km), Puebla de Sanabria (84 km) and Villafranca del Bierzo (147 km).*

PUEBLA DE SANABRIA

A modern building simply decorated with marble floors and wooden panelling.
ADDRESS: *Puebla de Sanabria, Zamora.*
TELEPHONE: *(988) 62 00 01.*

Parador Príncipe de Viana

CAPACITY: *83 beds. 39 double and 5 single rooms. (It will soon be expanded to 46 double rooms.)*
CATEGORY: *Three stars.*
AMENITIES: *A bar, library, central heating, garden, Convention hall, casino and telephone.*
AUTHOR'S POINTS: *2.*
THE NEAREST PARADORS: *Benavente (84 km), Verín (98 km), Zamora (110 km), León (154 km) and Villafranca del Bierzo (187 km).*

MONTERREY

A modern building set on a steep vine-clad hill on the outskirts of Verín.
ADDRESS: *Castillo de Monterrey, Verín, Orense.*
TELEPHONES: *(988) 41 00 75 and 41 00 76.*
CAPACITY: *45 beds. 22 double and 1 single rooms.*
CATEGORY: *Three stars.*
AMENITIES: *A bar, central heating, garage, garden, swimming pool and telephone.*
AUTHOR'S POINTS: *2.*
THE NEAREST PARADORS: *Puebla de Sanabria (98 km), Pontevedra (175 km), Tuy (178 km), Benavente (182 km), Bayona (199 km), Cambados (200 km) and Zamora (209 km).*

CENTRAL SPAIN

— TOUR SEVEN —

PARADOR DE SEGOVIA

A modern building set on a natural terrace with splendid views, on the outskirts of Segovia.
ADDRESS: *Apartado 106, Segovia.*
TELEPHONE: *(911) 43 04 62.*
CAPACITY: *155 beds. 75 double and 5 single rooms.*
CATEGORY: *Four stars.*
AMENITIES: *Air-conditioning, bar, central heating, garden, swimming pool, indoor, heated pool, Convention hall, sauna and telephone.*

Parador Condes de Alba y Aliste

AUTHOR'S POINTS: *3.*
THE NEAREST PARADORS: *Pedraza (36 km), Ávila (65 km), Tordesillas (116 km), Gredos (130 km), Toledo (158 km), Sigüenza (185 km) and Soria (194 km).*

PARADOR DE TORDESILLAS

A modern single-storey building, set in a pine forest.
ADDRESS: *Tordesillas, Valladolid.*
TELEPHONE: *(983) 77 00 51.*
CAPACITY: *138 beds. 65 double and 8 single rooms.*
CATEGORY: *Three stars.*
AMENITIES: *Air-conditioning, bar, central heating, garden, swimming pool. Convention hall and telephone.*
AUTHOR'S POINTS: *1.*
THE NEAREST PARADORS: *Zamora (65 km), Benavente (82 km), Salamanca (85 km), Ávila (110 km), Segovia (116 km), León (152 km), Ciudad Rodrigo (173 km) and Fuentes Carrionas (190 km).*

CONDES DE ALBA Y ALISTE

A 15th-century palace on a quiet square, where beautiful cloisters surround a central courtyard.
ADDRESS: *Plaza de Cánovas, Zamora.*
TELEPHONE: *(988) 51 44 97.*
CAPACITY: *54 beds. 25 double rooms and 2 singles.*
CATEGORY: *Four stars.*
AMENITIES: *A bar, central heating, garage, garden, swimming pool, Convention hall and telephone.*
AUTHOR'S POINTS: *3.*
THE NEAREST PARADORS: *Salamanca (62 km), Benavente (65 km), Tordesillas (66 km), Puebla de Sanabria (110 km) and León (135 km).*

ENRIQUE II

This 14th-century castle dominates the town with its massive walls and impressive gateways.
ADDRESS: *Plaza del Castillo, 1, Ciudad Rodrigo, Salamanca.*

Parador Carlos V

Parador de Gredos

TELEPHONE: *(923) 46 01 50.*
CAPACITY: *54 beds. 26 double rooms and 1 suite.*
CATEGORY: *Three stars.*
AMENITIES: *Air-conditioning, central heating, garden, Convention hall and telephone.*
AUTHOR'S POINTS: *4.*
THE NEAREST PARADORS: *Salamanca (89 km), Zamora (151 km), Tordesillas (183 km), Trujillo (206 km) and Guadalupe (288 km).*

— TOUR EIGHT —

RAIMUNDO DE BORGOÑA

Situated in part of the town walls, the Parador occupies a 15th-century palace with a modern extension.
ADDRESS: *Marqués de Canales y Chozas, 16, Ávila.*
TELEPHONE: *(918) 21 13 40.*
CAPACITY: *121 beds. 59 double and 3 single rooms.*
CATEGORY: *Three stars.*
AMENITIES: *An elevator, bar, central heating, garden, Convention hall and telephone.*
AUTHOR'S POINTS: *3.*

THE NEAREST PARADORS: *Gredos (65 km), Segovia (65 km), Salamanca (97 km), Tordesillas (110 km) and Toledo (184 km).*

PARADOR DE SALAMANCA

A modern white building overlooking the magnificent golden-bricked city of Salamanca.
ADDRESS: *Teso de la Feria, 2, Salamanca.*
TELEPHONE: *(923) 22 87 00.*
CAPACITY: *206 beds. 94 double and 10 single rooms and 4 suites.*
CATEGORY: *Four stars.*
AMENITIES: *Air-conditioning, elevator, bar, central heating, garage, garden, swimming pool, Convention hall and telephone.*
AUTHOR'S POINTS: *2.*
THE NEAREST PARADORS: *Zamora (62 km), Tordesillas (85 km), Ciudad Rodrigo (89 km), Ávila (97 km) and Trujillo (258 km).*

CARLOS V

One of the oldest castles in Spain, built in the 14th-century.
ADDRESS: *Apartado 15, Jarandilla de la Vera, Cáceres.*

TELEPHONE: *(976) 56 01 17.*
CAPACITY: *82 beds. 39 double and 4 single rooms.*
CATEGORY: *Three stars.*
AMENITIES: *Air-conditioning, bar, central heating, garden and telephone.*
AUTHOR'S POINTS: 3.
THE NEAREST PARADORS: *Oropesa (66 km), Trujillo (103 km), Gredos (107 km) and Guadalupe (108 km), Ávila (145 km), Nérida (193 km) and Zafra (253 km).*

PARADOR DE GREDOS

A peaceful, isolated parador surrounded by snow-covered mountains.
ADDRESS: *Navarredonda, Ávila.*
TELEPHONE: *(918) 34 80 48.*
CAPACITY: *150 beds. 73 double and 4 single rooms.*
CATEGORY: *Three stars.*
AMENITIES: *A bar, library, central heating, garage, garden, Convention hall and telephone.*
AUTHOR'S POINTS: 3.
THE NEAREST PARADORS: *Ávila (65 km), Oropesa (103 km), Jarandilla de la Vera (107 km), Toledo (160 km) and Ciudad Rodrigo (171 km).*

—— TOUR NINE ——

CASTILLO DE SIGÜENZA

A magnificent castle with stone archways and wooden ceilings.
ADDRESS: *Sigüenza, Guadalajara.*
TELEPHONE: *(911) 39 01 00.*
CAPACITY: *166 beds. 74 double and 3 single rooms.*
CATEGORY: *Four stars.*
AMENITIES: *Air-conditioning, bar, central heating, Convention hall and telephone.*
AUTHOR'S POINTS: 4.
THE NEAREST PARADORS: *Santa María de Huerta (64 km), Soria (100 km), Alcalá de Henares (100 km), Chinchón (150 km) and Teruel (185 km).*

SANTA MARÍA DE HUERTA

Spacious, comfortable motel-style building.
ADDRESS: *Santa María de Huerta, Soria.*
TELEPHONE: *(975) 32 70 11.*
CAPACITY: *78 beds. 38 double and 2 single rooms.*
CATEGORY: *Three stars.*
AMENITIES: *Air-conditioning, bar, central heating, garage, garden, Convention hall and telephone.*
AUTHOR'S POINTS: 1.
THE NEAREST PARADORS: *Sigüenza (64 km), Soria (104 km), Alcañiz (220 km), Santo Domingo de la Calzada (255 km) and Sos del Rey Católico (268 km).*

ANTONIO MACHADO

A stylish modern building set on the very brink of the hill overlooking the river.
ADDRESS: *Parque del Castillo, Soria.*
TELEPHONE: *(975) 21 34 45.*
CAPACITY: *64 beds. 30 double and 4 single rooms.*
CATEGORY: *Three stars.*
AMENITIES: *A bar, central heating, garage, garden, Convention hall and telephone.*
AUTHOR'S POINTS: 1.
THE NEAREST PARADORS: *Sigüenza (100 km), Santa María de Huerta (104 km), Calahorra (116 km), Olite (142 km), Santo Domingo de la Calzada (151 km) and Segovia (194 km).*

—— TOUR TEN ——

PARADOR DE CHINCHÓN

Once a convent, this elegant building is filled with ornate furnishings.
ADDRESS: *Avda. Generalísimo, 1, Chinchón, Madrid.*
TELEPHONE: *(91) 894 08 36.*
CAPACITY: *76 beds. 36 double rooms and 2 suites.*
CATEGORY: *Four stars.*
AMENITIES: *Air-conditioning, bar,*

Parador de Chinchón

AUTHOR'S POINTS: 4.
THE NEAREST PARADORS: *Alcalá de Henares (50 km), Toledo (69 km), Sigüenza (150 km) and Alarcón (153 km).*

—— TOUR TEN ——

CONDE DE ORGAZ

A spacious modern building with breathtaking views, situated on the outskirts of Toledo.
ADDRESS: *Paseo de los Cigarrales, Toledo.*
TELEPHONES: *(925) 22 18 50 and 22 18 54.*
TELEX: *47998 RRPT.*
CAPACITY: *142 beds. 67 double and 8 single rooms.*
CATEGORY: *Four stars.*
AMENITIES: *Air-conditioning, bar, central heating, garage, garden, swimming pool, Convention hall and telephone.*
AUTHOR'S POINTS: 3.
THE NEAREST PARADORS: *Oropesa (112 km), Manzanares (123 km), Almagro (143 km), Segovia (158 km), Gredos (160 km), Jarandilla de la Vera (177 km), Ávila (184 km) and Guadalupe (202 km).*

PARADOR DE MANZANARES

A large modern hotel.
ADDRESS: *Manzanares, Ciudad Real.*
TELEPHONE: *(926) 61 04 00.*
CAPACITY: *100 beds. 50 double rooms.*
CATEGORY: *Three stars.*
AMENITIES: *Air-conditioning, elevator, bar, central heating, garden, swimming pool, Convention hall and telephone.*
AUTHOR'S POINTS: 1.
THE NEAREST PARADORS: *Almagro (35 km), Bailén (122 km), Toledo (123 km) and Albacete (154 km).*

PARADOR DE ALMAGRO

A vast 15th-century convent with sixteen courtyards and patios.
ADDRESS: *Almagro, Ciudad Real.*
TELEPHONE: *(926) 86 01 00.*
CAPACITY: *104 beds. 48 double and 6 single rooms and 1 suite.*
CATEGORY: *Four stars.*
AMENITIES: *Air-conditioning bar, typical wine-cellar, central heating, garden, swimming pool, Convention hall and telephone.*
AUTHOR'S POINTS: 3.

Parador Castillo de Sigüenza

THE NEAREST PARADORS:
Manzanares (35 km), Bailén (130 km), Toledo (143 km), Jaén (167 km), Úbeda (169 km), Albacete (190 km), Alarcón (248 km) and Guadalupe (345 km).

TOUR ELEVEN

PARADOR VIRREY TOLEDO

A medieval castle with large courtyard.
ADDRESS: *Plaza del Palacio, 1, Oropesa, Toledo.*
TELEPHONE: *(923) 43 00 00.*
CAPACITY: *86 beds. 42 double and 2 single rooms.*
CATEGORY: *Four stars.*
AMENITIES: *Air-conditioning, elevator, bar, central heating, Conventional hall and telephone.*
AUTHOR'S POINTS: *4.*
THE NEAREST PARADORS: *Jarandilla de la Vera (66 km), Guadalupe (90 km), Trujillo (102 km), Gredos (103 km) and Toledo (112 km).*

ZURBARÁN

Once a 15th-century hospice, the rooms look onto a central courtyard with Moorish-style gardens.

ADDRESS: *Marqués de la Romana, 10, Guadalupe, Cáceres.*
TELEPHONES: *(927) 36 70 75 and 36 70 76.*
CAPACITY: *80 beds. 40 double rooms.*
CATEGORY: *Three stars.*
AMENITIES: *Air-conditioning, bar, central heating, garage, garden, swimming pool and telephone.*
AUTHOR'S POINTS: *4.*
THE NEAREST PARADORS: *Trujillo (82 km), Oropesa (90 km), Jarandilla de la Vera (108 km), Mérida (131 km), Zafra (191 km) and Toledo (202 km).*

PARADOR DE TRUJILLO

This parador is the old convent of Trujillo, a charming town in the midst of wild heathland rimmed by distant mountains.
ADDRESS: *Plaza de Santa Clara, Trujillo.*
TELEPHONE: *(927) 32 13 50.*
CAPACITY: *92 beds. 45 double rooms and 1 suite.*
CATEGORY: *Four stars.*
AMENITIES: *Air-conditioning, bar, central heating, garage, garden, Convention hall and telephone.*
AUTHOR'S POINTS: *3.*

Parador Zurbarán

THE NEAREST PARADORS:
Guadalupe (82 km), Mérida (90 km), Oropesa (102 km) and Jarandilla de la Vera (103 km).

VIA DE LA PLATA

This Baroque 15th-century convent faces onto a quiet square, a short walk from the centre of Mérida.
ADDRESS: *Plaza de Queipo de Llano, 3, Mérida, Badajoz.*
TELEPHONE: *(924) 31 38 00.*
CAPACITY: *99 beds. 49 double and 1 single rooms.*
CATEGORY: *Four stars.*
AMENITIES: *Air-conditioning, bar, library, central heating, garage, garden, Convention hall and telephone.*
AUTHOR'S POINTS: *2.*
THE NEAREST PARADORS: *Zafra (60 km), Trujillo (90 km), Guadalupe (131 km) and Jarandilla de la Vera (193 km).*

HERNÁN CORTÉS

This parador is a 15th-century palace, beautifully decorated with cool white marble, painted ceilings and a magnificent two-storey Renaissance patio.

ADDRESS: *Plaza de María Cristina, Zafra, Badajoz.*
TELEPHONE: *(924) 55 02 00.*
CAPACITY: *50 beds. 22 double and 6 single rooms.*
CATEGORY: *Three stars.*
AMENITIES: *Air-conditioning, bar, central heating, garden, swimming pool, Convention hall and telephone.*
AUTHOR'S POINTS: *3.*
THE NEAREST PARADORS: *Mérida (60 km), Trujillo (150 km), Guadalupe (191 km), Córdoba (195 km) and Carmona (225 km).*

EASTERN SPAIN

TOUR TWELVE

COSTA BRAVA

A low white building overlooking a beautiful sandy beach, light and airy interior.
ADDRESS: *Aiguablava, Gerona.*
TELEPHONE: *(972) 62 21 62.*
CAPACITY: *156 beds. 69 double and 18 single rooms.*
CATEGORY: *Four stars.*
AMENITIES: *Air-conditioning, elevator, bar, central heating, gymnasium, garden, swimming pool, beach, Convention hall, sauna and telephone.*

Parador de Almagro

Parador Via de la Plata

Parador Hernán Cortés

Parador Costa Brava

AUTHOR'S POINTS: *4.*
THE NEAREST PARADORS: *Vich (177 km), Cardona (233 km) and Tortosa (327 km).*

PARADOR DE VICH

Styled as a traditional Catalan farmhouse this isolated parador overlooks a beautiful lake.
ADDRESS: *Vich, Barcelona.*
TELEPHONE: *(93) 888 72 11.*
CAPACITY: *56 beds. 25 double and 6 single rooms.*
CATEGORY: *Four Stars.*
AMENITIES: *Air-conditioning, elevator, bar, garage, garden, swimming pool, Convention hall, telephone and tennis.*
AUTHOR'S POINTS: *3.*
THE NEAREST PARADORS: *Cardona (100 km), Seo de Urgel (151 km), Aiguablava (177 km) and Tortosa (262 km).*

DUQUES DE CARDONA

Set in a 9th-century castle with an ancient tower built in the 2nd century.
ADDRESS: *Cardona, Barcelona.*
TELEPHONES: *(93) 869 12 75, 869 13 00 and 869 13 50.*
CAPACITY: *123 beds. 58 double and*

7 single rooms.
CATEGORY: *Four stars.*
AMENITIES: *Air-conditioning, elevator, bar, central heating, Convention hall and telephone.*
AUTHOR'S POINTS: *3.*
THE NEAREST PARADORS: *Seo de Urgel (93 km), Vich (100 km), Artíes (205 km), Viella (212 km), Tortosa (231 km) and Aiguablava (233 km).*

—— TOUR THIRTEEN ——

PARADOR SEO DE URGEL

This parador built in the 14th-century, has a preserved Romanesque cloister covered by a glass roof, which is now a lounge.
ADDRESS: *Seo de Urgell, Lérida.*
TELEPHONE: *(973) 35 20 00.*
CAPACITY: *144 beds. 60 double and 24 single rooms.*
CATEGORY: *Three stars.*
AMENITIES: *Air-conditioning, elevator, bar, central heating, garage and indoor, heated pool.*
AUTHOR'S POINTS: *1.*
THE NEAREST PARADORS: *Cardona (93 km), Artíes (124 km), Viella (131 km), Vich (151 km) and Aiguablava (326 km).*

PARADOR VALLE DE ARÁN

A hunting-lodge style Parador, with its circular lounge providing sweeping views across three valleys.
ADDRESS: *Viella, Lérida.*
TELEPHONE: *(973) 64 01 00.*
CAPACITY: *251 beds. 116 double and 19 single rooms.*
CATEGORY: *Three stars.*
AMENITIES: *An elevator, bar, central heating, garage, garden, swimming pool, Convention hall and telephone.*
AUTHOR'S POINTS: *3.*
THE NEAREST PARADORS: *Artíes (7 km), Seo de Urgel (131 km) and Vielsa (163 km).*

DON GASPAR DE PÓRTOLA

A modern building constructed in the local style, set in the mountains.
ADDRESS: *Artíes, Lérida.*
TELEPHONES: *(973) 64 08 01 and 64 08 02.*
CAPACITY: *80 beds. 40 double rooms.*
CATEGORY: *Four stars.*
AMENITIES: *Air-conditioning, bar, central heating, garage, Convention hall and telephone.*
AUTHOR'S POINTS: *3.*
THE NEAREST PARADORS: *Viella (7 km), Seo de Urgel (124 km), Vielsa (170 km), Cardona (205 km) and Vich (290 km).*

MONTE PERDIDO

A granite building in the style of a hunting lodge, set high in the mountains.
ADDRESS: *Valle de Pineta, Bielsa, Huesca.*
TELEPHONES: *(974) 50 10 11 and 50 10 36.*
CAPACITY: *32 beds. 16 double.*
CATEGORY: *Three stars.*
AMENITIES: *A bar, central heating, garage, garden, playground, Convention hall and telephone.*
AUTHOR'S POINTS: *3.*
THE NEAREST PARADORS: *Viella (163 km), Artíes (170 km), Sos del Rey Católico (304 km) and Olite (343 km).*

—— TOUR FOURTEEN ——

COSTA DEL AZAHAR

A two-storey building in the form of a square, situated by the coast.
ADDRESS: *Avda. de Papa Luna, 3, Benicarló, Castellón.*
TELEPHONE: *(964) 47 01 00.*
CAPACITY: *201 beds. 93 double and 15 single rooms.*
CATEGORY: *Three stars.*
AMENITIES: *Air-conditioning, bar, central heating, garage, garden, swimming pool, beach, telephone and tennis.*

Parador Valle de Arán

Parador La Concordia

AUTHOR'S POINTS: 2.
THE NEAREST PARADORS: *Tortosa (52 km), Alcañiz (145 km), El Saler (153 km), Teruel (234 km), Jávea (245 km) and Alarcón (303 km).*

CASTILLO DE LA ZUDA

A modern granite construction. The bedrooms have large wooden balconies with fine views.
ADDRESS: *(Apartado 157), Tortosa, Tarragona.*
TELEPHONE: *(977) 44 44 50.*
CAPACITY: *155 beds. 73 double and 9 single rooms.*
CATEGORY: *Four stars.*
AMENITIES: *Air-conditioning, bar, central heating, garden, play ground, swimming pool, Convention hall and telephone.*
AUTHOR'S POINTS: 2.
THE NEAREST PARADORS: *Benicarló (52 km), Alcañiz (106 km), El Saler (205 km), Cardona (231 km) and Vich (262 km).*

LA CONCORDIA

A magnificent castle with a grand stone staircase, terracotta floors and walls decorated with heraldic flags.
ADDRESS: *Castillo de Calatravos, Alcañiz, Teruel.*
TELEPHONES: *(974) 83 04 00 and 83 04 04.*
CAPACITY: *22 beds. 10 double and 2 single rooms.*
CATEGORY: *Three stars.*
AMENITIES: *A bar, central heating and telephone.*
AUTHOR'S POINTS: 3.
THE NEAREST PARADORS: *Tortosa (106 km), Benicarló (145 km), Teruel (162 km), Santa María de Huerta (220 km) and Soria (253 km).*

PARADOR DE TERUEL

A traditional style parador with marble floors, high ceilings and simple white decor.
ADDRESS: *(Apartado 67), Teruel.*
TELEPHONE: *(974) 60 25 53.*
CAPACITY: *124 beds. 58 double*

rooms and 2 suites.
CATEGORY: *Three stars.*
AMENITIES: *Air-conditioning, elevator, garage, garden, swimming pool, Convention hall, telephone and tennis.*
AUTHOR'S POINTS: 1.
THE NEAREST PARADORS: *Alcañiz (162 km), El Saler (163 km), Sigüenza (185 km), Santa María de Huerta (198 km), Alarcón (220 km), Benicarló (234 km), Albacete (240 km) and Jávea (255 km).*

TOUR FIFTEEN

MARQUÉS DE VILLENA

One of the finest castles in the region built during the early years of Moorish occupation.
ADDRESS: *Avda. Amigos del Castillo, Alarcón, Cuenca.*
TELEPHONE: *(966) 33 13 50.*
CAPACITY: *21 beds. 10 double and 1 single rooms.*
CATEGORY: *Three stars.*
AMENITIES: *An elevator, central heating, garden and telephone.*
AUTHOR'S POINTS: 3.
THE NEAREST PARADORS: *Albacete (90 km), Chinchón (153 km), El Saler (186 km), Teruel (208 km), Toledo (211 km) and Manzanares (212 km).*

LA MANCHA

A modern building with terracotta tiles and mellow wooden furniture on the outskirts of Albacete.
ADDRESS: *La Mancha, Albacete.*
TELEPHONE: *(967) 22 94 50.*
CAPACITY: *137 beds. 67 double and 3 single rooms.*
CATEGORY: *Three stars.*
AMENITIES: *Air-conditioning, bar, central heating, garden, swimming pool, Convention hall, telephone and tennis.*
AUTHOR'S POINTS: 1.
THE NEAREST PARADORS: *Alarcón (90 km), Manzanares (154 km), El Saler (209 km), Úbeda (210 km) and Jávea (262 km).*

COSTA BLANCA

A typical modern Spanish hotel with balconies for every bedroom looking onto beautiful beaches.
ADDRESS: *Jávea, Alicante.*
TELEPHONE: *(965) 79 02 00.*
CAPACITY: *130 beds. 65 double rooms.*
CATEGORY: *Four stars.*
AMENITIES: *Air-conditioning, elevator, bar, library, central heating, garage, garden, swimming pool, Convention hall and telephone.*
AUTHOR'S POINTS: 2.
THE NEAREST PARADORS: *El Saler (92 km), Puerto Lumbreras (247 km), Albacete (262 km) and Mojácar (308 km).*

LUIS VIVES

A long building hidden among the pines next to a long sandy beach, and near the lagoon of La Albufera.
ADDRESS: *El Saler, Valencia.*
TELEPHONE: *(96) 323 68 50.*
CAPACITY: *116 beds. 58 double rooms.*
CATEGORY: *Four stars.*
AMENITIES: *Air-conditioning, bar, central heating, football field, garage, golf, garden, swimming pool, beach, Convention hall, telephone and tennis.*
AUTHOR'S POINTS: 2.
THE NEAREST PARADORS: *Jávea (92 km), Benicarló (153 km), Teruel (163 km), Tortosa (205 km) and Albacete (209 km).*

SOUTHERN SPAIN

TOUR SIXTEEN

PARADOR DE GIBRALFARO

Constructed in a regional style, with tall elegant arches, this parador stands on a wooded hillside next to Gibralfaro castle.
ADDRESS: *Gibralfaro, Málaga.*
TELEPHONE: *(952) 22 19 02.*
CAPACITY: *23 beds. 11 double and 1 single rooms.*

CATEGORY: *Three stars.*
AMENITIES: *A bar, central heating and telephone.*
AUTHOR'S POINTS: 3.
THE NEAREST PARADORS: *Torremolinos (10 km), Nerja (51 km), Antequera (51 km), Granada (134 km), Córdoba (178 km) and Carmona (188 km).*

PARADOR DE ANTEQUERA

A modern building set in peaceful gardens with lovely views over the plain.
ADDRESS: *Parque de María Cristina, Antequera, Málaga.*
TELEPHONE: *(952) 84 02 61.*
CAPACITY: *110 beds. 55 double rooms.*
CATEGORY: *Three stars.*
AMENITIES: *Air-conditioning, bar, central heating, garden, swimming pool, Convention hall and telephone.*
AUTHOR'S POINTS: 1.
THE NEAREST PARADORS: *Málaga (51 km), Torremolinos (61 km), Granada (95 km), Nerja (102 km) and Córdoba (127 km).*

LA ARRUZAFA

A modern parador set in the old gardens of Abderramian I.
ADDRESS: *Avda. de la Arruzafa, Córdoba.*
TELEPHONE: *(957) 27 59 00.*
CAPACITY: *163 beds. 80 double and 3 single rooms.*
CATEGORY: *Four stars.*
AMENITIES: *Air-conditioning, elevator, bar, library, central heating, garden, swimming pool, Convention hall, telephone and tennis.*
AUTHOR'S POINTS: 2.
THE NEAREST PARADORS: *Jaén (104 km), Bailén (105 km), Carmona (109 km), Antequera (127 km), Úbeda (144 km), Málaga (178 km), Torremolinos (188 km) and Nerja (229 km).*

ALCÁZAR DEL REY DON PEDRO

This parador stands on the site of one of the old defending castles of Seville

Parador Gibralfaro

Parador Alcázar del Rey Don Pedro

converted into a palace by Pedro I of Castille.
ADDRESS: *Carmona, Sevilla.*
TELEPHONE: *(954) 14 10 10.*
CAPACITY: *110 beds. 51 double and 8 single rooms.*
CATEGORY: *Four stars.*
AMENITIES: *Air-conditioning, elevator, bar, central heating, garden, swimming pool, Convention hall and telephone.*
AUTHOR'S POINTS: *3.*
THE NEAREST PARADORS: *Cordoba (109 km), Arcos de la Frontera (120 km), Antequera (137 km), Mazagón (147 km), Cádiz (154 km) and Ayamonte (185 km).*

TOUR SEVENTEEN

COSTA DE LA LUZ

This single-storey parador enjoys sweeping views over the river, sea and Portuguese countryside.
ADDRESS: *El Castillo, Ayamonte, Huelva.*
TELEPHONE: *(955) 32 07 00.*
CAPACITY: *40 beds. 20 double rooms.*
CATEGORY: *Three stars.*
AMENITIES: *Air-conditioning, bar, central heating, garden, swimming pool, Convention hall and telephone.*
AUTHOR'S POINTS: *1.*
THE NEAREST PARADORS: *Mazagón (85 km), Carmona (185 km), Arcos de la Frontera (247 km), Cádiz (281 km) and Córdoba (294 km).*

CRISTÓBAL COLÓN

This low white building, hidden amongst pine trees, overlooks the shores of the Atlantic Ocean.
ADDRESS: *Mazagón, Huelva.*
TELEPHONE: *(955) 37 60 00.*
CAPACITY: *46 beds. 23 rooms.*
CATEGORY: *Three stars.*
AMENITIES: *Air-conditioning, bar, central heating, garden, swimming pool, Convention hall and telephone.*
AUTHOR'S POINTS: *3.*
THE NEAREST PARADORS: *Ayamonte (85 km), Carmona*

(147 km), Cádiz (243 km) and Zafra (258 km).*

HOTEL ATLÁNTICO

Overlooking the sea this parador is built in the established style of Mediterranean hotels and is famous for its view of spectacular sunsets.
ADDRESS: *Duque de Nájera, 9, Cádiz.*
TELEPHONE: *(956) 22 69 05.*
CAPACITY: *306 beds. 153 double.*
CATEGORY: *Three stars.*
AMENITIES: *Air-conditioning, elevator, bar, central heating, garage, garden, swimming pool, Convention hall, snack bar and telephone.*
AUTHOR'S POINTS: *2.*
THE NEAREST PARADORS: *Arcos de la Frontera (63 km), Carmona (154 km), Mazagón (243 km), Torremolinos (255 km), Málaga (265 km) and Ayamonte (281 km).*

CASA DEL CORREGIDOR

This parador was formerly the mansion of Gonzalez de Gameza, and is now a comfortable hotel.
ADDRESS: *Plaza de España, Arcos de la Frontera, Cádiz.*
TELEPHONE: *(956) 70 05 00.*
CAPACITY: *44 beds. 20 double and 4 single rooms.*
CATEGORY: *Three stars.*
AMENITIES: *Air-conditioning, bar, library, central heating and telephone.*
AUTHOR'S POINTS: *4.*
THE NEAREST PARADORS: *Cádiz (63 km), Carmona (120 km), Antequera (144 km), Málaga (195 km), Torremolinos (205 km), Córdoba (229 km) and Granada (239 km).*

GOLF PARADOR

This parador is surrounded by a splendid golf course and quiet sandy beach.
ADDRESS: *Torremolinos, Málaga or Apartado no. 324, Málaga.*
TELEPHONE: *(952) 38 12 55.*

CAPACITY: *78 beds. 38 double and 2 single rooms.*
CATEGORY: *Four stars.*
AMENITIES: *Air-conditioning, bar, library, central heating, golf, garden, swimming pool, beach, Convention hall, telephone and tennis.*
AUTHOR'S POINTS: *1.*
THE NEAREST PARADORS: *Málaga (10 km), Nerja (61 km), Antequera (61 km) and Granada (134 km).*

TOUR EIGHTEEN

PARADOR DE NERJA

Built on the clifftop this parador overlooks Burriana, one of the finest beaches on the Costa del Sol.
ADDRESS: *Nerja, Málaga.*
TELEPHONE: *(952) 52 00 50.*
CAPACITY: *117 beds. 57 double and 3 single rooms.*
CATEGORY: *Four stars.*
AMENITIES: *Air-conditioning, bar, central heating, garden, swimming pool, beach, Convention hall, telephone and tennis.*
AUTHOR'S POINTS: *3.*
THE NEAREST PARADORS: *Málaga (51 km), Torremolinos (61 km), Antequera (102 km), Granada (106 km), Sierra Nevada (141 km) and Mojácar (253 km).*

REYES CATÓLICOS

Set on the shores of the Mediterranean, this parador is ideal for water sports and fishing enthusiasts.
ADDRESS: *Mojácar, Almería.*
TELEPHONE: *(951) 47 82 50.*
CAPACITY: *187 beds. 89 double and 9 single rooms.*
CATEGORY: *Four stars.*
AMENITIES: *Air-conditioning, bar, central heating, garden, swimming pool, telephone and tennis.*
AUTHOR'S POINTS: *2.*
THE NEAREST PARADORS: *Puerto Lumbreras (60 km), Granada (214 km), Sierra Nevada (249 km), Nerja (253 km), Albacete (291 km), Jávea (307 km) and Málaga (317 km).*

PUERTO LUMBRERAS

Quiet and comfortable with a restaurant overlooking a garden shaded by lemon trees.
ADDRESS: *Puerto Lumbreras, Murcia.*
TELEPHONE: *(968) 40 20 25.*
CAPACITY: *112 beds. 52 double and 8 single rooms.*
CATEGORY: *Three stars.*
AMENITIES: *Air-conditioning, bar, central heating, garage, garden;*

Parador Cristóbal Colón

Parador Casa del Corregidor

Parador de Puerto Lumbreras

Parador El Adelantado

swimming pool and telephone.
AUTHOR'S POINTS: 1.
THE NEAREST PARADORS: Mojácar (60 km), Granada (197 km), Úbeda (208 km), Cazorla (216 km), Albacete (231 km), Sierra Nevada (232 km) and Jávea (247 km).

EL ADELANTADO

A secluded mountain parador surrounded by verdant forests and rare plants.
ADDRESS: Cazorla, Jaén.
TELEPHONE: (953) 72 10 75.
CAPACITY: 68 beds. 34 double rooms.
CATEGORY: Three stars.
AMENITIES: A bar, library, central heating, garage, garden and telephone.
AUTHOR'S POINTS: 4.
THE NEAREST PARADORS: Úbeda (70 km), Bailén (109 km), Jaén (127 km), Granada (224 km) and Albacete (236 km).

CONDESTABLE DÁVALOS

A magnificent 16th-century palace displaying the artistic wealth of the Spanish Renaissance.
ADDRESS: Plaza de Vázquez Molina, Úbeda, Jaén.

TELEPHONE: (953) 75 03 45.
CAPACITY: 50 beds. 25 double rooms.
CATEGORY: Three stars.
AMENITIES: A bar, library, central heating, garage, Convention hall and telephone.
AUTHOR'S POINTS: 3.
THE NEAREST PARADORS: Bailén (39 km), Jaén (57 km), Cazorla (70 km) and Albacete (210 km).

─── TOUR NINETEEN ───

PARADOR DE BAILÉN

A spacious airy building in an area rich with Spanish history.
ADDRESS: Bailén, Jaén.
TELEPHONE: (953) 67 01 00.
CAPACITY: 168 beds. 82 double and 4 single rooms.
CATEGORY: Three stars.
AMENITIES: Air-conditioning, bar, central heating, garage, garden, swimming pool, Convention hall and telephone.
AUTHOR'S POINTS: 1.
THE NEAREST PARADORS: Jaén (37 km), Úbeda (39 km), Córdoba (105 km), Cazorla (109 km), Almagro (120 km), Manzanares (122 km), Granada (134 km), Sierra

Nevada (169 km) and Carmona (214 km).

CASTILLO DE SANTA CATALINA

Built in the style of a medieval castle this parador overlooks both the city of Jaén and the surrounding mountains.
ADDRESS: Jaén.
TELEPHONES: (953) 26 44 11.
CAPACITY: 80 beds. 37 double and 6 single rooms.
CATEGORY: Four stars.
AMENITIES: Air-conditioning, bar, library, central heating, Convention hall, telephone and Café-bar with mountain views.
AUTHOR'S POINTS: 4.
THE NEAREST PARADORS: Bailén (37 km), Úbeda (57 km), Granada (97 km), Córdoba (104 km), Cazorla (127 km) and Sierra Nevada (132 km).

SAN FRANCISCO

This old Franciscan convent is situated in the grounds of the Alhambra, and is now one of the most beautiful and romantic paradors.
ADDRESS: Alhambra, Granada.
TELEPHONE: (958) 22 14 40.
CAPACITY: 67 beds. 32 double and

2 single rooms.
CATEGORY: Four stars.
AMENITIES: Air-conditioning, bar, central heating, garden. Convention hall, telephone and outdoor café overlooking the Alhambra.
AUTHOR'S POINTS: 4.
THE NEAREST PARADORS: Sierra Nevada (35 km), Antequera (95 km), Jaén (97 km), Nerja (106 km) and Málaga (124 km).

PARADOR DE SIERRA NEVADA

High on the slopes of Europe's southernmost ski resort this chalet-style parador overlooks the valley below.
ADDRESS: Monachil, Granada.
TELEPHONES: (958) 48 02 00 and 48 02 04.
CAPACITY: 82 beds. 20 double, 2 single and 10 quadruple rooms.
CATEGORY: Three stars.
AMENITIES: A bar, central heating, garage, Convention hall, telephone and tennis.
AUTHOR'S POINTS: 2.
THE NEAREST PARADORS: Granada (35 km), Antequera (130 km), Jaén (132 km), Nerja (141 km), Málaga (159 km) and Torremolinos (169 km).

Parador Condestable Dávalos

Parador San Francisco

Index

Holidays for the discerning

MUNDI COLOR IBERIA

The Spain of Mundi Color . . . the historic, authentic land where traditional elegance combine with a simple charm and friendly people.

Castles, Monasteries, Manor Houses, Convents and Palaces. These are the unique Paradores of Spain awaiting the pleasure of your company.

Ideas to delight . . . fly and drive or stay put. Historic cities or wonderful wildlife holidays. Two centres, two islands or a relaxing short break. And the expertise to handle your 'tailor made' requirements.

MUNDI COLOR HOLIDAYS
276 Vauxhall Bridge Road, London SW1V 1BE Telephone 01-834 3492